HOW TO BECOME A SCHIZOPHRENIC

# How To Become
# A
# Schizophrenic

*The Case Against Biological Psychiatry*

**Second Edition**

## John Modrow

*Apollyon Press*
Seattle, Washington

*To*

*Steve & Rahn*

*Fellow Voyagers*

Copyright © 1992, 1996 by John Modrow
All rights reserved
Printed in the United States of America.


Apollyon Press
P.O. Box 16052
Seattle, Washington 98116

## Publisher's Cataloging in Publication

Modrow, John.
    How to become a schizophrenic: the case against biological
       psychiatry / John Modrow
    p. cm.
    Includes bibliographical references.
    Includes index.
    Preassigned LCCN: 92-71410.
    ISBN 0-9632626-7-X

    1. Schizophrenia—Social aspects. 2. Schizophrenia—Genetic aspects.
    I. Title. II. Title: The case against biological psychiatry.


RC541.M63 1996                         616.898'2

Sometimes I aint so sho who's got ere a right to say when a man is crazy and when he aint. Sometimes I think it aint none of us pure crazy and aint none of us pure sane until the balance of us talks him that-a-way. It's like it aint so much what a fellow does, but it's the way the majority of folks is looking at him when he does it.

William Faulkner
*As I Lay Dying*

# TABLE OF CONTENTS

## PART I
## A RECIPE FOR MADNESS

## PART II
## THE MAKING OF A SCHIZOPHRENIC

# PREFACE TO THE SECOND EDITION

Since the publication of the first edition of this book, I have received a number of letters and phone calls from the parents of schizophrenic patients asking about alternatives to biological psychiatry with its psychoactive drugs and other physical treatments. This book does not promote or discuss any cure or nostrum for schizophrenia and there are some people who think that this is its chief weakness. Consequently, I have asked Dr. Bertram Karon, one of the world's foremost advocates of psychotherapy as a treatment for schizophrenia, to write a Foreword to the second edition of this book.

I, however, have little interest in any purported cure for schizophrenia simply because I know from personal experience that being labeled schizophrenic can cause a hundred times as much suffering as the so-called "illness" itself. Being labeled a schizophrenic can lead to being incarcerated and injected with potent neurotoxic drugs that often cause such irreversible brain diseases as tardive dyskinesia, tardive dementia, and the supersensitivity psychosis. It can lead to one's total psychological devastation — to being indoctrinated with the utterly demoralizing notion that one is a defective, biologically inferior person with an incurably sick mind. Finally, it can lead to one being viewed and treated by others as if one is not fully human.

How then are we to help "schizophrenics"? The answer is simple: *Stop the lies!* Stop spreading dehumanizing myths about these people. If this answer seems unsatisfactory, one must bear in mind that we can help schizophrenic persons only to the extent that we are able to understand the true nature of their problems. However, we will be able to understand their problems only to the extent that we are able to shed all the misconceptions we have concerning "schizophrenia."

In this present edition I have updated the research, straightened out innumerable bad sentences, and completely rewritten certain portions of the narrative section — particularly the first few pages of chapter 2. Other than this, no other changes have been made.

One thing more. Throughout this book one will encounter such phrases as "he became 'schizophrenic,'" "she was 'schizophrenic,'" and other similar language. Just as I have tried to avoid awkward phrases and sentences by using the pronoun "he" when the more inclusive "he or she" would be more appropriate, so I've found it easier to write as if "schizophrenia" actually exists in order to avoid tying myself in semantic knots. Actually I have about much belief in the reality of "schizophrenia" as I have in the reality of witchcraft or demoniac possession.

John Modrow
June 1996

# FOREWORD

# IN SEARCH OF TRUTH

Neither schizophrenic patients nor their families are typically given accurate information today. The psychoeducational model (which teaches schizophrenics and their families what is known about schizophrenia so that they can cope better) is now widely advocated in the United States. But, to be helpful, the information must be accurate.

The most important scientific finding about schizophrenia learned in the last 15 years concerns the long-term prognosis. Every study anywhere in the world which has followed schizophrenic patients for more than 25 years has found that approximately 35 percent fully recover and another 35 percent function independently are self-supporting with some possible residual symptoms. These are empirical findings not tied to any particular theory of causality. Nor do different diagnostic formulations, including DSM-III-R, make any difference in the long-term prognosis.

Further, the benign prognosis is not the result of modern treatments. In Switzerland, where the diagnosis of schizophrenia was first clinically described and where accurate population records were available, it has been found that this benign long-term course of schizophrenia has been true for patients diagnosed since 1900. But no one had attempted to seek out and analyze the data until recently.

Patients and their families are still taught the pessimistic formulation of Eugen Bleuler, who first described schizophrenia: the patient will never get better; or, the patient will temporarily remit but get sick again, and, in the long run, become a chronic patient (the latter "revolving door syndrome" is believed to be the usual course in the era of modern medications). But, Manfred Bleuler, Eugen Bleuler's son, who (like his father) spent his professional career treating and researching schizophrenia, was the first to report the better long-term prognosis: "My father and I were misled by the fact that the only patients we saw in the long run were those who never left the hospital or those who came back." However, his father's pessimistic formulations are still to be found in most textbooks.

The second hopeful fact that has been replicated consistently is that children of schizophrenics who are raised by their schizophrenic parent, with environmental factors and possible genetic factors working in the same direction, have only one chance in five of ever becoming schizophrenic. This information, too, is usually withheld from families and patients.

Why is such hopeful information withheld from patients and families? Either because the professionals may not yet know it, even though it has been in the literature for years and there is no contradictory information, or because it makes professionals feel guilty.

If schizophrenics have no realistic hope of recovery, then it is sensible to medicate and forget the patients. Medication does make patients more bearable in the short run and improves their behavior and adjustment to a ward or board and care home. If the medication has a risk of producing long-term brain damage (and it does), that really is not important since the patients do not have a hopeful long-term future anyway. But if at least one-third are going to fully recover and two-thirds socially recover, then it is a serious matter to produce brain damage. Moreover, it is a crime to ignore these patients. And there is evidence that, whatever the short-term benefits, the long-term consequences of maintained medication may be to preclude full recovery.

Economics does not determine all of human behavior, but it is an influencing factor. Most American medical schools today do not regularly include training in psychotherapy as part of the curriculum in psychiatry. There has always been a split in American psychiatry between the biological psychiatrists and the psychotherapeutic psychiatrists, with the biological psychiatrists being more numerous since their training is briefer and they earn a larger income. Departments of psychiatry have become dependent on research grants which are far more abundant in biological psychiatry; hence, the faculties are primarily biological psychiatrists who teach what they know. The income differential has become so great that a study commissioned by the American Psychiatric Association has recommended that reasonable psychiatrists will not practice psychotherapy since they cannot make more than $100,000 annually, whereas one can easily earn three times that if one only evaluates and medicates. Such an economic differential makes it hard for psychiatrists to want to take the extra time and trouble to learn to do psychotherapy, particularly with difficult patients.

The chair of a prestigious department of psychiatry once chided the head of another psychiatric residency program: "You have a strange residency. You teach your residents to talk to these patients. We teach our residents to medicate these patients, but never to talk to them."

A well-known biological psychiatrist said, in reaction to a paper of mine, "It isn't true that I don't talk to schizophrenics because I'm afraid of them. I don't talk to them because it's well known that talking to them makes them sicker." He was objecting to the idea that professionals avoid talking with schizophrenics because it makes professionals anxious —

they feel the patient's terror and they don't want to. They recognize that the patient is no different from them except that the patient's life has been worse, and they don't want to know what it feels like to be schizophrenic or that they themselves could be schizophrenic if life were bad enough.

The truth, of course, is that appropriate psychotherapy has been shown to be more effective than medication, or even the benign spontaneous long-term prognosis. My controlled study in Detroit with inner-city schizophrenics; Revere, Rodeffer, Dawson, and Bigelow's study with chronic hospitalized patients in Washington, D.C.; Benedetti & Furlan's study of patients in Italy and Switzerland; Alanen's study in Finland; and Schindler's study in Austria: these are among the better studies showing what appropriate psychotherapy can do. But all that psychotherapy has to offer is understanding and a corrective relationship. Both of these are attainable outside psychotherapy — only with greater difficulty. (There are studies — using psychiatrists untrained in working with schizophrenics, supervised by therapists untrained in working with schizophrenics — which find that therapy is less helpful than medication. Free copies of the book describing one such study have been given away to any psychiatrist, administrator, or interested party who would accept it by the manufacturer of the medication used. Consequently, that study is widely cited.)

In John Modrow's book, the professional or interested layman who has never spoken to a schizophrenic at length can have the luxury of listening at length to a particularly honest and self-revealing story of a schizophrenic patient's life, told with all the details; this account does not withhold information even if it may be consistent with an alternative view besides the one held by the author. Thus, a Procrustean biological psychiatrist could re-interpret this life history as showing the development of a physical disorder causing mental symptoms: it would be a work of great bending and fitting, but it could be done. Nonetheless, this life history makes best sense when understood as the story of a human tragedy, engendering unnecessarily great suffering. The good part is that the author has found his way out of his private hell, and made something valuable out of his suffering. He has gone to the psychiatric literature to find out how much of what he was told by professionals was true and how much is not true on the basis of current scientific knowledge. After all, scientific journals are not secret documents but available at any good university or medical school library to anyone who cares to read them. Reality, as revealed in the scientific knowledge to date, is much easier to live with than the partial knowledge of professionals who may spend more time reading the *Wall Street Journal* than professional journals, or who only read journals that are committed to one point of view — the one they believe because it is convenient.

In a careful and readable form, the author summarizes this literature in a way that professionals, families, and patients all will find enlightening and useful. It is sad that this patient had to learn for himself the nature of his difficulties — namely, that he is just a human being in trouble — but it is ennobling that despite bad and discouraging treatment he was able to understand himself and others, and share that acquired knowledge in an accurate and helpful way.

Bertram P. Karon, Ph.D.
Professor of Clinical Psychology
Michigan State University

# ACKNOWLEDGMENTS

During the nearly twelve years I have been researching and writing this book, several persons have given me valuable criticism, advice, and encouragement. I wish to thank: Dan Borgström, Dick Doane, John Munson, Dave Neff, David Piff, and Greg Price. I am especially grateful to Rahn Porter for discussions concerning Hans Selye's general adaption syndrome, and to Shaindell Goldhaber for her infinite patience in preparing this manuscript. Ted Clifford and William Morrill have also been of help in preparing this manuscript.

I am deeply grateful to Dr. Theodore Lidz who has read the entire manuscript and provided a valuable eleven-page critique. However, the views expressed in this book are solely my own and not those of Dr. Lidz or anyone else.

I also want to thank Caroline Klumpar for the superb job she has done in editing the second edition of this book.

Finally, I would like to thank various persons who must remain anonymous — individuals who have shared their experiences and insights with me, and who have helped motivate me to write this book.

# INTRODUCTION

Like any worthwhile endeavor, becoming a schizophrenic requires a long period of rigorous training. My training for this unique calling began in earnest when I was six years old. At that time my somewhat befuddled mother took me to the University of Washington to be examined by psychiatrists in order to find out what was wrong with me. According to my mother, those psychiatrists told her: "We don't know exactly what is wrong with your son, but whatever it is, it is very serious. We recommend that you have him committed immediately or else he will be completely psychotic within less than a year." My mother did not have me committed since she realized that such a course of action would be extremely damaging to me. But after that ominous prophecy my parents began to view and treat me as if I were either insane or at least in the process of becoming that way. Once, when my mother caught me playing with some vile muck I had mixed up — I was seven at the time — she gravely told me, "They have people put away in mental institutions for doing things like that." Fear was written all over my mother's face as she told me this. Another similar incident occurred sometime before Christmas when I was nine years old. I was sitting under the Christmas tree eagerly examining one of my presents. Suddenly, a vivid mental picture formed in my mind and I told my father that I "knew" what was inside the package I was holding. My father was shocked at my pretended psychic ability. He sternly told me that people who make such claims deserve to be locked up in a booby hatch. Such treatment upset me so much that I began to act a little odd. The slightest odd behavior on my part was enough to send my parents into paroxysms of apprehension. My parents' apprehensions in turn made me fear that I was going insane.

My paternal great grandmother died at Northern State Hospital at Sedro Wooley, Washington, a state institution for the insane. Increasingly, as time passed by, my mother began to view me as a virtual reincarnation of my great-grandmother destined for the same fate.

As a child I was told the most remarkable tales about my great-grandmother — or "Old Gram" as my family called her. One such tale was that Gram literally drove her husband to utter despair and suicide, and then, in the most cold-blooded way, set about making her husband's suicide appear accidental in order to collect his insurance money. When my grandfather had been unaccountably missing for nine years, Gram attempted to have him declared legally dead so she could collect his army insurance. Family legend has it that when her son turned up alive

1

and well Gram was infuriated at the prospect of her not being able to collect his insurance. Several years later, Gram launched a slanderous campaign against my grandfather which nearly cost him his job with the city. Gram told everyone who would listen to her that my grandfather was stealing vast sums of money from the city and that he was neglecting and mistreating his own mother. She was able to persuade several clergymen to contact my grandfather at work and talk to him concerning his "sinful activities." Toward the end of her life, after she had been thrown out of several nursing homes for being a troublemaker, Gram showed up at my grandfather's doorstep and wished to move in with him. When my grandfather refused to take his mother into his home, Gram threatened to get a knife and stab him through the heart. Obligingly, Gram repeated her threat in front of a judge at a commitment hearing. She died soon after being committed to Northern State Hospital.

Such tales made quite an impression on me, for in countless subtle ways my mother led me to believe that I was a person very much like my great-grandmother. My mother's favorite refrain was that I was a person totally incapable of thinking of anyone but myself. This, of course, had been the primary distinguishing characteristic of my great-grandmother. Whenever some minor thoughtless or inconsiderate act on my part made her angry, my mother, like a prosecuting attorney, would meticulously go over every similar incident in my past in order to establish that these were no mere isolated instances, but instead pointed to some deep and unalterable flaw in my character. She would tell me that even from my earliest years I had been a selfish, unloving and nearly inhuman creature and that I was steadily getting worse. Immediately prior to my schizophrenic breakdown my mother explicitly told me — and had me totally convinced — that I had been flawed from the moment of conception: my fate had been sealed by my genes.

My fate had been sealed not by my genes, but by the attitudes, beliefs, and expectations of my parents. This is not to suggest that my parents deliberately drove me insane or that they are cruel people worthy of condemnation. My parents tried to perform the duties of parenthood as best they could, but they had serious psychological problems of their own. Also I find it extremely difficult to condemn my parents for behaving as if I were going insane when the psychiatric authorities told them that this was an absolute certainty. Indeed, had my parents failed to respond with an appropriate amount of alarm to what these "experts" told them, they could be accused of a callous lack of concern. In the same way I find it hard to blame my mother for believing I had inherited my great-grandmother's insanity when it is a widespread misconception, particularly among mental health professionals, that schizophrenia is a genetically transmitted disease.

Psychiatry, with its pseudoscientific doctrines of inherited insanity and its incompetent practitioners with their self-fulfilling prophecies, together with my parents' gullibility and other personal limitations had in effect driven me insane.

I believe it is a fact beyond all reasonable dispute that I had been victimized by a series of events — not by a disease. And I believe this can be demonstrated to be true of all people who have been labeled schizophrenic. To label a person schizophrenic explains nothing. As an explanation for socially deviant behavior, schizophrenia is very similar to the ancient notion of demoniac possession. Demons and schizophrenia: both are thoroughly mysterious entities which make people do *bad* things. Both hypotheses are impossible to verify. Both are exterior to the personality — that is, it isn't the person thinking, acting, etc., but the demon or illness causing the person to act. Both provide a rationale for the social control and the mistreatment of individuals. Both explanations obscure the real social and psychological causes of behavior. And in both cases the person is consistently taught to misunderstand himself.

In part I, "A Recipe for Madness," I reveal the social and psychological ingredients necessary in order to produce a schizophrenic. Contrary to popular belief, a considerable amount is known concerning the etiology of schizophrenia. Owing to the brilliant work of such men as Harry Stack Sullivan, Theodore Lidz, Gregory Bateson, R. D. Scott and P. L. Ashworth, W. Ronald D. Fairbairn, Anton Boisen, and many others, it is no longer necessary to invoke the medical model with its intellectual crudities in order to explain the behavior of certain individuals designated as schizophrenics. Unfortunately, up until now this knowledge has existed only in an extremely fragmentary form. However, by utilizing the discoveries of the above men, not only have I been able to achieve a remarkable understanding of my own admittedly bizarre experiences, but I have also been able to forge the insights that I have gained from understanding myself into a comprehensive theory capable of explaining the experiences of all persons who have been diagnosed as schizophrenic. In the first part of this book, I will explain step by step, in great detail, just how and why people become schizophrenic.

Part II, "The Making of a Schizophrenic," is a narrative of the first sixteen years of my life from my earliest memories up until my schizophrenic breakdown in 1960 and subsequent recovery in early 1961. Since I believe with Scott and Ashworth that schizophrenia, rather than being an illness, is actually the culmination of a series of progressively worsening personality disorders spanning three or four generations, in order to tell the story of my schizophrenic breakdown it is necessary to go back two or three generations: one cannot fully understand the true nature of my emotional difficulties without first understanding what sort of people my immediate ancestors were. This story of my descent into madness is essentially a dramatic illustration of the theories and principles formulated in the first section of this book.

In part III, "The Medical Model Reexamined," I decisively refute various pseudoscientific slanders which have been perpetrated against schizophrenics by members of the psychiatric profession. Ironically, some of the world's greatest psychiatrists, including C. G. Jung, Harry Stack Sullivan, and R. D. Laing have had schizophrenic episodes similar to mine. Yet according to the psychiatric establishment, such persons — myself included — must be considered biologically inferior people who suffer from either (a) a brain defect, (b) a biochemical defect, (c) a genetic defect, or any combination of these three factors. However, each of these three allegations has been subjected to the most devastating criticisms by biologists and other competent professionals. Until now this information has lain dormant in technical journals and has never before been made available to the general public.

However, I will do more than merely criticize the notion that schizophrenics are biologically inferior. I will cite hard facts which prove beyond a reasonable doubt that schizophrenia cannot possibly be a disease. For instance, it has recently been established by Courtenay M. Harding of the University of Vermont, as well as by other researchers, that over a long-term basis even the most profoundly disabled schizophrenics generally make good recoveries. This simple fact is nearly impossible to explain if we assume that schizophrenia is a disease due to either a brain lesion or an inborn metabolic defect. For this very reason many psychiatrists insist that schizophrenia is an incurable disease. Yet it is precisely the psychiatrists who make such claims — and not we so-called "schizophrenics" — who are the ones hopelessly divorced from reality!

In the third part of this book I also explore in detail the social functions of the medical model. The medical model (or disease hypothesis) is universally accepted because it serves the needs of so many people, including psychiatrists, the parents of schizophrenics, and society in general. The medical model helps psychiatrists by assuring layman and psychiatrist alike that psychiatrists are *legitimate* medical practitioners treating a *real* illness, and therefore are fully entitled to a doctor's high status and high pay. Similarly, the medical model helps the parents of schizophrenics by reassuring them that schizophrenia is a disease much like diabetes or cancer — a disease for which no one is responsible. The medical model also helps society in general by providing a disguised form of social control in which, without trial or due process, certain troublesome individuals can be locked up, forcibly drugged, and shocked into brain damage. Such a procedure is justified on the grounds that (a) this procedure is a benevolent medical intervention designed to help these people and (b) schizophrenics are biologically inferior people who fully deserve such vicious treatment. Obviously, the medical model benefits everyone except the persons whom it is ostensibly designed to help: the schizophrenics.

It is my conviction that we are able to help schizophrenic persons only to the extent that we are able to understand the true nature of their problems. Furthermore, it is also my conviction that we are able to understand the real problems of schizophrenics only to the extent that we abandon the medical model.

# PART I

## A RECIPE FOR MADNESS

# 1

# THE ENVIRONMENT OF THE SCHIZOPHRENIC

Before I explain how people become schizophrenic it is only reasonable to ask: what is schizophrenia? Although innumerable theories exist that purport to explain the exact nature and origin of schizophrenia, schizophrenics, as people, can be viewed only in one of two ways: as basically similar to other people, or as basically different. The dominant view is that of the medical model, which asserts that schizophrenics are so different from other people that they must be studied and treated as if they were alien creatures; that the actions, beliefs, and experiences of schizophrenics are not manifestations of their humanity, but of a mysterious and terrifying disease; and that schizophrenics constitute a genetically distinct group of inferior and dangerous people who must be kept locked up and/or drugged to the point of stupor. The other — or heretical — view emphasizes the fact that the so-called "symptoms" of schizophrenia are mental traits common to all mankind which have been exaggerated in schizophrenics due to environmental stress; that if any person were to be put through the same types of stress that schizophrenics have undergone, that person would become a schizophrenic; that "schizophrenics," as such, do not exist, but rather they are human beings who have undergone terrifying, heartbreaking, and damaging experiences, usually over a long period of time, and as a consequence are emotionally disturbed — often to the point of incapacitation. I have adopted this latter view.

My view that schizophrenia is not a disease is shared by an increasing number of authors including Thomas Szasz,[1] Laing and Esterson,[2] Sarbin and Mancuso,[3] and many others.[4] Moreover, despite a recent and deplorable trend, psychiatry itself has been gradually abandoning the medical model throughout most of the twentieth century. For instance, in the early years of this century, Sigmund Freud discovered psychological causes for phenomena once believed to be caused by disease. Furthermore, as far back as 1906, Adolf Meyer* argued that schizophrenia was not a disease entity but merely the result of a deterioration of habits.[5] Building upon the foundations laid by Freud and

---

*Adolf Meyer (1866-1950) is usually considered the founder of modern American psychiatry.

Meyer, Harry Stack Sullivan was able to construct a coherent and convincing theory of schizophrenia as a grave disorder in living, traceable to specific traumatic incidents in the individual's life. A logical extension of Sullivan's approach are the studies that have been done on the families of schizophrenics by researchers at Palo Alto, California,[6] Harvard University,[7] Yale University,[8] the National Institute of Mental Health,[9] and in Great Britain,[10] France,[11] West Germany,[12] and Finland.[13] These researchers have demonstrated that schizophrenia is not a disease entity which can be localized within a single individual but is instead merely a part of a larger pattern of disturbed family relationships. Some examples are as follows:

*The Abbot Family*. Mr. and Mrs. Abbot appeared to be very sensible and ordinary people. Their daughter, Maya, had been diagnosed as a paranoid schizophrenic with delusions of reference. Maya's major clinical symptom — her "ideas of influence" — consisted in her belief that she influenced other people and was influenced in turn in ways she could neither understand nor control. It took over a year of investigation to find out that her parents were, in fact, influencing Maya in a very strange way. Mr. and Mrs. Abbot would regularly conduct "telepathy experiments" on Maya without her knowledge. This they would do by using agreed upon nonverbal signals to communicate with each other in Maya's presence in order to see if Maya would be able to pick this up. It was their belief that Maya possessed special powers.

The Abbots are very typical of the parents of schizophrenic children. On one hand, they are extremely intrusive and are disinclined to permit Maya to have any autonomy whatsoever. On the other, they are totally impervious to Maya's needs, perceptions, and feelings. They interpret Maya's wish for autonomy and her bitter resentment at its being thwarted as merely a symptom of her "illness."[14]

*The Ferris Family*. Roger Ferris has been diagnosed as schizophrenic. In his family, his parents mutually manipulate each other in order to maintain a facade of optimism and harmonious amiability. Discussion of emotionally sensitive topics in his family is strictly taboo. When either of his parents would discuss such a subject, the other parent would remain silent for days or even weeks on end. One of Roger's main symptoms is his long periods of silence which deeply worry his parents. Nevertheless, Roger is the only member of his family who would openly discuss such topics as sex. His parents wish Roger would keep silent on this subject.

That Roger was able to obtain a job as a salesman while he was still severely disturbed was viewed by both his parents as a miraculous sign of his sudden recovery. Though Roger selected the job himself, Mr. Ferris, in a private agreement with the employer, had promised to pay part of Roger's salary on the condition that he be hired. Roger, however, was left with the impression he had gained that job through his own effort. Mr. Ferris had also agreed to secretly follow Roger on his rounds in case he should need help. One of Roger's "delusions" was his belief that he was being watched.

Mrs. Ferris' manner in relating to Roger as evidenced in her body language and tone of voice was clearly sexually provocative. Roger's other delusion concerns his sexual seduction of older women.[15]

*The Dolfuss Family.* Emil Dolfuss, a 26-year-old schizophrenic man, had been returned from the Orient by consular authorities where he had been living out his religious delusions of saving the world. When he arrived at the psychiatric institute, he was formally dressed, ostentatious in his bearing, and very correct and grandiloquent in his speech. He expected everyone around him to obey his commands. While at the institute, his behavior gradually deteriorated, and he soon discarded his formal attire and went about dressed in his shorts.

He became catatonic. While in this state, his behavior consisted largely of rituals borrowed from various Eastern religions. Emil would hoard food in his room. He would also periodically gorge himself on meat then go on a strictly vegetarian diet. Emil worshipped light as something sacred and was terrified of darkness. At times Emil would kneel and pray before his sister, Adele, whom he believed was a goddess. Sometimes Emil thought he too was a god.

Emil Dolfuss came from a very interesting family whose style of life was suggestive of European nobility. All members of this household had to be formally dressed as they sat down to eat dinner together. Mr. Dolfuss was a wealthy manufacturer and inventor who spent most of his time when he was home in his bedroom studying Eastern religion and philosophy while dressed only in his underwear. Mr. Dolfuss believed he was a reincarnation of the Buddha. From his studies, Mr. Dolfuss conceived a bizarre religious cult which was shared by his entire family, including his domestic servant. One ritual of Mr. Dolfuss' religion was the ceremonial lighting of candles. Before this ritual, Mr. Dolfuss would deliver a long speech concerning the holiness of light. Mrs. Dolfuss believed Mr. Dolfuss was a great man, and that her sole purpose in life should be to serve him. She was also a food faddist. The nursemaid worshipped Mr. Dolfuss as a demigod. She treated Emil as if he were a prince and would alternate between spoiling and harshly disciplining him. She often slept with him.[16]

These examples clearly show that schizophrenia is not a disease but merely a reaction to and expression of a disturbed family environment. That schizophrenia is strictly a learned response, originating in how the parents communicate and in how the family interacts as a whole, has been most impressively demonstrated by Lyman C. Wynne and his coworkers at the National Institute of Mental Health.[17] They have exhaustively studied a thirty-five family sample consisting of twenty families with an overtly schizophrenic member, nine families with a borderline schizophrenic member, and six families with a severely neurotic nonschizophrenic member. All members of these thirty-five families were given a comprehensive battery of psychological tests, including the Rorschach, Thematic Apperception, Draw-a-Person, Sentence Completion, Minnesota Multiphasic Personality Inventory, the Proverbs Test, and the Object Sorting Test. In addition to those tests, each patient was given a clinical rating of one to five corresponding to the severity of his or her mental disorder.

The results of the parents' tests were sent to a psychologist, Dr. Margaret Thaler Singer, at the University of California at Berkeley, three thousand miles from where those tests were originally conducted. From the results of their parents' tests, Dr. Singer predicted the patients' diagnosis, their form of thinking, and the severity of their mental disorder. Dr. Singer correctly predicted the diagnosis of seventeen of the twenty overtly schizophrenic patients. She also accurately predicted the diagnosis of the nine borderline schizophrenic patients and the six nonschizophrenic patients, making only two errors in their diagnoses. Dr. Singer also predicted with similar accuracy the patients' form of thinking (such as amorphous, mixed, fragmented, or constricted) and the severity of their mental disorder. In each of these three predictive tasks the level of significance was better than .001. However, in blindly matching the test results of the patients with that of their parents, Dr. Singer was phenomenally accurate and achieved a level of significance of .000002.[18]

Since the sufferings and mental disorders of the schizophrenic patient can be seen as a protest against an intolerable living situation, some psychiatrists such as R. D. Laing[19] and Martti Siirala[20] view him or her as the sanest member of the family. Their views find confirmation in the experimental findings of Elliot Mishler and Nancy Waxler, two Harvard University psychiatrists, who write:

> It is a matter of great importance that differences between parents of schizophrenic children and parents of normal children are more striking than are differences between schizophrenic patients and normal children serving as research controls.[21]

Rather than merely establishing correlations between the mental disorders of parents and their schizophrenic offspring, Gregory Bateson and his associates are among those researchers who have actually helped explain how these parents produce schizophrenia in their children. According to Bateson, schizophrenia is caused by a no-win situation that he has called the *double bind*. This double bind situation is composed of five essential ingredients, which are:

1) Two or more persons.
2) Repeated experience.
3) A primary negative injunction.

4) A secondary injunction which contradicts the first. This contradiction is not obvious because (a) this secondary injunction is more abstract than the first and (b) it is usually communicated nonverbally. However, like the first, this secondary injunction is enforced by punishment, or by other behavior which threatens the individual's security.

5) A physically, financially, or emotionally dependent victim incapable of escaping from the field.

One of the simplest and most basic double bind situations is described by Bateson as follows:

1) A child whose mother becomes anxious and withdraws if the child responds to her as a loving mother. That is, the child's very existence has a special meaning to the mother which arouses her anxiety and hostility when she is in danger of intimate contact with the child.

2) A mother to whom feelings of anxiety and hostility toward the child are not acceptable, and whose way of denying them is to express overt loving behavior to persuade the child to respond to her as a loving mother and to withdraw from him if he does not.

3) The absence of anyone in the family, such as a strong and insightful father, who can intervene in the relationship and support the child in the face of the contradictions involved.[22]

However, the above description should not be taken to imply that the mother is solely responsible for causing schizophrenia. In many instances it is the father who is the major disturbing influence in the family — as the case of Mr. Dolfuss, the megalomaniac who believed he was a reincarnation of the Buddha, aptly illustrates.

Moreover, since most parents of schizophrenics are well-meaning people who have been handicapped by their own upbringing, it is a gross injustice, as well as an oversimplification, to hold them responsible for causing their children to become schizophrenic. According to a number of investigators including R. D. Scott and P. L. Ashworth, schizophrenia must be viewed as the culmination of a series of progressively worsening personality disorders spanning three or four generations.

In their profoundly illuminating paper, "The Shadow of the Ancestor: A Historical Factor in the Transmission of Schizophrenia," Scott and Ashworth report several cases in which a parent has perceived the patient in terms of his or her experience with a mad relative.[23] In some cases this parent viewed the patient as a virtual reincarnation of the mad relative destined for the same fate.[24] Due to his or her experience with, and involvement in, a relative's madness, this parent has a secret fear of going mad. Prior to viewing the patient in terms of the mad relative, some parents admitted "looking for it" both in themselves and in their children before centering their attention exclusively upon the patient.[25]

When these parents project their own fear of going insane onto the patient, three things happen. First, these parents no longer fear going insane themselves since the patient has become the carrier of this fear.[26] Second, the parents then proceed to view and treat this child as if he or she were either insane or in the process of going insane.[27] Third, this kind of treatment creates a self-fulfilling prophecy in which the parent's fear produces first anxiety, then psychotic panic in the child.

I find Scott and Ashworth's paper extremely significant since it suggests that schizophrenia is actually transmitted through the *belief* that madness is inherited rather than by heredity itself. However, I think these authors have overlooked two things. First, it is not necessary for a parent to have had a mad relative in order to fear going insane. This parent could be unstable for a number of reasons. For instance, a mother could undergo a postpartum psychotic episode and as a result acquire a lifelong fear of madness which she then projects onto her child. Second, this same mother may then view her child as a virtual reincarnation of a mad relative *of her spouse*. This more effectively distances her from the onus of insanity than if she were to view this child in terms of one of her own relatives. Furthermore, this maneuver could be a covert way of calling into question the sanity of her own husband and thereby castrating him as a man. I suspect this is a common pattern in families which Lidz has described as "schismatic."

The acknowledged pioneer in the family studies of schizophrenia is Theodore Lidz, now professor emeritus at Yale University, whose studies concerning schizophrenia have earned him four major scientific awards.[28] Very early in his career Dr. Lidz extensively studied patients whose mental disturbances were due to brain lesions, metabolic disorders, and toxic conditions. Dr. Lidz soon came to the conclusion that his schizophrenic patients were in an entirely different category from the former patients in that they suffered no loss of memory, orientation, or intellectual potential.[29]

The core of Dr. Lidz's investigation centers around seventeen families in which at least one member was schizophrenic. No group of families has ever undergone such a prolonged and intensive scrutiny for any purpose as have those families. Over a period of years, Dr. Lidz and his associates were able to compile such a mass of intimate and minute detail on each and every member of those families as to be the envy of any novelist. Although the number of these families is relatively small, hundreds of other families were also studied in a less intensive way by

Lidz and his coworkers at the Yale Psychiatric Institute. These families all had such grave deficiencies and distortions as to be frankly "schizophrenogenic" in nature.

Two predominant patterns characterize such schizophrenogenic families, patterns which Lidz terms the "schismatic" and the "skewed." According to Lidz, the schismatic family is marked by open marital discord, one in which

> ...both spouses were caught up in their own personality difficulties, which were aggravated to the point of desperation by the marital relationship. There was chronic failure to achieve complementary of purpose or role reciprocity. Neither gained support of emotional need from the other... Each spouse pursues his needs or objectives, largely ignoring the needs of the other, infuriating the partner and increasing ill-will and suspiciousness. A particularly malignant feature of these marriages is the chronic "undercutting" of the worth of one partner to the children by the other. The tendency to compete for the children's loyalty and affection is prominent; at times to gain a substitute to replace the affection missing from the spouse, but at times perhaps simply to hurt or spite the marital partner.[30]

> Commonly, the child of such divisive families is caught in a bind because she finds that trying to please either parent provokes rebuff and rejection by the other. She may internalize her irreconcilable parents as irreconcilable introjects leading to splits in her superego and her ego. In her attempt to salvage the parents' marriage and retain two parents, a child may accept the role of the family scapegoat... and behave in ways that seem to be the cause of the parental strife, masking their incompatibility, but at the cost of failing to invest her own developmental needs.[31]

Lidz describes the skewed family as follows:

> In the skewed family the focus of attention is apt to fall upon the mother who is termed "schizophrenogenic," a mother who is impervious to the needs of other family members as separate individuals and is extremely intrusive into her son's life. Yet, the very poor model the father provides the son and his inability to counter the mother's aberrant ways in rearing the children are also critical. Although the mother has serious difficulties in being close and maternal to her son when an infant, she soon becomes overprotective, unable to feel that the child can even exist without her constant concern and supervision. She does not

differentiate her own anxieties, needs, and feelings from those of the child. The mother seeks completion through her son, and... wishes to have him live out the life she feels has been closed to her...[32]

As an example of such a schizophrenogenic mother, Lidz tells of a very domineering woman author who at an interview would answer questions specifically addressed to her husband and would scarcely let him get in a word of his own. She was a woman with the fixed idea that her daughter was a literary genius who would some day be world famous. However, her daughter's real needs, personality, and aspirations were a matter of complete and total indifference to her. For this mother, her daughter merely existed to fulfill her own frustrated literary ambitions. She told Dr. Lidz she wished her daughter would become a great novelist and follow in the footsteps of her idol, Virginia Woolf. Upon hearing this Dr. Lidz warily commented, "But Virginia Woolf had psychotic episodes and committed suicide."[33] Without hesitation the mother replied, "It would be worth it."[34]

A few weeks after that interview Dr. Lidz visited that woman's daughter in the hospital while he was making his rounds. He noticed several novels by Virginia Woolf in the patient's room and asked her about them. She replied in a lifeless voice, "Mother sent them — she has a thing about Virginia Woolf."[35] As the months passed, the patient spoke of her despair over her own literary ineptness, of her resentment at having to live out her mother's ambitions, and of her desire for a marriage in which she could help her husband assert himself. After she had recovered from her psychosis her mother took her home. There, while living in her mother's home, she relapsed and committed suicide.[36]

In all the families investigated by Dr. Lidz, either one or both parents were so egocentric as to be unable to differentiate their own needs and feelings from those of their child. In skewed families, one parent — usually, but not always, the mother — seeks completion through her child and is incapable of viewing him as anything but an extension of herself.* Instead of learning to master events or to recognize his own feelings or needs, the child's energies and developing capabilities go principally into supporting his mother's precarious emotional balance, and into bringing meaning and fulfillment to her life.[37] Thus, the child's emerging individuality is stymied by his subservience to his mother's needs; he comes to view the world almost exclusively through his mother's eyes, unable to clearly distinguish his own feelings and needs

---

*Throughout this book, I occasionally use the pronoun "he" when "he or she" would be more appropriate. I have done this to improve the clarity of the passages involved and to prevent the use of awkward phrasing. No sexism is intended.

16

from those of his mother.[38]

In schismatic families there is constant discord because both parents are markedly egocentric and treat each other, as well as their children, as mere functions of their own needs. The child is often caught up in the conflict, trying to unite the parents and sometimes succeeding only at the cost of becoming a scapegoat on which the parents can hang their own inadequacies, thus concealing their own fundamental incompatibility. In this case, too, the child's development as an individual is stunted and sacrificed to save his parents. Because of their egocentricities, the parents can usually maintain their emotional equilibrium by projecting their own inadequacies onto the child. But the child's situation is far graver. Whereas the parents can maintain their stability by distorting reality in accordance with their own needs, the child, in order to feel wanted by the parents, must deny or repress his own feelings and needs and distort reality in accordance with his parents' needs.[39] Thus the child's orientation is parent-centered more than it is egocentric.[40] But in viewing things according to his parents' needs the child is stripped of his ego defenses and is made emotionally vulnerable even as he strengthens his parents' defenses.[41] This explains why the parents of schizophrenics often become emotionally disturbed as their children begin to improve.[42]

Often people who have been labeled "schizophrenic" are viewed as a genetically distinct subspecies of infrahumanity, or at least as horrendously defective persons. But their defect has its origins in their love for their parents, a love so deep that they are led to sacrifice their needs, their individuality, and ultimately their sanity for the sake of their parents.[43] The children who become schizophrenic are always the ones who are closest to their parents.[44] By contrast, so-called "invulnerable" children, i.e. children who come from clearly schizophrenogenic homes who yet evince superior adjustment, keep their physical and emotional distance from their parents.[45]

This concludes my description of the schizophrenic's family environment. I will now describe how this environment affects or modifies the schizophrenic's inner world.

# 2

# THE INNER WORLD OF THE SCHIZOPHRENIC

As I have already mentioned, those children who become schizophrenic distort reality in accordance with their parents' needs rather than their own, and in so doing they become stripped of ego defenses vital to maintaining their own sanity. According to Harry Stack Sullivan, it is precisely this stripping of their ego defenses which makes such people vulnerable to schizophrenic breakdowns.

Of all psychiatrists, Harry Stack Sullivan has made the most valuable contributions to the understanding of schizophrenia. Moreover, he has also sought to discredit the many dehumanizing myths about schizophrenia which, unfortunately, still linger on. Central to Sullivan's thought[1] is his observation that there is nothing to be found in schizophrenic thinking which is not to be found to some extent in the thinking of more normal people. Freud before him had emphasized the pathology of everyday normal thinking. It is perhaps Freud's most fundamental discovery that normal people are continually distorting reality in order to bolster their self-esteem. This self-deception is completely involuntary and is expressed through such Freudian defense mechanisms as repression, reaction-formation, projection, and rationalization. However, failure to employ such defense mechanisms — or security operations, as Sullivan calls them — can have grave consequences.

According to Sullivan, schizophrenia occurs with the total collapse of those security operations upon which we depend to maintain our self-esteem.[2] When such defensive — or self-deceptive — measures fail altogether, the individual goes into an intense state of panic and simply comes "unglued," so to speak.[3] In this panic state, the individual has a terrifying vision of himself as a person of no value or worth. Painful memories once repressed rise and come flooding into awareness with a gruesome, hallucinatory vividness. As if in a trance, he suddenly "realizes" that at no time in his life had he ever been a person who was fully human. And, worst of all, comes the realization that as an individual he will always be hopelessly and irredeemably flawed, that any action on his part would only be meaningless and futile, and that things will only continue to get worse as he is inexorably swept to his destruction.[4]

Such a demoralized panic state can be induced in several ways. Three of the most common ways are as follows. In the first way, a person is subjected to very severe and often cruel disparagement by people who are significant to him and on whose good opinion he is largely dependent for his self-esteem. This sort of treatment usually has a history extending from infancy up until some especially hurtful incident produces an out-and-out panic state.[5]

The second way panic can be induced has its origin in the psychological immaturity of the schizophrenic. In the last chapter it was noted that the psychological development of schizophrenics is stunted due to their subservience to their parents' needs. However, sometime in adolescence these persons must begin functioning as adults, and their inability to do so can trigger a series of emotional crises which may lead to a full-blown panic episode. In this regard, it has been noted that schizophrenic episodes often occur when such persons have risen to their level of incompetence due to a job promotion, leaving home for the first time, graduating from college, or upon marriage or parenthood.[6]

The third way panic can be produced is by the intrusion into a person's awareness of certain abhorrent cravings, feelings, or thoughts.[7] Often specified examples of such are incestuous, homosexual, or homicidal impulses and thoughts. Such impulses and thoughts are felt to be inimical to the person's values and ideals, and to the person's conception of himself. They often cause an intense panicky revulsion and the conviction that one must be subhuman to harbor them. But in and of themselves these sorts of experiences will not cause anyone to become schizophrenic unless that person's security operations no longer function in an adequate way.[8]

At this point, it must be noted that although people have been known to face death with calmness, resignation, and sometimes even with joy, no one can experience anything but abject terror as his or her mind disintegrates into madness. The panic state immediately proceeding schizophrenia is the most appalling and devastating experience that any person can undergo — it is a disorganizing and transitory state, wholly incompatible with life.*

As an individual proceeds into a panic state, five things occur as a result: a splitting of the personality, a drastic narrowing of interests, insomnia, the return of the repressed or split-off portion of the personality which invades and takes over the ego, and the formation of an explicit delusional system.

---

*Some schizophrenic individuals apparently never undergo such panic episodes. Instead they experience a slow and gradual wearing down of their personalities — a process indistinguishable from brainwashing. What I suspect happens during the course of this slow process is that the individual undergoes dozens — perhaps hundreds — of mini-panic episodes.

The splitting of the personality resulting from a panic state has two aspects. One aspect of this splitting is described by W. R. D. Fairbairn as follows. When a parent's intolerably cruel behavior produces a panic state in the child, this child, in order to feel emotionally secure, will idealize his parent and delude himself by believing that his parent's cruel behavior toward him is really his own fault, so that he need only change and become "good" and he will be loved. This child, therefore, takes upon himself the burden of his parent's badness, which is to say he internalizes his parent's badness as a living presence within himself. In so doing, this child has bought a measure of outer safety at the cost of inner peril, for thereafter he will be menaced by a "fifth column" of internal persecutors.[9]

The other aspect of this splitting is described by Harry Guntrip as follows. Due to an especially traumatic panic-producing incident, the emotional core of the personality withdraws from external reality into the safety of the inner world, leaving the conscious ego with a feeling of depletion and loss. In this state, the individual feels drained of all emotion, interest, energy, and zest. Feeling distressingly cut-off from life, he often experiences the world as if it were sealed off from him behind glass. It is not uncommon in this state for everything to seem a little unreal: colors and other sensations seem duller or less intense; flowers, trees, and other forms of vegetation sometimes appear fake, as if made of plastic; other people are often experienced as lifeless automatons; and not infrequently, the person himself feels numb and unreal as if he were, in Guntrip's words, "an empty shell out of which the living individual has departed to some safer retreat."[10]

Another result of panic is that the individual undergoes a drastic narrowing of interests — he becomes increasingly absorbed in a narrow circle of ideas to the exclusion of all else. Faced with a future that seems to offer no promise or hope, the individual retreats from external reality into the inner world and memories of a happier past. This person may also immerse himself in highly esoteric religious ideas or be constantly reading and thinking about a historical personage whom he greatly admires and increasingly identifies with. These obsessive ruminations serve to reduce this person's anxiety by taking his mind off panic-producing thoughts. As long as this individual is forever thinking about Jesus, Hitler, karma, astral spirits and the like, homicidal impulses, incestuous cravings, and other abhorrent thoughts or tendencies will be kept from his awareness.

In addition to shielding the individual against panic-producing thoughts and tendencies, these obsessive ruminations also serve to ward off feelings of depersonalization.[11] Because the emotional core of this person has been split off from his conscious awareness, he experiences a distressing feeling of inner deadness and is unable to respond to his environment in a meaningful way. Since the individual is unable to achieve a sense of personal identity either by relating to other people in a satisfying way or by being in contact with his emotions, his thoughts become the only available means by which he can feel he is alive or real. Descartes' famous dictum, "I think, therefore I am," ("Cogito, ergo sum,") expresses perfectly this person's struggle to hold on to a sense of personal identity. Inasmuch as these obsessive thoughts are necessary, both to bolster the individual's faltering sense of identity and at the same time to protect him against anxiety and panic, they have a marked tendency to become highly addictive: in the end, this person is literally unable to stop thinking or to get any sleep; *his ruminations continue nonstop 24 hours a day.*

It is nearly universal for schizophrenics to be virtually unable to sleep for as much as one or two months immediately prior to the onset of their psychosis.[12] During this period of time important biochemical changes take place. When a panic episode occurs, catecholamines (adrenaline, noradrenaline, and dopamine) are produced in superabundance causing a hyperaroused state.[13] Moreover, since panic-producing thoughts are always threatening to break into awareness, this hyperaroused state continues along with the increased production of catecholamines, and leads to a prolonged wakefulness.[14] This loss of sleep is by itself enough to produce illusions, visual hallucinations, and other psychotic symptoms in ostensibly normal people.[15] "In most cases," writes Anton Boisen in regard to schizophrenia, "this...loss of sleep..[is] carried to the point where the boundaries are lost between sleeping and waking. In this condition, a man is half awake when he ought to be asleep and half asleep when he ought to be awake."[16] Due to his increasing fatigue, this individual's focus of attention is narrowed even further. "In any case," Boisen continues,

> "...there is preoccupation and absorption so intense that the individual lapses into an abnormal condition suggestive of auto-hypnosis or trance. The conscious self is plunged into the lower strata of the mental life and finds himself surrounded by elemental and archaic thought forms. The individual thus feels himself in a strange new world in which previous experience and accepted standards of value do not apply."[17]

As Bateson and his associates have noted, a variety of phenomena encountered in schizophrenia — hallucinations, delusions, alterations of the personality, amnesias, and so forth — can also be produced in normal people on a temporary basis by hypnosis.[18] However, the psychological dynamics causing the altered states in hypnosis and schizophrenia are quite different. The narrowing of attention occurring in hypnosis is a wholly voluntary effort on the individual's part in order to assume the role of a hypnotized person, whereas the narrowing of awareness occurring in schizophrenia is a defense mechanism actuated by panic. Furthermore, the relaxation or mild trance induced by hypnosis is hardly the zombie-like trance produced jointly by prolonged sleep deprivation and intense self-absorption. But as different as the underlying psychological mechanisms are in both cases, the altered states resulting in schizophrenia must still be considered a form of self-hypnosis — a form of *involuntary* hypnosis many magnitudes more powerful than a hypnosis produced by conventional means.

Since the process terminating in schizophrenia can be viewed as a form of hypnosis, it follows that in order to understand schizophrenia, we must first understand how hypnosis works. In this regard, I find that Ronald E. Shor's article, "Hypnosis and the Concept of the Generalized Reality-Orientation" sheds considerable light upon the genesis of schizophrenia. Shor defines the concept of the generalized reality-orientation as the "...usual state of consciousness...characterized by the mobilization of a structured frame of reference in the background of attention which supports, interprets, and gives meaning to all experiences."[19] According to Shor, as the individual becomes completely absorbed in a narrow circle of ideas, the more generalized reality-orientation in which these ideas reside fades "like a weak Ground behind an attention-compelling Figure."[20] Furthermore, when the generalized reality-orientation fades:

> (a) experiences cannot have their usual meanings; (b) experiences may have special meanings which result from their isolation from the totality of general experiences; (c) special orientations...can function...as the only possible reality for the subject in his phenomenal awareness as a result of their isolation from the totality of general experience.[21]

Moreover:

> ...as usual reality-orientation fades, its derivative distinctions between wishes, self, other, imagination and reality fades with it, as do many inhibitions, conscious fears and defenses, and primary-process material and primary-process modes of thought can flow more easily into awareness, and *if* they do, a new kind of orientation is created which shares some of the qualities of the dream.[22]

Always on the periphery of this individual's consciousnesses as he begins his descent into madness lurk Fairbairn's "internal persecutors" waiting to flow into his field of awareness the instant his guard is down. To the extent that their actual external existence is inconsistent with the individual's usual view of reality, these internal persecuting presences will be kept at bay, but as the person's reality-orientation fades, these presences come to seem more real and are able to flow more easily into his awarenesses. When this happens, the individual panics and narrows his focus of attention even further in order to exclude these persecuting presences from his awarenesses. However, this creates a vicious circle: the more the individual narrows his focus of awareness, the more his generalized reality-orientation fades and makes him increasingly vulnerable to internal persecutors, which in turn necessitates a further narrowing of awareness. After each assault by these "internal persecutors," the individual's ego retreats more and more behind a fortress that becomes increasingly empty, until at last, in the words of C. Peter Rosenbaum: "The moat is empty; the bridge is down; the sentinels fail to stand guard. The unconscious storms into consciousness, and the waking dreamer of Jung is to be seen."*[23]

Randy, a close friend of mine, provides a striking example of how it is possible to literally hypnotize oneself into madness. Randy fervently believes that homosexuals are "degenerate scum." However, Randy himself has strong homosexual tendencies that he is able neither to fully control nor to openly acknowledge. Randy also has another problem, in that he is 36 years old, works at a menial job as a dishwasher, and feels that his life has been a total failure. Like everyone else, Randy has a need to think well of himself, but for him this is a very difficult task.

Through the years, I have watched Randy gradually change. I have noticed that although Randy is a voracious reader, nearly every book he has read in the last several years has been about either Hitler, the Nazis, or the Holocaust. I have also noticed that Randy, who used to be a very mild-mannered and happy-go-lucky person, has now become quite a hater. First, Randy acquired an obsessive hatred for homosexuals. He later expanded his hate list to include liberals, Communists, feminists, and Jews. Finally, one day I saw a picture of Hitler hanging in his room. When I asked Randy about this picture he told me that it reminded him of his own father.

Randy has recently told me that *he spends every conscious moment of his existence thinking about Hitler*. He has also told me that he has noticed many parallels between his own life and Hitler's. Both he and Hitler were army veterans whose highest rank in the service had been that of corporal. Both he and Hitler were unsophisticated provincials. Both were failed artists. And both he and Hitler were men of vast intellect who were, nevertheless, looked down upon, despised, and rejected by men

---

*C. G. Jung once wrote: "Let the dreamer walk about and act as though he were awake and we have at once the clinical picture of dementia praecox." Quoted in Silvano Arieti, *Interpretation of Schizophrenia*, p. 23.

who were their "natural" inferiors. The fact that Hitler had been a virtual tramp until he was thirty years old is a constant source of inspiration for Randy, for he believes that by his iron will alone he will someday, like Hitler, be able to overcome impossible odds and become a great historical figure.

Today, Randy believes himself to be a God-inspired genius destined to establish a Fourth Reich, consisting of all the English-speaking countries of the world. Randy has offered me a cabinet post in his administration if I help him take power. He told me I could be either his Goering or his Goebbels. More recently, Randy has announced, "I am Hitler, my father was Hitler, and you are Hitler." He thereupon threw his arms around me and told me, "I love you, man, I love you."

Another example of this insidious autohypnotic process is Paul. After undergoing an intense panic episode, Paul suddenly developed an obsessive interest in mysticism and the occult. For nearly three years, Paul's main activities consisted of reading occultist literature and practicing various mystical disciplines in order to achieve an altered state. Gradually, the world in which Paul lived ceased to be like the world we are familiar with and became more and more like the world described by various occultist authors. Paul became so adept at inducing altered states, that one day he was able to achieve a state of total enlightenment. In this enlightened state, Paul was contacted by "spirits" who told him that he was a messiah destined to save the world.

If I were to write Paul's biography, I would title it *The Power of Wishful Thinking*. While in high school, Paul had used the technique of self-hypnosis with great success to improve his performance as an athlete. It is my opinion that Paul had also used self-hypnosis to improve his performance as a schizophrenic. When Paul asked my opinion concerning his spiritual revelations — which seemed to me to be nothing more than a hodgepodge of every occult book he had ever read — my reply could be summarized in four words: "garbage in — garbage out."

As individuals such as Randy or Paul proceed into a panic state, terror floods their entire being as they view themselves as loathsome, inhuman creatures whom nobody could possibly respect. In this profoundly demoralized and despairing state, these individuals desperately clutch at any idea or notion which would provide them with a feeling of dignity or self-respect. But as we have seen, the panic state did not last long before these persons began to undergo a striking cognitive transformation very similar to a religious conversion. For example, not only did Randy view himself as a total failure, but he also experienced strong homosexual tendencies that made him despise himself. But eventually, Randy was able to acquire a new self-image — he believed he was a God-inspired genius destined to rule the entire English-speaking world. Similarly, Paul once viewed himself as "a hopeless case" and as "all washed up." However, he later came to see himself as an immensely important person endowed with a sacred mission.

Often this cognitive transformation takes a paranoid form in which the person imagines sinister enemies lurking in the shadows. For example, about a year and a half after he had his first contact with the "spirit realm," Paul told me he was being harassed by a group of Satanists. They would gather beneath his apartment window and shout up at him, "You are a vegetable!" Paul explained to me that every special or creative person has a group of Satanists harassing them. This is because Satanists are so internally dead and so totally devoid of any creative spark that they are full of envy and malice toward people who are creative and internally alive. As Paul explained, such harassment was an attempt on the part of the Satanists to break him down psychologically so he would become an internally dead zombie indistinguishable from them.

Paul betrayed almost no anxiety as he told me this. In fact, his morale was extremely high. However, this had not always been the case. Immediately prior to his full-blown psychosis, when he was going through a very demoralized period in his life, Paul had voiced his concern that he was intellectually deteriorating and that some day he would end up as a complete vegetable. Paul's psychosis seemed to have totally revitalized him by enabling him entirely to wash his hands of his own perceived inadequacies by transferring them out of his own awareness and onto the external environment. Here it was no longer he, Paul, who was the vegetable but they, the Satanists. His perception that the Satanists were harassing him was proof in his own mind that he was really a superior and very creative person. Thus, through this process, a once demoralizing belief was transformed into a source of strength and pride.

Far from being a disease, schizophrenia, according to Harry Stack Sullivan, is actually a very purposive and meaningful attempt by the individual to cope with a catastrophic loss of self-esteem. This loss of self-esteem is in turn caused by the fact that those security operations (self-deceptive measures) by which we distort reality in order to maintain our self-esteem are defective in people who become schizophrenic. But no one can accuse psychiatrists of being defective in this way, for they truly possess magnificent powers of self-deception and are fully capable of believing they are legitimate medical practitioners treating a real illness, schizophrenia.

# PART II

# THE MAKING OF A SCHIZOPHRENIC

# 1

# MOTHER

One night, a few days after giving birth to my older brother, my mother was visited by an apparition. It was white, luminous, and shaped like a human figure but without any arms or legs. The specter appeared in the doorway and came floating in toward my brother, who lay in his crib beside my mother. The apparition circled my brother's crib several times and left. It never came back.

The next night, my mother was visited by an even more sinister presence. This consisted of a luminous white cloud which came floating in and descended upon her as she lay in bed. My mother felt a crushing weight on her chest as this shapeless and glowing presence settled on top of her. She tried to scream but was totally paralyzed with fear, unable to move or even breathe. Every night for nine months my mother had to endure this wakeful nightmare.

During this time my mother was living alone. My father was in the Army and it was in the midst of World War II. In addition to her hallucinations, my mother also had strange and vivid dreams in which it seemed as if she were fully awake and levitating a foot or two over her bed. She also had the paranoid belief that people passing on the street were constantly watching her and looking in her windows. She kept her window shades down and her curtains closed at all times. My mother was terrified to go out of her apartment alone, but after nine months the paranoid fog in which she was living lifted, and she again felt fine.

According to my mother, during those nine months of her postpartum distress her body underwent changes similar to a second pregnancy. But, although metabolic and endocrinal changes do account for some of the vulnerability to such postpartum reactions, most researchers who have studied this phenomenon believe, for several reasons, that such reactions are triggered mainly by psychological rather than physiological causes. One reason is that there exist at least 12 well-documented cases of women undergoing severe postpartum reactions upon the adoption of a child.[1] A British psychiatrist, W. H. Trethonan, has also found that 11 to 14 percent of the fathers report symptoms similar to the expectant mother, sometimes including abdominal bloating.[2] This phenomenon, known as the *couvade syndrome*, is caused by the anxiety aroused by the father's identification with the maternal role.

Frederick T. Melges, a Stanford University psychiatrist, has found that conflict over assuming the mothering role to be the major stress in 68 percent of the cases of postpartum mental disorders. Dr. Melges has also found that this conflict usually centers around the patient's ambivalent identification with her own mother: 88 percent of the women he studied experienced either major or moderate difficulties in this area. These women often find themselves in a bind in that in wanting to be good mothers they often find themselves imitating and identifying with their own mothers — the only maternal model or guide they have for caring for their own infant. However, these women do not want to be like their own mothers whom they feel rejected them. And they are especially ashamed when they find themselves rejecting their infants as they themselves were rejected by their own mothers. As a result, they often become extremely confused; they alternate between feeling helpless without their own mothers as models and feeling ashamed when they are like their own mothers.[3]

At first glance, Melges' findings do not seem to describe my mother's problems, since my mother was not ashamed, but proud, of her own mother. My maternal grandmother came from a prominent aristocratic Norwegian family — a family that was instrumental in choosing a king for Norway when it became an independent republic in 1905. Before my grandmother immigrated to the United States she had begun a career as an operatic singer, having studied under a student of the composer Edvard Grieg. My mother disputes this and insists her mother had studied under Grieg himself. (According to my grandmother she had met Grieg only once, and briefly at that.)

Shortly after beginning her operatic career my grandmother began receiving letters from her mother's sister who was living in the United States. Her aunt pleaded with her to come live with her in the United States where she claimed she not only could continue her musical career but also would find far greater opportunities for success. My grandmother was the oldest of ten children and although her family had servants it was still her responsibility to look after her younger brothers and sisters. Finding her family responsibilities onerous and stifling, my grandmother began to find her aunt's promises alluring. She therefore decided to immigrate to the United States and live with her aunt. This was done against the advice and express wishes of her mother.

My grandmother's aunt lived on a desolate farm in North Dakota. Her only motive in luring my grandmother to come live with her was so that she could exploit her as free labor on her farm. My grandmother was stuck. On one hand, she had insufficient funds to return to Norway; on the other, she was too proud to admit to her mother that she had made a mistake or to complain that her mother's sister was mistreating her. For nearly three years my grandmother was a virtual slave to her aunt.

My grandmother settled in North Dakota in 1912. Three years later she married a local farmer. They had four children, a boy and three girls. My mother was the oldest daughter. She was five years younger than her brother and three to six years older than her sisters. In 1928, the year in which their youngest child was born, my grandparents lost their farm and moved from North Dakota to Everett, Washington, a small industrial city thirty miles north of Seattle. There my grandfather secured employment at the local gas works.

In 1934, my grandfather was struck and killed by a speeding automobile as he was crossing a city street. Sometime before this he had canceled his company life insurance policy, resenting it as an unnecessary deduction from his paycheck. All my grandmother received from the motorist who struck and killed her husband was an apology. This left her absolutely destitute in the midst of the Great Depression with three daughters to support. (Her son had already left home.)

In order to support her family, my grandmother worked sixteen hours a day, primarily as a tole painter creating Norwegian folk art. She also wove rugs on a large loom in her attic which she later sold. Occasionally, when there was a demand for it, she did beadwork for Norwegian folk costumes. For a while she worked as a seamstress for a welfare agency making clothes for poor people. A few years later, she worked as a house cleaner and as a cook. During these years my grandmother virtually abandoned her family, having no time to give anything but material support.

From the time my mother was eleven years old she had to single-handedly raise her two younger sisters and perform all the household chores. She never saw her mother at all except on Sundays when they had meals together. My grandmother, who was a gentle woman capable of forgiving her aunt for mistreating her, still possessed a deep bitterness concerning her tragic and wasted life. She also possessed a martyr's complex. When my mother failed to meet her responsibilities, she would castigate her by constantly reminding her of the many sacrifices she had made on behalf of the family.

My mother must have resented this. But since she loved and respected her mother so greatly and had such sympathy for her mother's plight, she could hardly be aware of any anger or hostility toward her mother without undergoing intense guilt. My mother virtually worshipped my grandmother. Yet beneath these feelings of love and respect that she had for her mother — feelings which I regard as genuine and not as mere reaction-formations — there lurked a subterranean hate, a feeling totally dissociated from my mother's awareness.

The birth of my brother and the necessity to assume the mothering role must have caused my mother's long buried feelings of resentment and hostility toward her own mother to erupt into her field of awareness with devastating results. My mother's hallucinations, strange dreams, and beliefs have their counterpart in the emotional conflicts that she was going through. The luminous white cloud that enveloped my mother was an expression of the confusion and perplexity that her emotional conflicts engendered; its crushing weight as it settled on top of her was the burden of her sense of guilt for feelings she must have felt were totally unacceptable and unnatural. Torn by conflicting emotions, she first would experience herself as being crushed by a weight on top of her, then as floating weightlessly above her bed. Her belief that she was being watched and that people were looking in her windows was merely the projection of her own feelings of guilt.

After my younger sister's birth, my mother underwent an even more serious postpartum reaction. For nine months my mother was extremely weak and depressed and would have crying spells for no apparent reason. With great effort she would climb the stairs, only to wonder, when she had reached the top, why she had done so. During this time my aunt had to raise my sister since my mother was unable to take care of her. She was afraid, in her words, that she would "drop the baby." Also during this time my mother had heart palpitations and was afraid of dying of a heart attack. The physician who examined her could find nothing organically wrong with her heart. Yet it was evident that her heart was malfunctioning and her doctor warned her that another pregnancy would undoubtedly kill her.

My mother maintains that unlike her first, her second postpartum experience had affected her only physically but not mentally. But this was simply untrue. When my sister was born I was only five years old, but even at that early age it was evident to me that something was wrong. For nine months my mother simply could not cope with raising my sister. Every afternoon she would decide that my brother and I were tired and needed a nap. She would herd us up the stairs and tell us that Arthur Godfrey would announce over the radio when we could come down. "He knows that you are up there," she would tell us, "and he will tell you when you can come down." We would go to our room and glumly sit on our beds and listen to the radio. Arthur Godfrey never got around to acknowledging our existence. I wondered why.

Once during this same period, I remember sitting at the dinner table when we were having guests over for the evening. As she was serving dinner, my mother told everyone present that the comedian Bob Hope was one of our family's oldest and dearest friends and that she was expecting him any minute now. She kept pacing from the kitchen to the dining room and nervously glancing at her watch. A strange make-believe atmosphere prevailed. Nobody seemed to regard this as the least bit out of the ordinary. Needless to say, Bob Hope was unable to make it to our home that evening.

My mother did not undergo a postpartum depression after I was born. At first, this may seem somewhat paradoxical in that it was I rather than my brother or sister who later in life encountered severe emotional difficulties. Yet the psychological conflicts engendered by the birth of my siblings must also have existed after I was born. In my brother's and sister's cases, my mother had undergone nine months of intense emotional distress, but, as a result, she had been able to work through and thoroughly resolve the conflicts attendant upon her assuming the mothering role. In my case, my mother never underwent such a catharsis. Thus, she was never able to resolve the psychological conflicts accompanying my birth, and so these conflicts continued indefinitely and this had devastating consequences as far as I was concerned.

Exactly why my mother never underwent a postpartum depression after my birth remains a mystery to me. Perhaps my birth had an altogether different meaning to my mother than that of my siblings. For instance, I had a twin who was stillborn six weeks after conception.* Possibly this or some other factor caused my mother to view my birth as having a special or sinister significance.[4]

I think that as an infant and as a small child my mere presence must have stirred up very strong and unpleasant emotions in my mother. Each time my mother confronted me she was also confronting a dark side of her own mind: thoughts and feelings of a profoundly disturbing nature. Unable (or unwilling) to claim such thoughts and feelings as her own, my mother projected them onto me and viewed me as an abnormal child. Rather than view herself as a mother who could not adequately nurture and love her child, my mother chose to view me as an abnormally cold child who rejected her love.

In 1982, upon being asked why she had me examined by the psychiatrists at the University of Washington, my mother told me she was prompted to do so for two reasons. To quote her exact words, these reasons were: "You would never let me love you," and "Other people made you ill." Since I had been hearing those two complaints for as long as I could remember, my mother's answer hardly came as a surprise!

I think I can locate the exact moment in time when the notion finally crystallized in my mother's mind that I wouldn't let her love me. One evening when I was about four and a half years old, I was in the kitchen with my parents when suddenly, feeling playful and affectionate, my mother grabbed me and started bouncing me on her knee. As my mother bounced me on her knee, she teased me by repeatedly calling me "Dubbe Dubbe." My mother's behavior infuriated me, since I believed she was

---

*Medical model fanatics will, of course, claim that all my problems stem from prenatal brain damage. However the fact remains that I was born without any physical defects and without any physical or mental disabilities.

making fun of me and treating me like a baby. (My mother constantly reminded me that "dubbe dubbe" were the first syllables I had spoken as an infant.)

However, to fully explain how I interpreted my mother's behavior, it is first necessary to relate an incident which happened about a year previous to the one just described. As my mother was dying of cancer, she told my sister the following story. One afternoon, my mother and paternal grandmother were sitting together at the kitchen table talking. The back door leading into the kitchen was open and I was sitting in the doorway with my back turned toward them, holding my knees and rocking back and forth in silent self-absorption. As I sat with my back turned toward them, light was streaming in through the doorway, and was forming what appeared to be a halo around my head. To my mother at that moment I appeared to be the image of sweetness and innocence itself. My mother smiled at my grandmother and pointed to me. My grandmother misinterpreted my mother's smile and rushed toward me, picked me up in her arms, and yelled at my mother, "Don't you dare make fun of your son!" I then fixed an accusing look upon my mother which haunted her for the rest of her life.

Now as my mother was bouncing me on her knee and calling me Dubbe Dubbe, I interpreted her behavior not as playful affection but as outright mockery. Totally enraged, I screamed at her to stop calling me Dubbe Dubbe. However, ignoring my request and my feelings as well, my mother continued calling me Dubbe Dubbe. Finally, I broke away from my mother's arms and jumped off her lap. She then made a playful lunge at me and grabbed my chest — a place where I am extremely ticklish. I tore my mother's hands off my chest and pushed them away. When my mother attempted to grab my chest again, I prevented this by slapping her hands and pushing her away.

My mother seemed fascinated by my behavior. After I prevented her from tickling me again, she called my father over to witness my behavior. Then, with my father watching, my mother again attempted to grab my chest. When I stopped her from doing this, she turned to my father and said in a voice touched with awe, "Isn't that strange!"

From that incident — and possibly from other similar incidents in which I objected to my mother's teasing and molesting behavior — the idea became fixed in my mother's mind that I was an unnaturally cold child who rejected her love. "You would never let me love you" was a favorite litany of my mother's which she endlessly repeated to me down through the years.

My mother's other reason for viewing me as an abnormal child stemmed from an incident which must have occurred sometime in 1949 when I was about four years old. This incident involved my becoming enraged for no apparent reason and chasing a boy out of the yard who wanted to play with me. From that singular event, my mother came to the bizarre conclusion that other people made me ill! I myself have no memory of that incident. Perhaps for some reason I happened to dislike that particular boy. What I do remember, however, is that like other children I did have playmates whose presence I enjoyed. I never drove my friends away — nor did my mother ever claim that I did. Yet as recently as 1982, my mother would still point to that *one* instance of my chasing away that boy as irrefutable proof that other people made me ill!

When my mother told me that other people made me ill, I understood her to mean that the entire human race, with the exception of herself, made me sick. This statement of hers conveyed simultaneously the covert suggestion that I was a defective person who was incapable of growing up and going out into the world, and a covert plea for me to never abandon her and to remain her helpless little baby for the rest of her or my life.

On a number of occasions, my mother made fully explicit her desire that I not grow up and leave her. In this regard, I remember my mother making her wishes perfectly clear to me one afternoon in the autumn of 1951, not long before she took me to the University of Washington. At that time, we were alone in the car together riding down Walnut Street in Everett, and she was telling me how certain women do not want to see their children grow up and leave home. As she was telling me this, her manner was somewhat cold and distant as it almost always was when she was speaking to me. My mother then told me that she was very much like the women she had just been telling me about: that she had always felt a certain closeness toward me and would like to keep me with her for the rest of her life and would feel very unhappy if I were to grow up and leave her. I felt very happy and flattered that my mother wanted me always to live with her, and I assured her that I would never leave her. "Are you sure about that," my mother then asked me, "because the consequences of your never leaving me might not be altogether pleasant for you." With an ardor that comes from being emotionally starved, I told my mother that I would always want to live with her, no matter what the consequences.

That I was emotionally starved was certainly the case, for although my mother undoubtedly loved me, she was, nevertheless, unable to communicate this love. I know of no incident in my childhood when my mother ever gave me her complete and undivided attention. However, for reasons I have already explained, this was not also true of the way she treated my siblings.

The following incident, which occurred when my brother was in the second grade and I was in kindergarten, epitomizes the respective ways my mother treated my brother and me. One afternoon, upon coming home from school and walking into the kitchen, my brother was happily eating a roll of multicolored candy wafers. These particular wafers were of a variety which my brother had never tasted before. After my brother greeted my mother and walked over to where she stood, he launched into a meticulous description concerning the unique taste of the candy wafers he had just eaten. As my brother spoke, my mother gazed lovingly into his face, and seemed to savor and relish his every word. I stood in the kitchen absolutely spellbound, watching this scene as if witnessing a miracle: at no time in my life had my mother ever bestowed such attention on me.

The next day in a vain attempt to duplicate this miracle, I myself purchased a package of those unique candy wafers, tasted them, and then proceeded to recite to my mother the exact magical words which had once compelled her rapt and loving attention. For this effort of mine, I received the usual treatment. My mother simply walked away. She did not even acknowledge my existence.

Such treatment by my mother had the ultimate effect of making me more dependent upon her: because my mother was never emotionally available, I needed her that much more.

# 2

# THE WITCH DOCTOR'S CURSE

It was a bleak and overcast November morning when I traveled with my mother to the University of Washington for my psychiatric examination. Of this momentous trip, which occurred in 1951 when I was in the first grade, I can still vividly remember certain details while others have receded into a gray obscurity. First of all, I remember feeling intense anxiety as I rode down the highway with my mother. I could tell by the tense and worried expression on her face, by her emotional distance and secretive air, that something was seriously wrong. Her evasive replies to my questions as to where we were going and the purpose of our trip did nothing to alleviate my fears. Then, as we arrived at our destination, I remember my mother leading me through a maze of imposing neo-Gothic buildings, down a flight of stairs and across a street into a sprawling three-story complex which somewhat resembled a penitentiary.

My next memory is one of standing outside an office at the end of a dimly lit hallway, being interrogated by a psychiatrist. This psychiatrist stood behind a lectern and appeared to be reading questions out of a book. Each time he asked me a question, he would fix upon me an impersonal but very intense and penetrating stare. He asked me a number of bizarre questions such as whether I believed that I was being poisoned, whether I thought I was being controlled by radio waves, and so forth. Being asked these kinds of questions was hardly a pleasant experience!

All day the university psychiatrists administered tests to me which were expressly designed to pinpoint some specific type of mental abnormality. They probably gave me every personality test that was then in current use. They even gave me an intelligence test — a test I was unable to complete.

I remember being alone in a room where I had been given the task of arranging different colored blocks so that they would match various preselected patterns. Although I worked at this task as best I could, I was just too upset to concentrate. Something seemed horribly *wrong*. The bizarre questions the psychiatrist had asked me kept going through my mind. As I pondered their possible implications, recollections of my mother's alarming secrecy and emotional aloofness returned to haunt me.

I looked up at the windows high above me and found they were covered with bars. An eerie light filtered down through the windows, lending the entire room an aura of oppression and gloom. While gazing up at those windows, a feeling of dread overcame me as the suspicion entered my mind that my mother might be planning to abandon me.

This wasn't the first time my mother had taken me to see a psychiatrist. About a year previously, she had done so following an incident which occurred while we were in the Everett Public Library.

While in the library I saw a man in a wheelchair with his back turned toward me. Since I had never seen a wheelchair before I thought it was a vehicle similar to a wagon or a tricycle. I walked over to the man and began to push his wheelchair.

When my mother saw what I was doing she became totally enraged. She interpreted my actions as a serious attempt to throw the man out of his wheelchair. She grabbed me and shook me violently. "I'm taking you to see a psychiatrist!" she screamed at me as she hustled me out of the library.

My mother drove all the way to Vancouver, Canada — over a hundred miles from where we lived — in order to have me examined by a psychiatrist. (That psychiatrist was probably recommended by our family doctor who had business associates in Vancouver.)

However, the psychiatrist never examined me. He must have realized that my mother had grossly overreacted and that I had had no serious intention of harming the man in the wheelchair. Moreover, in view of my age — I was only in kindergarten at that time — he probably knew I simply had no real understanding of what I had been doing. He might even have suspected that if anyone needed psychiatric help, that person was my mother.

However, things were considerably different when the university psychiatrists examined me. From the results of the tests they gave me, they came to the conclusion that I was an extremely disturbed child. Moreover, although they didn't know exactly what was wrong with me, they also concluded that I was disturbed to such an extent that I was in need of institutionalized care. They recommended to my mother that she have me placed in a special school for emotionally disturbed children located somewhere in California.

However, the annual cost of my staying at that school was two and a half times what my father earned in an entire year. Consequently, if I had to be put in an institution, that institution would had to have been a state mental hospital since that would have been the only place my parents could have afforded.

It is possible — as Theodore Lidz has suggested — that those psychiatrists might have wanted to have me institutionalized in order to protect me from being psychologically damaged by my mother.[1]

However, if this were in fact the case, then their suggestion in regard to my institutionalization had exactly the opposite of its intended effect, for in mother's eyes it seemed to lend all the authority of modern medical science to her preconceived belief that I was an abnormal child. And it was precisely this belief — and the attitudes and behavior stemming from this belief — that made my mother such a disturbing person to live with.

According to my mother, the psychiatrists told her that unless I received immediate psychiatric care I would become completely psychotic within less than a year. However, the prognostication of my becoming "completely psychotic within less than a year" probably represents one of my mother's embellishments. It is unlikely that the psychiatrists actually told her that. Still they must have told my mother something of a similar nature. They must have warned her that something terrible would happen to me unless she had me institutionalized — a warning that ultimately became a self-fulfilling prophecy.

To an extent unusual even for a small child, how I viewed myself depended upon how my mother viewed me. I remember being perpetually filled with anxiety and self-doubt because my mother never gave me the slightest indication that she had any expectation of my becoming a worthwhile and competent person. For that very reason, I was constantly asking her what kind of person she expected me to be when I grew up.

Shortly after the psychiatrists at the University of Washington recommended that I be institutionalized, I received a brutal and unwelcome reply to my questions as to what my mother expected of me. This unpleasant event happened while I was at home, standing in my back yard. My mother walked over to where I was standing, and in a hysterical and quavering voice, told me that I must not ever feel that I was under any obligation to compete with my brother, since that would be impossible. She told me, moreover, that I would never be anything remotely like my brother — and that this was perfectly satisfactory as far as she was concerned. As my mother was telling me this, she gave me a look which would have been appropriate had I been grotesquely mutilated in a car accident which had rendered me a hopeless vegetable. That look by itself had a certain eloquence which no words could possibly match. But my mother's words were fantastically destructive nonetheless. Had she set about to deliberately damage my self-esteem to such an extent that it would require the most extravagant delusions of grandeur on my part simply to look into a mirror without screaming, my mother could not have delivered a finer or more effective speech. As my mother spoke, I stood there absolutely stunned, not wanting to know or comprehend what she was telling me. From that day on, I never again asked my mother what she expected of me.

Moreover, after the university psychiatrists had made their pseudoscientific pronouncement in regard to my miserable fate, my mother conferred with Mrs. Hatch, who was my first grade teacher at Washington Elementary School in Everett. While I sat dejectedly thumbing through a comic book, my mother and my teacher discussed the wisdom and feasibility of having me locked away in a mental institution. Although I didn't fully comprehend what they were talking about, I did understand that there was supposedly something mysteriously wrong with me, and for this reason my mother was considering having me sent away. It was as if I were a piece of damaged merchandise that my mother was planning to ship back to the manufacturer.

My mother finally decided against having me committed since she realized that such a course of action would have been extremely damaging to me. However, the damage had already been done, for thereafter she never viewed or treated me as if I were a wholly sane person.

However, not only did my mother view me as if I were in imminent danger of going crazy, she was also busy poisoning my entire environment by actively proselytizing everyone around her to view me in a similar way. For example, one afternoon as I was walking home through the alley, I saw my mother talking to one of our neighbors over the backyard fence. I received the distinct impression that they were talking about me, for when I approached, my mother looked embarrassed and immediately stopped talking and went back into the house. After giving me a curious look, the woman who had been talking to my mother began to tell me a story. The story concerned a boy who had jumped off a mountain cliff and killed himself because he was under the delusion he could fly. As this woman told her story, she scrutinized me with a concerned and pitying look. She concluded her story with the comment, "There are people like that, you know," and gave me a significant look which suggested unmistakably that I was the kind of person she was talking about.

I gaped at this woman in utter astonishment. It was agonizingly apparent to me that my mother had told her that I was crazy. I turned around and walked back down the alley. I was horribly upset. As I wandered through the back alleys, vivid images raced through my mind. I imagined I was looking down from the top of a mountain. Just as I was about to fly through the air like Peter Pan, the neighbor lady grabbed me and pulled me toward her with a look on her face at once solicitous and pleading. Upon my imagining this, thousands of tiny needles seemed to be prickling me up and down my spine. In the back of my mind lurked the dreadful suspicion that I might really be crazy.

These doubts concerning the soundness of my own mind so disturbed me that for two or three nights I was unable to sleep. As I lay awake at night, incredibly vivid thoughts and images kept coursing through my mind. It seemed as though I were having the most wonderfully inspired thoughts. One such "inspired" thought involved my using a toy wrench — one of my Christmas presents — to turn on a fire hydrant and flood the street. I also vaguely remember conceiving of a plan for some kind of mechanical contrivance. What exactly this device was, I cannot now recall, but at the time I considered it a marvelous invention. During these sleepless nights the most delightful images flowed through my head. Among the images were beautiful and intricately shaped cookies of the purest and most radiant colors: violet, pink, turquoise, and blue. That I could imagine cookies of such unusual colors seemed proof to me that I was immensely clever. As puerile as these "ideas" of mine were, they nevertheless served a therapeutic purpose: they reassured me that I had a good mind. Consequently, in a few days I had calmed down to the point where I was pretty much my old self again.

The above events occurred about six weeks after undergoing my psychiatric examination at the University of Washington. At that time my father was in the Army and was stationed overseas. He had re-enlisted shortly after the outbreak of the Korean War. (Since my father was in the Army Reserves he would have been drafted anyway.) For a period of two years — from September 1950 to September 1952 — my father was away from home most of the time.

During this two year period my family moved around quite frequently. In November 1950, we moved to California where my father was temporarily stationed before he was shipped overseas. We stayed first at Santa Barbara, then at Oxnard, before returning to Everett in March 1951. Then sometime in late March 1952 — in anticipation of rejoining my father in Japan — my mother sold the house, and we moved into an apartment complex near Everett's Forest Park. We stayed at this apartment complex for about five months before moving to Japan.

To a large extent, my memories of living near Forest Park are pleasant ones. At that time Forest Park deserved its name, for the park was virtually surrounded by wilderness. I would spend hours on end happily wandering through the woods near where I lived picking huckleberries and thimbleberries, and daydreaming. Moreover, through these woods ran a brook stocked with trout. In addition to exploring the forest, I also enjoyed fishing in this stream with my brother.

In the early 1950s, Everett maintained an impressive zoo at Forest Park, not more than a quarter mile from where I lived. By taking a trail that wound through some of the most beautiful parts of the forest, I would walk to the zoo. Before this trail led out of the woods, it broadened into a straight path. On the right side of this path as one walked out of the forest were the animals: lions, tigers, leopards, hyenas, wild boars, an elephant, and other animals. This path led straight to the monkey house where there was a large collection of monkeys, apes, and birds. I especially remember the peacocks: every night before I went to sleep I heard their unearthly cries.

However, during this same period of time I also remember having some very unpleasant experiences, especially while attending school. Due to a very slight and temporary hearing impairment, I was placed in a special class consisting of twelve students in which the teacher gave each student very personalized attention. This was at Garfield Elementary School in Everett. What made going to this school so incredibly unpleasant for me was the fact that my teacher, Eliza Clark,* not only knew of the alleged psychiatric prophecy in regard to my impending psychosis, but evidently believed in it as well. It was not long before I was made acutely aware of the fact that my teacher believed I was crazy. This disturbed me to such an extent that in no time at all I was able to live up to her expectations. Therefore, in addition to teaching me how to read, write, and do arithmetic, Miss Clark also gave me very sound and practical lessons on how to become a schizophrenic. Below is an evaluation sheet written by Miss Clark, dated May 12, 1952. I view this document as a sort of Schizo Progress Report:

John Modrow

*Diagnosis*: Great emotional disturbance of mixed origin. Great insecurity and fear of failure present. Need to strike out at people and withdraw from them obvious. Hearing loss small.

*Social Evaluation*: Greatly disturbed child. Alternately strikes out at everyone and withdraws completely from group. Wants to make friends seemingly, but unable to successfully [sic] approach children.

*Emotional Evaluation*: John is under observation at the U. of W. Psychiatric Clinic at this time.†

*Speech*: Negative. Voice weak when addressing group... fear of being heard and of drawing criticism???

*Physical*: Appears frail. Poor appetite reported. Fatigues easily.

---

*Not her real name.

†I had been under psychiatric observation for one day only, and that was back in either late November or early December, 1951. In Miss Clark's mind, it was probably inconceivable that someone as supposedly "disturbed" as myself would not be under some sort of continual psychiatric observation or care.

Seldom appears happy... Looks worried and tired most of the time.

*Goal*: To provide acedemic [sic] work on his present level for goo [sic] success to build self-confidence. To provide small group cooperative activities. To provide some auditory and speech reading training.

*Home Cooperation*: Good. Mother requested school help concerning John's deviate [sic] behavior at home and at school. Was referred to the U. of W.

*Progress*: Some progress in identifying at times with the small group. Behavior swings from aggressive to great withdrawal... appears to be less of a swing to either extreme. Reading number work good.

*Remarks*: John needs expert psychiatric care. He should be placed in a slow-paced small group for successful work and chance to work thru inter-personal problems in group relationships. Hearing loss is slight, but should be checked periodically.

However, to fully appreciate what wonderful progress I had made in becoming a schizophrenic, it is necessary to compare the above document to one written eleven months earlier. On June 8, 1951, Lessie Baker, my kindergarten teacher at Washington Elementary School in Everett, wrote the following comments on the back of my report card:

John is obedient and courteous. He does not always listen, and follow given directions. John is slow to accomplish his work. John enjoys his friends, and gets along well in the group.

John was away from the group from Nov. 16, 1950 until March 12, 1951. This made it difficult for John to be aware of the continuity of our work.

Within less than one year I was transformed from an "obedient and courteous" boy who "enjoys his friends and gets along well in the group" to a "greatly disturbed child" who is "unable to success[ful]ly approach children" and who "alternately strikes out at everyone and withdraws completely from [the] group." How do we explain this sudden and dramatic metamorphosis? Although it is undeniable that I had undergone some significant change during this brief period of time, I nevertheless think that about 90 percent of this apparent change was due to the respective ways in which I was viewed and treated by these two different teachers. Because Miss Baker, my kindergarten teacher, knew me before the university psychiatrists had examined me and pronounced their dire verdict, she had no reason whatsoever to view or treat me as if I were anything other than a normal, well-adjusted child. Consequently, I got along just fine with both Miss Baker and my fellow classmates. My relations with Miss Clark were another thing altogether. I found Miss Clark's mental attitude and way of dealing with me both infuriating and deeply alienating.

However, it wasn't just Miss Clark who was at fault — or even the misconceptions or preconceived ideas she got from my mother or the university psychiatrists, which were the source of her inhuman attitude toward me — but rather the entire situation in which I found myself. For reasons which I hope to have made clear, I was, generally speaking, a somewhat less self-confident boy in the first grade than I had been in kindergarten. This, together with the fact that I had moved around a lot while I was in the first grade and kindergarten, made it difficult for me to form friendships with other students. Moreover, in addition to being a very quiet and solitary boy, I also appeared to be physically frail. But to appear physically weak and socially isolated is almost a sure way to attract the attention of bullies.

So it was in my case. One day as soon as the teacher left the room, a husky boy confronted me and called me a "weirdo." He then attempted to twist my arm behind my back. But unfortunately for him, I was considerably stronger than I looked. In no time at all, I had this boy in a full nelson. Soon this "tough guy" was whimpering like a baby.

I told that boy that I would release him on the condition that he would leave me alone. He meekly assented. Then, with his eyes still moist with tears, he found Miss Clark and told her that I had picked a fight with him.

Miss Clark's eyes flashed with indignation over what I had done to that poor inept bully. She was in no mood to listen to what I had to say when I tried to explain what had happened. Turning her back on me, Miss Clark explained to my assailant that I wasn't in my right mind and that such behavior was only to be expected of me. She then told him to take me up to the principal and tell him what I had done.

I was too stunned to do anything other than submit to that degrading ordeal.

This exquisitely subtle lesson in the art of human relationships was not lost on my adversary. He now knew that he could make the most unfounded and whimsical accusations against me and be instantly believed. So a few days after the above incident, for no apparent reason he left his desk, walked up to the teacher, and whispered something in her ear. Although I had no idea what he told Miss Clark, I could tell by the outraged expression on her face that it must have been a whopper. Again Miss Clark delegated to that sane and responsible student the duty of escorting me to the principal's office.

However, this time I wasn't in a submissive mood. When that liar approached me, I smashed him in the face and sent him reeling. As several students attempted to subdue me, I exploded in an ecstasy of rage and attacked everyone who came near me — throwing chairs and overturning tables in the process.

Finally, the teacher grabbed me and held me long enough to enable two students to get a firm grip on each of my arms. Miss Clark then ordered those boys to take me to the principal.

I struggled with them all the way to the principal's office. I was panic-stricken. It seemed as though everyone had suddenly ganged up on me.

The hallway down which those boys were leading me had handrails running the entire length of its sides. Every few feet I would make a desperate lunge at one of those handrails and hold on to it tenaciously. Repeatedly, the boys would have to pry my hands from the handrail and continue leading me — sometimes even dragging me — down the hall. They had to virtually carry me up a flight of stairs. It probably took them close to twenty minutes to get me to the principal's office.

Fortunately, the principal never spoke to me or betrayed the slightest interest in me whatsoever. When I entered his office, the principal gave me a quick glance and beckoned me to sit in a chair. Finally, when he felt that I had calmed down sufficiently to re-enter my class, he gave me a signal that I could leave.

I remember going to the principal's office only twice. This was due to the fact that I was able to intimidate my enemy to such an extent that he left me alone and stopped telling lies about me. Consequently, as Miss Clark has noted, my behavior swings from aggression to great withdrawal tended to become less extreme.

By and large, Miss Clark treated her pupils as if they were miniature adults. For instance, as I have already mentioned, she would delegate to her pupils the responsibility of taking me to the principal's office. However, in Miss Clark's mind there must have existed a sharp dichotomy between me and the rest of her students. By countless nonverbal cues, Miss Clark gave me the distinct impression that she did not consider me a sane or responsible person. Whenever she spoke to me she always had a certain condescending air. It was as if I really weren't a student at all, but rather some student's kid brother who had wandered into the classroom and was merely being tolerated.

Furthermore, although it was painfully evident to me that I had been placed in Miss Clark's class because there was supposed to be something wrong with me, it had never been adequately explained to me just what this "something" was. I thought I could hear perfectly. From the way Miss Clark treated me, I began to suspect that I had been placed in her class because there was something mentally wrong with me.

This suspicion seemed confirmed by the mere presence of a classmate whom I considered exceedingly odd and repulsive. This student was a pathetic girl who always had two rivers of snot oozing from her nose. She also had a severe speech impediment, possibly due to cerebral palsy. To my utter mortification, whenever she saw me, she would emit a joyful but weird sound and rush up to me and begin hugging me. No matter how much I tried to discourage her, she always insisted on sitting next to me. Deep down I harbored a fear that possibly this girl instinctively recognized that she and I were "two of a kind."

In short, I hated every moment I spent in Miss Clark's class. It was impossible for me to walk into her classroom without feeling humiliated. Moreover, my internal state can easily be inferred from the physical description Miss Clark had furnished of me:

Poor appetite reported. Fatigues easily. Seldom appears happy...
Looks worried and tired most of the time.

This description is typical of anyone who has undergone stress over a prolonged period of time. What these stresses were in my case has already been described.

In conclusion, one final clarification needs to be made. Miss Clark alludes to my mother requesting school help due to my alleged "devia[nt] behavior at home and at school." I have already explained what my so-called deviant behavior at home consisted of: namely, my mother's belief that I wouldn't let her love me and that other people made me ill. But what did my deviant school behavior consist of? This is a very interesting question which merits a long and detailed reply.

My troubles at school began one afternoon as I was walking with my brother and several of his friends. We were walking somewhere in our neighborhood when suddenly we were confronted with a gang of boys approximately my brother's age. My brother and his friends seemed terrified and immediately adopted a meek and submissive posture by sitting down on the grass.

However, with my brother and his friends present, I saw no cause for alarm. After all, we weren't outnumbered. Therefore, with the intention of rallying my brother and his friends behind me, I walked up to the leader of the gang — a wiry boy whose reddish-brown hair was trimmed into a butch — and demanded that he leave us alone. But my brother and his friends wouldn't budge. To my chagrin, my behavior only intensified their alarm. For several seconds everyone present glowered at me menacingly.

Seeing that I was now thoroughly intimidated, the boy to whom I spoke seemed somewhat satisfied. Before he left, he told me that someday when my friends weren't by my side, he would be seeing me again.

The next morning as I was walking to school, I noticed I was being followed by the same group of boys whom I had encountered the previous day. Since I was with other children, as was usually the case when I walked to school, they followed me from a discreet distance and had to content themselves with merely making threats.

But because I always walked home alone, those boys had ample opportunity to seriously menace me.

My brother refused to protect me. According to him, I was a "jerk" who probably deserved what he got.

Each day as I walked home from school, three boys always pursued me. Although this trio was invariably led by the boy with the reddish-brown hair, his assistants weren't always the same.

Of course, being menaced by those boys caused me a considerable amount of anxiety. Yet strangely enough, as time passed, I almost grew to like being chased by them: it became a sort of game of hide-and-seek with me. Somehow I always managed to elude my enemies by taking a different route home from school every few days.

Yet no matter which route I took home from school, they would always be waiting for me in the alley behind my home. By then, however, it was too late for them to risk harming me since I was too close to home. When my enemies appeared in the alley, I would experience a rush of vindictive pleasure, for then it would be my turn to harass them. I enjoyed taunting my enemies. Sometimes I would hurl rocks at them as well as insults. Once I managed to hit a boy in the kneecap with a large rock. As this boy writhed on the ground in agony, I showered him with insults, calling him, among other things, a crybaby, a weakling, a coward, and a sissy.

I had a unique method of taunting my enemies which never failed to drive them crazy. While facing my enemies and bending slightly toward them, I would clasp my right wrist in the palm of my left hand. Then raising my right hand up to my right eye and pointing my index finger at them as if I were sighting a rifle, I would rotate my index finger clockwise and sing, "nor nor, nor nor, nor nor, nor" to the tune of "Twinkle Twinkle Little Star." When I did this my enemies would literally jump up and down with rage and look as though they wanted to tear me limb from limb.

But my enemies were serious about wanting to cause me bodily harm. Since I was able to elude them until I was virtually in my own back yard, my would-be assailants decided to adopt a more direct tactic. Therefore, one afternoon just as school was letting out, they came barging into my classroom. Except for a few straggling students, the room was virtually empty. As soon as I saw those boys rush into the room, I charged them and began frantically hitting and kicking them. Because they had not expected such aggressive behavior from me, they were momentarily stunned, allowing me enough time to run out into the hallway and seek help.

I stopped a teacher, pointed at the boys, and told him that they were trying to hurt me. While the teacher stood nonplused, the boys scattered.

That intrusive incident was more than I could cope with. In desperation, I decided to talk to Mr. Lange, the principal of the school. However, I didn't know the names of the boys who were harassing me, and after listening to my story, Mr. Lange told me that he would be unable to help me until I furnished their names. I knew Mr. Lange would say this. Nevertheless, I continued to insist that he do something for me immediately because I felt that I was in grave danger.

For a while, Mr. Lange pondered what I told him with a troubled expression on his face. Then he brightened. "I could arrange for a girl to walk home with you," he told me, "that way they wouldn't dare try to harm you."

A *girl* walk home with me! The very idea was appalling — an affront to my macho pride. What would my enemies think of me if I did such a thing? Wouldn't they jeer at me and call me a sissy? That would be unbearable! In the last few weeks I had grown to have a peculiarly intimate relationship with my enemies. It mattered a great deal to me what they thought of me. I would rather they beat me to a bloody pulp then have them think that I was the sort of person who would hide behind a girl's skirt.

I flatly refused to have a girl walk home with me. Furthermore, I was unable to offer any reason for my refusal. The principal's suggestion had thrown me into such a state of consternation that I was totally incapable of articulating my feelings.

At first it appeared that Mr. Lange was unable to believe or fully understand what I had just told him. When my meaning finally became clear to him, I must have been transformed in his eyes from a harassed little boy to some kind of lunatic, for he gave me a look of naked hostility and ordered me to leave his office at once.

This, then, constituted my "deviant behavior" at school.

Sometime shortly after my leaving the principal's office, Mr. Lange called my mother and told her he had been having problems with me at school. He felt that there might be something mentally wrong with me. My mother wholeheartedly agreed. She asked Mr. Lange to recommend a place were I could undergo a psychiatric evaluation. Mr. Lange recommended that she take me to the University of Washington Psychiatric Clinic.

In this way, I was delivered into the hands of a far more sinister group of bullies than the ones who were already menacing me.

That one visit to the University of Washington Psychiatric Clinic probably damaged me more than any other event in my entire life. Although I could never remember myself as having been a very happy person, nevertheless, before the university psychiatrists had examined me, I had possessed a positive self-image: I had liked myself, and as a consequence, I expected acceptance from other people. Within less than a year after my psychiatric molestation, I had already begun to view myself as being an abnormal person.

However, if one views oneself as abnormal, one will have a tendency to act that way.

The two following series of events, which occurred while I was still living near Forest Park in Everett, illustrate how my increasingly blighted self-image affected my behavior. The first events are of a rather trivial nature. I recount them here mainly because they shed light on the significance of the second set of events — a chain of events concluded by an incident which I regard as a sort of dress rehearsal for my schizophrenic episode eight years later.

One peaceful day, as I was walking along the street in front of the apartment where I lived, I was approached by a boy approximately a year younger than myself. When he saw who I was, he suddenly became terrified and fled.

This happened repeatedly. Since the boy was a complete stranger to me, I was totally baffled by his behavior.

However, many years later, his behavior no longer seems so strange to me. The most probable explanation for his behavior is as follows. I was a member of a gang of boys who continually clashed with another gang over who would occupy an abandoned house. I supported my gang in battle by throwing so-called "dust bombs." A dust bomb is nothing more than dust wrapped in a piece of newspaper. Upon impact the dust bomb seems to explode, creating a dense cloud of dust which momentarily blinds the opponent. Apparently, the boy in question was struck by one of my dust bombs. He must have mistakenly concluded that I had some kind of personal animosity toward him, when, on the contrary, he was nothing to me but a faceless target.

As time passed by, that boy's fearful behavior began to amuse me. Whenever I saw him coming I would hide behind a bush or a telephone pole, then like a toy erupting from a jack-in-the-box, I would spring out at him and proclaim, "I am the bogeyman!" His reaction never failed to delight me. He would always burst into tears and run down the street screaming and crying.

I almost began to believe that I really was the bogeyman.

Once, upon seeing that boy coming my way, I was seized with a sudden compulsion to do something bizarre. I rushed into my apartment in search of a surrealistically inappropriate weapon with which to menace him. At first, I thought of hitting him over the head with an umbrella, but I soon rejected the idea since an umbrella could realistically be considered a weapon. In my frantic search I opened the refrigerator. When my eyes lit upon a cold wiener lying on a dish, I knew I had found the ideal weapon. I found the idea of hitting the boy over the head with a wiener simply irresistible because it seemed like such a weird thing to do. I therefore ran out of the apartment and broke the wiener over the boy's head.

After assaulting the boy with the wiener, the thought occurred to me that my action had been more mean than weird. Feeling somewhat ashamed of myself, I decided to leave the boy alone. However, more than ever, I yearned to do something *really* weird.

Not long after the wiener incident, my mother began to harass me. "All normal boys," she declared, "have hobbies. Why don't you have one?"

That question was more like an accusation than a question. Not only did the question answer itself, it suggested another question as well: if one is abnormal, then why act otherwise? Partly as a result of my mother's suggestion, I decided to take up a hobby of my own. But rather than adopting a "normal" hobby such as collecting bottle caps or stamps, I chose to collect my own turds. My turd collection wasn't very extensive — only two turds. Yet for my purposes two turds were enough; for as much as I liked my own turds, what really thrilled me was the *concept* of collecting turds.

I went into the bathroom and shat a large and perfectly formed turd into my hand. While savoring its warmth and rich aroma, I wrapped the turd in toilet paper and stuck it in my coat pocket. After washing my hands, I smuggled the turd out of the apartment. I then hid the turd behind a bush near our apartment's front entrance.

The next day after smuggling a second turd out of the apartment, I retrieved the first turd and headed toward a clump of trees near the edge of the forest. Upon arriving at my destination, I unwrapped the turds and plopped them into a discarded paint can. I urinated into the paint can and stirred the noisome mess with a stick. I then began to add other ingredients: red and black ants, a centipede, crushed leaves including nettles, dirt of different colors and textures, bits of rotten wood, termites, and a dead snake, making a "witches' brew" a la Macbeth.

Of course, I was aware of the fact that rather than going through all the trouble of smuggling turds out of the apartment, it would have been much easier and safer had I defecated directly into the paint can. But I felt that that would have been a grossly utilitarian act which would have eliminated all the adventure and fun. Besides, such behavior would have been almost normal, and thus beneath a true wizard.

As I was happily stirring my witches' brew, a boy who was an acquaintance of mine found me at my hide-out and asked me what was in the paint can. When I told him the ingredients he seemed delighted. He immediately dipped the stick he was carrying into the paint can and declared that he was going to touch a girl with the end of his stick. Before I could stop him, he took off after the girl.

I sensed that trouble was coming. And I was right. My witches' brew turned out to be a truly evil concoction. The poison from the crushed centipede, ants, and nettles caused a terrible rash to break out of the girl's forearm where the boy had touched her with his stick. Therefore, as a result of my sorcery, I became the victim of a literal witch hunt.

Yet it wasn't until a few days later, after I had nearly forgotten about the incident involving the paint can, that calamity finally struck. I was absent-mindedly strolling through a playground when I heard someone cry, *there he is!* and saw a motley group of about a dozen seemingly enraged and morally indignant children charging straight at me. This threw me into an instant panic. Those children looked as though they were going to tear me apart. As I fled in terror, I heard someone shrieking about my causing a horrible rash to break out on the girl's arm.

With the vigilantes still on my trail, I dashed down the hallway leading to my apartment. When I reached my apartment door, I was overcome with shame at the prospect of having to face my mother when the children came knocking at our door and telling their story. Feeling trapped between the condemnation of my mother and the fury of the onrushing mob, I adopted what seemed to be the only expedient.

Immediately across the hallway from our apartment, there was a small hinged door approximately two feet square which led down under the apartment building. I climbed down through this subterranean exit until my feet rested on the dirt beneath the building. I then waited fearfully in semidarkness, holding the door open a crack in order to keep my apartment door under surveillance.

Within seconds after I had hidden myself, the children came swarming past me and headed toward my apartment door. I heard somebody knock. My mother opened the door. Although it was apparent that someone was talking to my mother, I could hear nothing at all. After approximately a minute and a half, my mother closed the door and the children left.

When I was sure that all the children had left, I climbed out of my hiding place and hesitantly approached my apartment door. I lingered outside the door for close to a minute before I was able to steel myself sufficiently to enter the apartment and face my mother. Upon entering the apartment I found my mother standing in the living room with her back partially turned toward me, apparently deep in thought. Suddenly aware of my presence, she whirled around and gave me a look of intense loathing mixed with fear. She solemnly informed me that the children had just told her what I had done. My mother's voice quavered a little as she told me this. She continued looking at me with a gaze growing more intense and severe until at last it melted into a despairing helplessness.

Then, pulling herself together, my mother told me to sit down, that she had something to say to me. When we were seated my mother gravely told me, "They have people put away in mental institutions for doing things like that." Fear was written all over my mother's face as she told me this. Finally my mother dismissed me with the words, "Don't you ever do anything like that again." As my mother told me this there was a tone of hate in her voice which I had never heard before.

I left the apartment in a delirium of fear with the threat of my possible commitment still ringing in my ears. I headed toward my hideout near the edge of the forest, and found that it no longer felt like a refuge from the eyes of the world. I had an ominous feeling that someone was watching me. As this feeling took possession of me, I gazed off into the horizon and saw in my mind's eye a terrifyingly evil and powerful sorcerer looking down from a mountaintop high above the clouds. From far away, this sorcerer's eyes peered through the clouds like demonic searchlights, looking for me. When at last he saw me, I was transfixed with terror.

# 3

# FATHER

My father once said that children should be put into pickle barrels soon after they're born and placed in a deepfreeze; only after becoming adults twenty years later should they be taken out of the deepfreeze and thawed out. As facetious as my father's remark was, it accurately reflected his attitude toward children. My father never wanted children.

Yet, when one considers how he was raised, it is a wonder that he was as decent a father as he actually was.

My paternal grandparents met and were married in Andernach, Germany, in 1920. At that time my grandfather was in the Army serving as an interpreter for the American forces who were still occupying Germany. My grandmother was the youngest daughter of a German industrial mechanic. When my grandfather met my grandmother, she was working as a waitress in a restaurant owned and operated by one of her older sisters — a restaurant which catered to American servicemen.

My grandmother's father at first did not approve of the marriage. He told my grandfather that he would prefer that he marry one of his older daughters. After all, my grandfather had been married before and had a daughter, while my grandmother was a naive seventeen-year-old girl who had never had a boyfriend and who had never dated. Nevertheless, my grandfather was able to convince the old man that he would take good care of his daughter, and they were soon married.

My grandparents settled in the United States shortly after they were married. My grandfather worked for the Great Northern Railroad for about two years. Then, in late 1922, when my father was about a year old, my grandfather suddenly deserted his family and re-enlisted in the Army using an alias.

No one in our family knows for sure why my grandfather deserted his family. After all, my grandparents never quarrelled. The best guess is that my grandfather was trying to escape his domineering, sociopathic mother whom he greatly feared.

After my grandfather deserted her, my grandmother had a very difficult time supporting herself and my father. In the fall she worked in the fruit canneries in Everett, peeling and coring apples and pears. At other times she worked for wealthy individuals, frequently living in their homes as a domestic servant. My grandmother often found this kind of work extremely unpleasant. Her employers were frequently arrogant and domineering, and after an especially humiliating incident, she would simply announce that she was quitting and would walk out. Then, having no other place to go, she would seek shelter under her mother-in-law's roof.

My great-grandmother — or "Old Gram" as my family called her — was fond of having other people come and live with her. But Gram always demanded the total wages of anyone she took into her home, and my grandmother was certainly no exception.

Gram took care of and raised my grandfather's daughter whom he had fathered in an earlier marriage. (My grandfather's first wife died of influenza in 1918.) However, when my grandfather returned from the war, Gram presented him with an enormous bill for all the many services which she had rendered his daughter.

Gram grudgingly took my father into her home whenever one of my grandmother's employers refused to let him stay where his mother lived and worked. This was never a pleasant experience for my father. Once, when my grandmother was out of town, Gram threatened my father by telling him that she was going to have him put away in an orphanage.

Throughout most of his childhood my father never had a home in any meaningful sense. He was constantly being shuffled from house to house. He could never be sure for more than a day at a time where he was going to sleep.

But my father also had problems of a more serious nature. He was a severely neglected child. My grandmother — a rather cold woman who was very limited in her ability to express affection — was just too busy to care for him adequately.

In 1926 my grandmother moved to Hoboken, New Jersey, to live with one of her sisters. Her sister lived above a laundry which she managed. While in Hoboken my grandmother worked in a bakery and my father attended kindergarten. My grandmother stayed in Hoboken for a year, then moved back to Everett.

In 1929 my grandmother moved to Hoboken for a second time. This time she lived, together with my father, with a violin instructor who employed her as his domestic servant.

In early 1931, while my grandmother was still in Hoboken, Gram wrote to the Red Cross requesting information concerning her son. My grandfather had been missing for over eight years. Gram wished to have him declared legally dead so she could collect his army insurance. The Army had either to find my grandfather or pay out the insurance money. The Army found him and notified my grandmother in Hoboken.

In the spring of 1931, my grandfather rejoined his family in Hoboken. He offered my grandmother no explanations or apologies for deserting her. (Indeed, toward the end of his life, he told my grandmother he had no regrets at all for what he had done — that the eight years he had been away from her were the happiest years of his life!)

However, upon returning to Everett shortly after rejoining his family, my grandfather's happy years came to an abrupt end. There he, along with the rest of his family, moved in with — of all people — Gram!

My grandfather was fortunate in landing a job at the Scott Paper Company soon after his return to Everett. But his luck didn't last long. When payday arrived, Gram showed up at the company office to claim my grandfather's paycheck. Since it was company policy not to employ anyone whose wages had been garnished, my grandfather lost his job.

After losing his job at the Scott Paper Company my grandfather nearly starved. To put food on the table he grew vegetables in his garden, fished, baked bread from flour that had been given away, and did various odd jobs. After a while he started working for the Work Projects Administration (WPA), installing street pipes for the city. He began as a laborer on a part time basis, but he soon became a foreman. A few years later he went to work for the city street department — a job he stayed with until he retired.

For years my grandfather continued to live in his mother's home. As payment for this, she demanded that my grandfather sign over his paychecks to her — which he did. Like a child my grandfather had to abjectly beg his mother for money so he and my grandmother could go out and see a movie. Finding this intolerable, my grandmother finally persuaded my grandfather to find a home of their own.

In 1931, shortly after returning to Everett with his father, my father obtained a job as a paper boy. He was ten years old at the time. According to my grandparents, there were times when they would have to stand on the street corner and wait for my father to be paid before they could buy a loaf of bread. However, even when my grandfather's financial position had improved, he still continued to confiscate every cent my father made — just as Gram took every cent he made.

Once, when he was about twelve years old, my father saved fifty cents from his earnings to buy a leather belt which held .22 cartridges. In his spare time my father would go to the city dump and shoot rats with his pistol. With his fancy leather belt, my father thought he could do this in style. My grandfather thought otherwise. In a stern lecture he told my father that he had no right to waste money on such frivolities. He took my father's belt back to the store, and used the refund to treat himself and my grandmother to a movie.

My father held my grandfather in utter contempt — considering him among other things, "a pathological liar." However, my grandfather's lies were mostly of a trivial nature. For instance, my grandfather loved to embellish upon the stories that he told. He would often pretend that he was more knowledgeable than he actually was. And though my grandfather was a well-intentioned man, he seldom kept his promises. All these things exasperated my father.

My grandfather was deeply hurt by the fact that my father didn't look up to him or confide in him. But what most disturbed my grandfather was my father's propensity for mischief. For instance, my father once scuttled a barge by opening a valve and flooding the bilge with water. My father had no other motive for doing this than curiosity as to how long it would take the barge to sink. Another similar incidence occurred when my father saw a police car parked on a hill. He released the emergency brake and watched the car careen down the hill and smash into the side of a building.

Relations between my father and grandfather were never amiable. In 1938, after an especially bitter argument in which my grandfather refused to let my father use the car, my father ran away from home.

My father went to Astoria, Oregon, where he lived with a friend. It was my father's plan to support himself by working with his friend distributing newspapers.

However, my father's venture turned out to be a complete fiasco, for he and his friend were arrested by the police and charged with auto theft. (My father's friend stole a sheriff's car, and my father was charged as an accessory.)

The authorities notified my grandparents in Everett and they drove down to Oregon to attend the trial. Due to the fact that he didn't actually steal the car and was only a minor, my father received a one-month suspended sentence in which he was ordered to do community service. When a month had passed, my grandparents drove back down to Oregon and took my father home.

About two or three weeks after he returned from Oregon, my father decided to enlist in the Army because he felt he could no longer live at home. Since he was only seventeen at the time, he had to lie about his age in order to enter the Army.

My father saw no other alternative but to join the Army. He was intensely miserable living at home. Yet he was incapable of becoming economically independent due to the Great Depression and the fact that he had no marketable skills. Besides, he was failing in school owing to his chronic truancy and refusal to study.

Despite the fact that my father never liked the Army, he was an excellent soldier who impressed his superiors with his high intelligence. After my father had been in the Army for nearly four years, his commanding officer persuaded him to attend Officer's Candidate School and become an officer.

About a year prior to becoming an officer, my father wrote a letter to my mother proposing marriage. My father had met my mother, and seen her on a daily basis, when he was a paper boy. He became romantically involved with my mother while he was attending high school with her; and after joining the Army, he saw her as often as he could.

A few months prior to receiving my father's proposal, my mother had moved to San Francisco in order to escape marrying a man whom she considered too domineering. My mother had jilted this man a mere few hours before she was scheduled to marry him.

When she received my father's letter, she gladly accepted his proposal. My parents married in December 1941.

At the time he was married, my father had been out of the Army for three months and was working as a cashier at a Safeway in Everett. At that time he was also in the Army Reserves.

In April 1942, my father was inducted back into the Army and sent to Camp Hood, Texas, where he served as a training officer.

A few days before Christmas in 1942, my father and his fellow junior officers stood at attention before a colonel who enjoyed hectoring his troops. This colonel was a strange little man who always carried a riding whip in his hand. While two burly military policemen stood behind him, the colonel ordered his troops to make a contribution to charity. Then, slapping his whip into the palm of his hand to lend emphasis to his words, the colonel added menacingly, "and you *will* make that contribution, too."

Had the colonel merely asked my father to make a charitable contribution, he would have complied. But my father strongly objected to the colonel's attempt to intimidate him, so he flatly refused.

As a result, my father spent Christmas in the stockade.

He left the Army toward the end of 1945 with no intention of ever coming back. Yet he still retained membership in the Army Reserves. He probably did so out of consideration for my mother who loved being an officer's wife.

Upon returning to Everett in early 1946, my father drove an oil truck for the American Distributing Company. My earliest memories of my father date from this period of time.

Although he was not without a certain warmth, I remember my father as a rather stern man who related to my brother and myself as if we were a couple of army cadets. It was probably very difficult for my father to relate to us children in any other way. For this reason my father hardly interacted with my sister at all — for the most part, he simply ignored her. (My mother had to constantly explain to my sister that her father really loved her, but was unable to show it.)

As a small child, I was constantly running afoul of my father for some reason or other. For instance, once I was caught teasing my mother's old Scottish terrier by poking her with a stick as she crouched under the wood stove in the kitchen. A couple of times I was caught teasing my sister by twirling my finger at her and singing my nor-nor song. But my most usual offense was simply forgetting to do what I was told due to my chronic absent-mindedness and daydreaming.

At times when I had committed some petty offense, my father would gravely announce that he wanted to see me upstairs after dinner. Like a monarch seated upon a throne, my father would always be sitting on the toilet in the bathroom waiting for me. When I walked into the bathroom he always asked me why I deserved a spanking. I would then have to give a full confession of my sins or else risk an even more severe beating.

On a night in which I was going to be spanked, my brother was commiserating with me in the hallway outside the bathroom. Suddenly he had a brilliant inspiration. While my father was still waiting for me in the bathroom, my brother advised me to put on two or three additional pair of pants. After I had donned these extra layers of clothing, my brother stuffed my jeans with rolls of comic books and tied the bottom of my pant legs with cords to prevent the comic books from falling out.

Then, while clad in my protective armor, I waddled stiff-leggedly into the bathroom and confronted my father. Evidently, my father was amused, for I escaped a beating that night.

Unlike my mother, my father never discussed either his past or his most intimate feelings with me. However, one thing I have always understood about my father is that throughout most of his adult life he suffered from a deep sense of inadequacy due to his never finishing high school. This fact especially preyed upon my father's mind immediately prior to my schizophrenic episode.

Sometime in the late 1940s my father took up flying as a hobby, even going so far as to earn his instructor's license. He once told my mother that he considered learning how to fly an essential part of his education — which is to say, my father learned to fly because it increased his self-esteem and sense of competence as a human being.

My father often took my brother and me flying. However, the first time he took us flying he was somewhat disgusted by our behavior: we seemed more interested in the dials and gauges on the dashboard than in the experience of flying itself.

Once, when I was about five years old, my father took me with him on his rounds while he drove the oil truck. As he was filling the truck with oil near an industrial section of the Everett waterfront, I gazed upward in astonishment at the complex network of pipes spanning the oil tank and truck. All about me loomed a bewildering world of machinery and men at work.

For some time after the above incident, I had a recurring dream in which I floundered about in a sea of burning oil. I was always somewhere in the bay between a pier and an oil tanker. As I struggled to free myself from the flaming oil-laden water, I would become entangled in an arabesque of pipes stretching from the ship to the shore. Like metallic arms, these pipes would hold me down deep within the burning inferno.

Upon awakening from such dreams, I would lie awake during the night brooding. At a very early age it was apparent to me that life offered little more than an endless round of meaningless and deadening toil. I yearned to somehow break free from society and become a contemplative hermit. I desired to be anything — a drifter, a hobo, a tramp — anything but a functioning member of society.

In September 1950, my father re-entered the Army and was shipped overseas. He was stationed in Japan throughout most of the Korean War — serving in the artillery and receiving his field commission as a captain in June 1952, while on active combat duty in Korea.

While my father was overseas, he wrote home almost every day, and my mother has saved every one of his letters.

In one letter postmarked December 3, 1951, my father wrote:

Glad to hear John may get a chance to get looked at down at the U. of Wash. Would be nice to get it straight just what is the matter with him if anything!

However, in his next letter, my father seemed horribly distressed, for he had just received news he was being sent to Korea. In the letters which followed, it was obvious that my mother was shielding my father from what the university psychiatrists had told her, since he was suggesting she take me to a military hospital due to her being given the "run around" at the University of Washington.

When my father finally arrived in Korea in late January 1952, he wasn't immediately sent into combat; as a consequence, his life continued pretty much as usual. Then in late May — probably just after the unfortunate incident involving the paint can — my father finally received word of my impending psychosis. My mother apparently broke the news gradually, for on May 27, my father wrote:

Not much to write about honey! I've been waiting for an answer from you for 4 days. You said you took John to the U. I gather you would get the results etc. Now no letter!

Then on May 28:

I received your letter honey about John. I didn't know what to say for awhile — what to do, completely at a loss...I believe now knowing our problems we will be able to solve them in time if we try very hard. You will need the rest and relaxation too just as much as John. If you can be made happy, secure and relaxed John will go along with the group as a member of a happy family. Honey I so much wish I could have a long talk with you...

My father must have been pulled into combat almost immediately after writing those lines, for that was the last letter he wrote to my mother until after he left Korea in August 1952.

Upon moving to Japan in September 1952, I found my father somewhat better natured and more tolerant than usual. By that time he had pretty much reconciled himself to being in the Army. His plan was to stay in the Army just long enough to retire as a captain.

When I was at Camp Haugens, in Japan, a friend and I broke into a paint shed and proceeded to paint the army barracks with splotches of red, orange, blue, and green paint. The military authorities launched an investigation which was immediately quashed when it was learned that my partner-in-crime was the colonel's son.

My father's attitude toward this incident was fairly typical of him. With a broad smile on his face, my father told me: "You certainly picked the right friend to play with. You just keep playing with this friend of yours, and you'll never get into trouble."

Up until I was nine years old, my father never gave me the slightest indication that he regarded me as anything more than a perfectly normal boy. However, as he was increasingly beset by worries and onerous responsibilities, he began to project or focus his anxieties onto me. The more insecure he felt, the more obsessed he became with the idea of my impending psychosis.

**4**

## THE VOODOO CURSE CONTINUES
## AND IS TEMPORARILY DISPELLED

In September 1953, we moved back to the United States. For two months we stayed at a motel on North Broadway in Everett while my father awaited further orders from the Army. Then, in November, my father was stationed at Fort Lewis, Washington, where he resumed his military duties.

We moved to Fort Lewis on Thanksgiving day and ate dinner at an army mess hall where my father presided as officer of the day.

We were assigned quarters on the top floor of a two-story wooden barracks which housed three other families. This building was identical to innumerable other dilapidated wooden structures which made up a large section of Fort Lewis sometimes referred to as "Splinterville."

Upon assuming his duties at Fort Lewis, my father suddenly seemed to change. At first he seemed merely worried and tense. Later, he became increasingly withdrawn and severe: he began to act more like my commanding officer than my father. For instance, one afternoon as I was sitting on the couch absorbed in my own thoughts, my father advanced menacingly toward me and barked, "*Snap out of it!* If you were an adult and were to walk into a tavern with an expression like that on your face, you would get yourself killed." I had never known him to act this way before.

Another especially memorable instance of this sort — one which I have already mentioned — occurred shortly before Christmas when I was nine years old. I was sitting under the Christmas tree eagerly examining one of my presents. Suddenly a vivid mental picture formed in my mind and I felt that I "knew" what was inside the package I was holding. This in turn stimulated a number of pleasurable fantasies. While carried away by my imaginings, I told my father that I was able to tell what was inside all of the wrapped packages under the Christmas tree. My father was shocked at my pretended psychic ability. He sternly told me that people who make such claims deserve to be locked up in the booby hatch. He eyed me uneasily and added, "Just keep on talking like that and you'll end up there, too. I will guarantee you that."

To fully comprehend how my father's remark affected me, it is first necessary to understand the full implications of the fact that, as far as I could remember, my mother had never displayed any confidence in me. Although she was largely unconscious of what she was doing, since my earliest years she had been subtly conditioning me to regard myself as an inferior or defective person. This conditioning took place mostly on a nonverbal level and became especially intense and destructive just after the university psychiatrists had uttered their dire prophecy. The only thing that served to protect me against this insidious process was the fact that my father always viewed and treated me as if I were a perfectly normal child.

However, as soon as my father called my sanity into question, this one prop to my continued emotional security suddenly collapsed. Consequently, my mind began to become clouded with fears of my impending psychosis.

But I am not usually the sort of person who represses what he fears. Rather I tend to become hyperaware of what I fear in order to master it. So I began to confront my fear of going crazy *by acting crazy!* In so doing, I would constantly reassure myself that this was only make-believe and not real. Therefore I couldn't really be crazy. (When I actually became schizophrenic, I was still going through this mental hocus-pocus.)

So after my father's unkind remark, I began to act a little odd. For instance, one night while clad in tight-fitting pajamas, I put a pencil between my buttocks and held it in place by tightening my buttocks so that the pencil stuck out like a bee's stinger. Then I scampered around the apartment frantically flapping my elbows like wings, and making a farting sound. I was pretending to be a bumble-bee — or rather a lunatic who thought he was a bumble-bee.

I could see that my parents were alarmed by my behavior. It is even possible that I was being vindictive in acting as I did. Unconsciously, I might have been saying: "So you think I'm crazy? Well, this is the sort of behavior you can expect from me from now on."

In the months and years which followed, I began to accumulate an impressive repertoire of weird behavior. I developed a special "crazy walk," a "crazy laugh," and a number of odd mannerisms, gestures, facial expressions, and noises — all of which became increasingly chronic and compulsive in nature. I especially loved to mimic various cartoon characters such as Donald Duck and Elmer Fudd. I found that I could achieve the best results when I put myself in an altered state and actually "became" those characters.

Inky Dinky Mouse, whose identity I often assumed, was one of my own creations. When I became Inky Dinky, I would sometimes go as far as to sit on my haunches with my wrists curled downward and tucked under my chin like a mouse standing on its hind legs. Then, with my head bowed and my eyes closed, I would recite in a squeaky voice a list of imaginary enemies whom I feared, and give bizarre reasons for fearing them.

These performances were usually given for the benefit of my peers, who seldom appreciated them. One boy, who had just started to become friends with me, refused to have anything more to do with me after witnessing one of my Inky Dinky routines. My brother in particular was scandalized by my behavior. Since my odd behavior embarrassed him in front of his friends, he would no longer tolerate my presence.

I soon found myself virtually isolated. In my isolation, I began to live more and more in a world of fantasy. I became obsessed with the supernatural and constantly daydreamed about witches, ghosts, haunted houses, and the like.

More than anything else in the world, I wanted to visit a haunted house. Whenever I saw an old and abandoned building, I always endowed it with a certain aura of mystery and menace. There was a particularly ornate building in Everett which had a special place in my world of fantasy. By merely closing my eyes, I could visit this building in the dead of night, where deep within the crevices of its bottomless basement there always lurked an assortment of spooks and rattling skeletons.

I had remarkable powers of visualization. For instance, as I was thumbing through a history book while sitting at my desk at school, I saw a picture of the Cathedral of Notre Dame. I then had a vivid daydream of flying over this cathedral while riding on the back of a huge pterodactyl. As I was looking down from the flying reptile, I saw seven or eight monks in long brown robes tying three women to a stake in the center of a courtyard. Throngs of people were rushing into the courtyard in order to witness this spectacle. It was obvious that the women who were being tied to the stake were witches.

When I was in the fourth grade, I managed to make a number of friends. One of my closest friends was Warren, a morose boy who was still grieving his mother who had died two years previously. For some obscure reason Warren's father and stepmother never approved of me. Warren told me that they thought I acted rather odd or silly. He also told me that he agreed with his parents, and felt he had no alternative but to comply with their wishes and break off all relations with me.

However, I had no conscious awareness that I was acting strange. Apparently, by that time such behavior had become second nature to me.

There was a girl in my fourth grade class whom I considered the most beautiful girl I had ever seen. Her name was Carolyn, and not only was she beautiful, she looked and acted much older than she actually was. When I was in the classroom I never took my eyes off her.

Once, when the teacher had left the room, a boy named Ernie began playing too roughly with Carolyn and got her into a headlock. Recogniz-ing this as a wonderful opportunity to win points with Carolyn, I grabbed Ernie, twisted his arm behind his back, and made him apologize to Carolyn.

Carolyn thanked me for coming to her rescue and invited me to visit her at her home.

I visited her the following weekend. I found her sitting on the steps of her porch, holding her baby brother in her arms. She seemed glad to see me and invited me to sit beside her. She talked mostly about the baby and asked me if I wanted to hold him. Just to please her, I briefly held her baby brother. Although it was a rather short visit, when it was over I felt very happy and satisfied with myself.

But it was a short-lived romance. A few days later, in a harebrained attempt to impress Carolyn with my originality, I left a weird note on her porch. All that I can remember of its contents was that it contained a drawing of Waternose Foo Foo — i.e. a profile of a strange looking man with a dripping faucet for a nose. Carolyn wasn't impressed. The next time I saw her after leaving that note, she gave me a look filled with anger and disdain. That look was the last time she acknowledged my existence.

When I was in the fifth grade, I suddenly developed an intense sexual interest in girls. There was a girl in my fifth grade class, Kay, whose big, soft rear end I desperately longed to have physical contact with. However, I lacked the maturity and finesse necessary to persuade this girl to sit on my lap.

My solution to this dilemma was a rather crude one. I made a mental note of Kay's habits and found that she always spent the noon recess inside the gymnasium when the weather was cold. I could usually find her wandering around in this building in her socks — as were a number of other students. Now it occurred to me that the floor in this building was very slick, and that a girl could easily fall on her big butt if she wasn't careful. Furthermore, if this were to happen, it would be nice to have someone — me, for instance — underneath her to break her fall. With this in mind, I sauntered up behind Kay and suddenly lost my footing. In a feigned effort to restore my balance, I grabbed hold of Kay and pulled her down on top of me.

After this pleasureful sequence of events, I became very accident prone. However, following my second accident, Kay became much too vigilant to allow me to make another successful rendezvous with her derriere.

In addition to sexually harassing Kay, I was also constantly disrupting my fifth grade class with my weird noises and with my impersonations of Donald Duck and Elmer Fudd. Although I don't recall ever acting so obnoxiously before, my classmates must have appreciated my behavior: they elected me as their program chairman — a class officer responsible for providing entertainment at the end of each semester. Even my teacher Miss MacLachlan seemed to tolerate my behavior. (Possibly her tolerance stemmed from the fact that she was due to be married soon, and would be rid of us all long before the school year ended.)

Besides, Miss MacLachlan had a much more serious problem to contend with in the person of Karl,* who made me look like an angel in comparison. Whenever Miss MacLachlan asked Karl to do anything, he would always scream, "You damn sow! Stop persecuting me!" When Miss MacLachlan tried to assure Karl that no one was persecuting him, he would go crazy and shriek, "You're a goddamn liar! Everyone's always persecuting me!" As he said this, he would grimace and wring his hands. Sometimes he would burst into tears.

I liked Karl. Although I viewed him as mentally warped and never associated with him after school hours, I still considered him a valuable ally. Here, obviously, was a guy who would let nobody push him around!

Halfway through the school year, the permissive Miss MacLachlan was replaced by Mr. Roffler — a teacher who tolerated no nonsense. The first time a strange or objectionable noise issued from my lips, Mr. Roffler froze and fixed upon me a deadly stare. He then walked up to me and grabbed me gingerly by the scruff of the neck — much as if he were handling a sack of garbage and was afraid of soiling his hands — and escorted me to the principal's office.

The principal, Mr. Neff, stormed at me. He began to explain his philosophy to me in a very forceful way. His philosophy — which was hardly very original or profound — could be summed up in ten words: in every barrel there are always a few rotten apples. His job, as he saw it, was to locate those rotten apples and get rid of them before their rottenness ruined the entire barrel.

Mr. Neff thundered that, in his opinion, I was one of those rotten apples. "As far as I can see," he told me, "you have done absolutely nothing but make obscene noises and disrupt other students who are trying to study. There are students here who are trying to study because they want to make something worthwhile out of their lives. You seem to be incapable of understanding this. Perhaps you want to do nothing with your life but rot — which is fine with me. As far as I am concerned, you can go to hell. However, I will not allow you to drag others down to hell with you. I will not allow you to contaminate others with your rottenness and your filth! The next time you open that filthy mouth of yours, I am going to expel you from this school. Is that understood?"

"Yes, sir!"

"As things stand now, I see no other alternative but to call your mother and explain to her what you have been doing."

The principal's threat of calling my mother greatly alarmed me since

---

*Not his real name

I knew how she would react to such a call. Therefore I began to plead with Mr. Neff not to call my mother. I even gave him my word of honor that I would never misbehave again.

Although Mr. Neff wasn't convinced that I had suddenly turned over a new leaf, he nevertheless seemed satisfied that he had intimidated me enough and took no further action against me.

Two weeks after my encounter with the principal, I came across a rather crude sketch of soldiers defending the Alamo which another student had drawn and later discarded. Feeling that this picture didn't show enough detail to suit me, I drew a huge penis on one of the soldiers, and showed this "improved" drawing to Karl who gave an appreciative snicker. Then, having shown Karl the drawing, I tore it up and threw it into a wastepaper basket in the back of the room.

However, no sooner had I returned to my seat after throwing the picture away then Jose, a priggish little Puerto Rican boy, got up from his desk and walked to the back of the room. He then dove headfirst into the wastepaper basket and retrieved the compromising portion of the drawing. After placing the incriminating scrap of paper on the teacher's desk, he told Mr. Roffler who was responsible for it.

I knew that it would be useless arguing with an inexorable man like Mr. Roffler. As Mr. Roffler led me down the hallway toward my second encounter with Mr. Neff, I couldn't help but reflect how school with its unbending rules and regimentation was so very much like a mindless machine: if one isn't careful one could get caught in its gears and be ground to a bloody pulp.

I waited outside the principal's office while Mr. Roffler conferred with Mr. Neff behind a closed door. Suddenly, the door swung open and Mr. Roffler beckoned to me to come into the room and left.

When I entered the room, Mr. Neff gave me a furious look and glanced down at the scrap of paper lying on the desk in front of him. He then exploded into a tirade that lasted close to half an hour. He began his diatribe with such questions as: "Out of what sewer were you hatched? In which gutter have you been keeping your mind for all these years?" As he continued to work himself up into a kind of frenzy of moral indignation, questions, insults, accusations, and threats spewed from his mouth like bullets from a machine gun. According to Mr. Neff I was nothing but a filthy pervert who dirtied everything he touched.

"I am going to expel you," said Mr. Neff, "because I feel that I have a moral obligation to protect the students who are attending this school from your corrupting influence."

As I left his office, Mr. Neff's parting words to me were: "Won't your mother be proud of you when she finds out that the son she brought into the world is nothing but a dirty little pervert?"

I walked home in a daze, trying to reassure myself that what I had just been through was nothing more than a nightmare. Still, I knew the nightmare was alarmingly real.

Most of all, I dreaded how my mother was going to react to the news of my being expelled. I remembered how she behaved when I merely told her that I had quit the Cub Scouts. After I quit that boring organization, she harassed me for an entire week. She lectured me about being a "quitter" and told me that my quitting the Cub Scouts was a sure sign that I was going to be a complete failure in life.

If she acted this way when I quit the Cub Scouts, how would she act when she found out that I had been expelled from school?

When I walked in the door, I could tell by my mother's tranquil demeanor that Mr. Neff hadn't yet called. I curled up on the couch almost sick with apprehension. However I hadn't been lying on the couch for more than fifteen minutes before the phone rang. At that moment I hated the person who had invented the telephone.

"That was Mr. Neff," my mother icily informed me after she hung up the phone. "He tells me that you have been expelled from school."

For some obscure reason, my mother believed that such a mundane act as drawing a penis could only have been perpetrated by a hardcore sickie like my friend Karl, and that I was covering up for him. Every day she would come into my room in an effort to get me to declare my innocence of such a heinous act. Every time she did this, I felt as if I were being put through an emotional wringer. On one hand, I never denied doing what the school authorities claimed I did; nor would I even consider blaming Karl for an act which I had committed. Yet at the same time, since my mother attached such exaggerated significance to the act of drawing a penis, I was afraid to explicitly state that I had in fact done such a thing. Because I was unable to give straight answers to my mother's questions, she felt certain that I must be hiding something. So she kept after me.

This agonizing state of affairs lasted for about two or three weeks. Finally, while driving me home from the barbershop, my father nonchalantly asked me whether I had drawn a penis. When I confessed that I had, he simply told me not to do it again and let the matter drop.

As things turned out, I had not been expelled from school but merely given a one-week suspension. However, this had not been due to any leniency on Mr. Neff's part. Rather, I owe this favorable turn of events to Captain Devlin, an army psychologist, who had intervened on my behalf and was able to persuade the school authorities to reinstate me.

I had begun seeing Captain Devlin sometime in October not long after the beginning of the school year. On every Tuesday afternoon at one o'clock my mother would pick me up at school and drive me to the Madigan Army Hospital at Fort Lewis where Captain Devlin had his office. For me this was always a welcome reprieve from school, which I considered sheer torture.

However, as far as I was concerned, my visits to Captain Devlin were only the lesser of two evils, for I felt rather uncomfortable having this priestly looking man clad in a white smock examining my psyche. Still, I found Captain Devlin a pleasant enough man. Whenever I walked into his office, he always seemed glad to see me and would make me feel as comfortable as circumstances could possibly warrant.

Captain Devlin used two techniques in examining me. First, he would ask me questions. He always started with totally innocuous questions such as, "What did you have for breakfast this morning?" and gradually progressed to questions of a more personal nature. He questioned me extensively about my activities and attitudes.

For the most part, I was forthright in answering his questions, but I never volunteered any information. I believed that telling this man the wrong sorts of things could be dangerous.

Captain Devlin's other technique was to induce me to act in a spontaneous or playful way so he could scrutinize my behavior. He seemed to have an endless variety of games for me to play, for I never played the same game twice. Sometimes these games would be conventional ones like pool, sometimes they would be shrink games like building things with blocks, and sometimes I would be encouraged to improvise a game of my own.

Once, Captain Devlin led me down a hallway and into a room cluttered wall-to-wall with a huge variety of toys. He told me that I could play with any toy in the room. I ignored the toys and walked over to a blackboard on the wall. I rubbed the blackboard with a piece of chalk, then cleaned it with an eraser. I did this repeatedly until the eraser was saturated with chalk dust. I then walked over to Captain Devlin, raised the chalk-laden eraser to my mouth, and blew a cloud of chalk dust at him.

Captain Devlin glared at me and asked me why I did this.

This question and the severe manner in which Captain Devlin asked it made me extremely uneasy. I felt at a total loss as to what to say to him. I had certainly meant no harm. My blowing chalk dust had been a playful and unthinking act — one which I had done many times at school. However, in my confused and disturbed state of mind, one thing at least seemed clear: if I wasn't careful I could end up in a nut house.

I continued seeing Captain Devlin until the end of the school year. At our final meeting, Captain Devlin wrote his phone number on a slip of paper and gave it to me. He then told me I could call him any time I wanted to talk to him.

But I never called him. Although I rather liked Captain Devlin and felt that he was a well-intentioned and sincere man, I nevertheless was glad to be rid of him. Just as a priest is a representative of God and the hereafter, so Captain Devlin was a representative of another mysterious realm — of an ominous reality which I secretly dreaded and wanted no contact with.

During the eight months in which I was being examined by Captain Devlin, my mother began to drop subtle hints that I was a person very much like my great-grandmother who had died in a state mental hospital. Perhaps the mere fact that I was being examined by a psychologist was enough to convince my mother that I was mentally sick and that I had inherited my great-grandmother's madness or badness. (In my mother's mind, badness was equivalent to madness.)

While I was being examined by Captain Devlin, my mother was constantly telling me the most lurid and moralistic tales about Old Gram — some of which I have already described in the introduction. When she told me those stories she would adopt a grave and almost oracular manner very similar to that of a former neighbor of ours — the woman who told me about the boy who thought he could fly. My mother's stories always seemed to have an ominous but unstated moral: what happened to her could happen to you.

My mother held the most extraordinary beliefs in regard to the nature of heredity. For instance, she believed that everything a person could possibly be, including that person's moral character and eventual success or failure in life, was unalterably determined by that person's genes.

As to where or how my mother developed such views, I can only speculate. But plausible clues concerning the origin of my mother's fatalistic outlook exist nonetheless. For instance, she never had the feeling that she could exert any meaningful or significant control over her own life. Her feelings of powerlessness stemmed from at least three sources: from her restricted upbringing during Great Depression; from her alcoholism; and from the fact that her own life was tied to that of a man who was also an alcoholic and whose behavior — even when he was completely sober — often caused her considerable anxiety.

In addition to and partly as a consequence of her feelings of powerlessness, my mother also suffered from a lack of self-esteem. What pride she had in herself originated largely from factors totally beyond her control: from her status as an officer's wife and from her descent from her gifted and aristocratic ancestors. Inasmuch as this last factor — namely, her revered lineage — contributed to her self-esteem, it is easy to see how she could have developed a grossly exaggerated notion as to the importance of heredity.

Finally, my mother's mystical notions in regard to heredity might also have been influenced by her half-discarded belief in reincarnation. When my mother was very young she had repeated episodes of déjà vu, and as a result of these experiences, she developed a belief in reincarnation. As she became older, her déjà vu episodes became far less frequent,* and as a consequence, her belief in reincarnation diminished but was never entirely abandoned. It is wholly possible that as my mother's belief in reincarnation faded it underwent a pseudoscientific transformation: the genes replaced the soul as the vehicle through which a person's moral character and destiny are transmitted. In this way, I could be virtually a reincarnation of my great-grandmother even if we had both been alive at the same time.

Not being a mind reader, I cannot know with certainty just how my mother actually perceived me. But I am certain how I viewed myself. When I was in the fifth grade, I began to see myself as another manifestation of my great-grandmother. Yet I never believed in reincarnation. Rather the identification which I felt with my great-grandmother involved the recognition on my part of a certain terrible *sameness* between Gram and myself which determined our moral character and ultimate destiny.

That my mystical identification with my great-grandmother was a result of the indoctrination I received from my mother is also certain. The tales which my mother force-fed me about my sociopathic ancestor had but one motif: Gram was a person totally incapable of thinking about anyone but herself. Day in and day out, my mother constantly told me that I was a person who was totally incapable of thinking about anyone but myself. How could I fail to see a certain similarity between myself and Gram?

According to my mother, there was nothing superficial about this similarity: my alleged incapacity to think about anyone but myself stemmed not from any mere thoughtlessness on my part, but from some deep and unalterable flaw in my character. She often told me this when my misbehavior caused her to fly into a tirade.

Sometimes all it would take to trigger one of my mother's ferocious tirades would be to have the wrong sort of attitude or expression on my face. In the fifth grade I began to emerge as the family scapegoat. This pattern became especially pronounced immediately before my schizophrenic breakdown.

At the same time I was becoming a scapegoat within my own family,

---

*As far as I know, my mother had only one déjà vu episode after she reached adulthood. This singular event occurred in 1979, when she was visiting her relatives in Norway. Although my mother had never been in Norway before, the Norwegian villages and countryside seemed strangely and inexplicably familiar to her.

The phenomenon of déjà vu is usually thought to occur when illusively familiar surroundings or experiences have an associative link to memories which have been repressed due to a psychological conflict. In my mother's case, these repressed memories probably involved her ambivalent feelings toward her mother who had recently died.

I was also becoming something of a pariah among my peers. However, by no means was I the most notorious pariah in Fort Lewis: that distinction belonged to Billy, the chaplain's son, a handsome but effeminate-looking boy whom the other boys had nicknamed Billy Backbone. They called him this because they looked down on him as being a spineless weakling. When I first saw Billy, he was being chased by a gang of boys who were pelting him with ice cubes and mockingly calling him Billy Backbone.

I became friends with Billy while I was in the fourth grade, but I was never especially close to him. At that time I had a number of friends whose friendship I valued more than Billy's. I was therefore afraid to become too closely involved with Billy lest I jeopardize their friendship. Still, Billy seemed genuinely fond of me and wanted to become my best friend.

When I had reached the fifth grade, Billy began to haunt my doorstep. At first I was rather displeased by this turn of events because Billy could be disgusting at times. For instance, while standing on my front lawn, Billy defecated in his pants and squirmed and jiggled until two or three small round turds rolled out of his pant leg and onto the ground. Billy seemed quite proud of his skill in being able to do this without soiling his pants. He told me he used to practice this skill of his whenever he went into theaters and other public places.

Within a few weeks of when he started haunting my doorstep, Billy and I became the closest of friends. He made an excellent friend, for in addition to being loyal and trustworthy, he was also an intelligent and sensitive boy who was both interesting to talk to and fun to be with.

But, of course, Billy also had his faults. Perhaps his main fault was that he was just too sensitive. He was acutely aware of the fact that he was an outcast, and this caused him a great deal of mental anguish. He felt inferior and different — like one of the damned. Although he wasn't particularly religious and seldom talked about God, Billy was an intensely guilt-ridden person who was morbidly obsessed with the concepts of hell and sin — especially with sin.

Since we were so emotionally close and shared certain morbid tendencies, it was almost inevitable that Billy and I would influence each other in a thoroughly morbid way.

It is almost a law of human nature that the more inferior a person feels, the more that person feels a need to look down on someone else.

So it was in our case. Because we felt like pariahs, we needed a scapegoat to bolster our self-esteem. Therefore, one day during noon recess as I was walking with Billy across the school playground, Billy nudged me, pointed to a boy standing near the jungle gym, and said in a voice ringing with contempt, "That guy looks like he just crawled out from under a rock." There was no doubt about it, that boy looked strange. With his bowlegs, misshapen physique, and distorted facial features, he resembled nothing so much as a medieval gargoyle. His ultrathick glasses grotesquely magnified his popping walleyes. This, together with the idiotic grin on his face which revealed a set of snaggled teeth, gave him a distinct aura of subnormality. From the very moment our eyes lit upon that unfortunate creature who stood innocently before us, he was marked out as our personal scapegoat.

We both felt that it was our sacred duty to punish that weird looking boy for the crime of being different. To that end, Billy watched him carefully and found out where he lived. One night, we sneaked up in front of his home and let the air out of his bicycle tires.

It soon became apparent to us, however, that considering the enormity of that boy's crime, we had been much too lenient with him. Meanwhile, after I had procured a large coffee can, I suggested to Billy that we go out to urinate and defecate in that can, and dump the mess on our enemy's doorstep as a fitting gesture of our contempt. Billy enthusiastically approved of my idea.

I should have known better than to again practice the black art of anal sorcery, for in walking home on the night in which I had befouled my enemy's doorstep, I experienced the most uncanny feelings. Those feelings never left me as I walked in the door and sat down at the kitchen table to have supper. I felt almost certain that someone had observed me with Billy as I was pouring filth on the porch, and had phoned my parents and told them what I had done. Each time my father looked up from the table and gave me a grave and thoughtful look, I dreaded what he was going to tell me after supper was finished.

Although our foul deed was never unmasked, it soon became apparent to Billy and myself that we were our own worst enemies. For months on end, Billy agonized over what he had done. He kept harping about how sinful we were to commit such an indecent act. Listening to this day in and day out hardly enhanced my self-esteem. In the end, I began to hate Billy — and myself as well. In the back of my mind, I began to suspect that Mr. Neff was right about me: that I was nothing but a filthy pervert who dirtied everything he touched.

By my stupid act of defecating and urinating in a can and dumping its contents out onto a porch during the night, I had inadvertently reopened an old psychic wound. In so doing, my mother's nearly forgotten words, "They have people put away in mental institutions for doing things like that" came back to haunt me.

On my next visit to the psychiatric ward of the Madigan Army Hospital, Captain Devlin noticed that I was upset and asked me what was wrong. I just looked at him with fear and distrust. I wasn't about to incriminate myself. As it was, I knew that in merely coming to his office every week I already had one foot inside a mental institution. In my troubled and tormented state of mind, I felt certain that he would not hesitate to have me committed if I answered his question and told him what was bothering me.

For a variety of reasons, I began to lose confidence in myself when I was in the fifth grade. During this anxiety-ridden and demoralized period of my life, I did have one compensation, however: I had the most intense and meaningful dreams. In one recurring dream, I would be wandering through a forest when suddenly, I would experience feelings of intense joy and inner peace on coming across a certain secluded valley which no one else could possibly enter or reach. I would walk down into this valley, wade into a warm river which flowed through it, and float peacefully down the stream.

In many of my most mystical dreams, I would be wandering at night through a gloomy skid row section of a large city. To understand what significance such dreams had for me, it is first necessary to be aware of the fact that even in my wakeful state, old and dilapidated buildings always evoked in me a certain sense of mystery and suffering. As a boy I often walked through Seattle's skid row district with a portentous feeling that someday I too would end up in that infernal realm of the lost and the damned.

In my most frequent skid row dream, I would be standing on a fire escape outside a slum tenement in the middle of the night peering in a window. As I looked in the window, I would see a woman sitting alone in her bleak and bare room with her pale face turned toward mine. Although she looked straight at me, she was so lost in her somber meditations that she failed to notice me.

There was a certain saintly aura about this woman which I found riveting. The more I looked at her the more the feeling grew in me that she had undoubtedly discovered the key to the mystery of why people must suffer. Moreover, it also became evident that her knowledge of that dark secret was a terrible burden to her which was slowly destroying her.

As I continued to look ever more deeply into her eyes, she suddenly seemed apprehensively aware of my presence. This apprehensive expression on her face intensified and developed into a sinister look of unspeakable cruelty. As she leaned forward in her chair and was about to get up and approach the window, I could see that this woman was in the process of undergoing a terrifyingly evil transformation. However, as soon as I took my face away from the window, she settled back down in her chair and was again absorbed in her sorrowful contemplation.

Again in rapt wonder I peered in through the window at this mysterious woman. Again she became aware of my presence and began an ominous change. And again I prevented her diabolical metamorphosis from occurring by merely taking my face away from the window. I would repeatedly go through this cycle of looking and turning away every time I had this dream.

During the time I was having these dreams, I found it agonizing to have to wake up each morning and cope with another day. However, this was not a particularly pleasant time for my parents either.

Certainly not for my father. He had been anxiously awaiting Captain Devlin's verdict in regard to my mental status throughout the entire eight months I had been under observation. During the period of waiting, my father was in such a troubled state of mind that even my most innocuous deeds or comments sometimes frightened him. For instance, when I told him that one of my classmates resembled Bugs Bunny, my father became somewhat agitated and repeatedly said, "Just be yourself. Just be yourself." It was as if he were uttering a magical incantation in order to ward off the possibility of my undergoing some sort of horrific metamorphosis. Had I just made the claim that I was in fact Bugs Bunny or that I had just seen him walk in the door, my father's reaction would have been wholly appropriate.

At times, my father would wander into my room and deliver the most confused and moralistic sermons regarding my poor penmanship. At such times he would tell me that my cramped writing style revealed a flaw in my character: that I thought only of myself and not of the person who had to decipher what I wrote. Apparently, my father not only believed in graphology, but he also thought he could improve my moral character by getting me to improve my handwriting. As my father exhorted me to improve my penmanship, he seemed deeply troubled and concerned. Obviously, he was beginning to fear that there might be something seriously wrong with me. (Interestingly enough, according to my fifth grade report card, my penmanship was satisfactory.)

Of far more significance was the fact that after examining me for nearly eight months, Captain Devlin concluded that I was a perfectly normal boy.

Immediately after receiving this welcome news, my father warmly embraced me and said: "You have no idea of what a good friend you have in Captain Devlin. If it weren't for him, you wouldn't have been able to pass the fifth grade. But not only that, he also tells me that there's nothing wrong with you — that you're a completely normal boy.

"I'll have to admit I was beginning to get a little worried about you. But as I've told you before, you're very lucky to have been able to see Captain Devlin. He's a brilliant man, and a man whose judgment I respect very much. That's why it's a considerable load off my mind to have him tell me that there's nothing wrong with you."

That night as we sat alone together at the kitchen table, my father had a very long and serious talk with me. His talk covered a wide variety of topics including military science, primitive man and his struggle for survival, Selye's general adaption syndrome with its so-called "fight or flight" reaction, and voodoo death. My father explained to me how it is literally possible to frighten someone to death:

"In Haitian culture, belief in voodoo and black magic is so intense and unquestioned that if a voodoo priest were to curse someone and tell that person that he is going to die, that person will die. This is so because the victim himself accepts it as self-evident that he is going to die and panics. This causes a massive amount of adrenaline to flow so that that person's heart begins beating wildly and irregularly, and he dies."

My father looked at me thoughtfully and continued:

"In our culture we have the equivalent of witch doctors and voodoo priests in the person of the psychiatrist. Because psychiatrists are doctors, they are looked up to as if they were gods, and their opinions are seldom questioned. Therefore, just as a voodoo priest is able to inflict death by merely cursing someone, so a psychiatrist is capable of causing madness by merely telling someone that he is insane, or at least in the process of becoming that way. That is what is known as a self-fulfilling prophecy."

A note of anger crept into my father's voice as he continued:

"When you were in the first grade, you were given a battery of psychological tests at the University of Washington. Those psychiatrists at the university told your mother that you would become completely psychotic within less than a year unless we had you committed to a mental institution. There's no doubt in my mind that had we done just that, you would have been driven crazy.

"Those psychiatrists said that you would be completely crazy within less than a year. That was over four years ago. After studying the results of the tests that those psychiatrists gave you, and examining you for eight months, Captain Devlin couldn't find a single thing wrong with you.

"And believe me, as far as both your mother and I are concerned, there's absolutely nothing wrong with you."

However, my father's words could not undo the effects of four years of steadily escalating conditioning. Indeed, his merely mentioning the possibility of my being put away in a mental institution made me sick with fear. But he must have realized to some extent how I felt, for I found some comfort in the words which concluded his talk:

"Now, John, I know both your mother and I have treated you as if we had no confidence in you at all. Now that I think of it, I realize that we have often treated you badly. But that's going to change. From now on, you are going to find that things are going to be considerably different."

The sincerity of my father's words was amply borne out by the events that followed.

# 5

# A PREPSYCHOTIC INTERLUDE

Not more than a few days after my father's talk, I was in the house alone when I heard a knock at the kitchen door. When I opened the door, Linda, my sister's six-year-old friend, asked if my sister was home. I was somewhat annoyed by Linda's sudden intrusion. After affirming that my sister was home, I glumly escorted Linda into the kitchen, opened the oven door, and pointed to a large pork roast sizzling in the oven. "She's in here," I told her, "we're having her for dinner."

That night Linda almost had a nervous breakdown. She refused to believe that my sister was alive until she actually saw her in person.

Both of my parents — especially my father — thought the incident was hilarious. They were particularly amused by Linda's description of how serious I looked when I told her my sister was in the oven.

However, had I tried that same trick only a few days previously, my parents would have become nearly as hysterical as Linda. Almost overnight, as a result of Captain Devlin's giving me a clean bill of health, my parents began to see me in a different light.

This change was especially noticeable in my father, who immediately developed a much closer and more affectionate relationship with me. In his eyes, my eccentricities no longer appeared to be symptoms of my mental derangement but rather signs of my originality. He told me that as an adult he expected me to become either an "offbeat writer or an actor who plays character roles."

Unlike my father, my mother had a deep-seated need to view me as an abnormal person. Yet Captain Devlin's benign assessment of my mental status had the salutary effect of imbuing her with a certain amount of healthy skepticism in regard to the notion that I was in imminent danger of becoming psychotic. Consequently, like my father, my mother became much more relaxed around me. At that same time, she ceased being so overly critical of me.

All at once, I found my parents to be extremely pleasant people with whom to live. As they showed more confidence in me, I gradually began to regain some confidence in myself. With this newly acquired self-confidence and self-esteem, the odd behavior that began when my father had questioned my sanity diminished to a point where my brother was no longer ashamed to be seen with me. Not only that, I also began to make new friends. In brief, it seemed as if the voodoo curse the university psychiatrists had placed on me had finally been broken.

But this certainly was not the case, for the spell had not been broken but merely rendered dormant, where it waited to be activated by an unfortunate turn of events which was not long in coming.

While my father was stationed at Fort Lewis, he was constantly being called on the carpet for fraternizing with his men.

My father's habit of fraternizing with his men also infuriated my mother, who looked down on enlisted men as being strictly lowlife.

Nevertheless, my father was immensely popular with his men. They viewed him as their champion, for whenever any enlisted man got into trouble and was about to be court-marshaled, they could always count on my father to defend them in court.

When my father was in the Army, it was customary for regular army officers to act as defense attorneys whenever an enlisted man was due to be court-marshaled. For his part, the enlisted man had the right to be represented in court by any army officer he chose.

According to what my mother has told me, such trials were mere charades. Since the officers always stuck together, all the prosecuting attorney had to do in order to get a conviction was to point his finger at the defendant and say, "That man is guilty." No officer representing an enlisted man in court ever put up a decent defense.*

My father had nothing but contempt for this system. Whenever a GI chose my father to represent him in court, my father always put up such a good defense that the man was acquitted — even if it was obvious to everyone that he was guilty. Since my father never lost a case, he was in great demand as an army defense attorney.

One afternoon, about an hour before he was scheduled to represent someone in court, my father came staggering in the door so drunk that he was scarcely coherent. Upon seeing him in this condition, a look of incredulous horror appeared on my mother's face. However, as she recovered from her initial shock, her face became hard and stern. "You're stinking drunk!" she hissed at him.

"I'm not drunk," my father protested with a silly smirk on his face, "I'm just a little pixilated."

In rage, my mother picked up a vase and hurled it at my father. The vase missed his head by about a foot before it shattered against the wall. Then she began hurling accusations. She accused him, among other things, of being an irresponsible father who had never wanted to have children in the first place. "And now," she bitterly added, "being stuck with a rotten husband like you is enough to make me wish I never had

---

*This may have been true of Fort Lewis at that time, but I have learned from my father's letters that other officers also liked to "play hero."

any children!"

(This last remark greatly upset my sister. Afterward my mother had to explain to her that she was only saying those cruel things in order to shock her father into sobriety.)

Next I remember my mother grabbing my father roughly by the hair and leading him up the stairs — by then, we were living in newly constructed officer's quarters which had two stories — and into the bathroom where I could hear him yelling as she gave him a cold shower with his clothes on. Then she took off his wet clothes and dressed him as if he were a baby. After dressing him, she gave him several cups of hot coffee and hoped for the best as he walked out the door.

That day marked the end of my father's career as an army officer.

Yet it wasn't until about six weeks later — sometime after his being court-marshaled — that my father was formally discharged from the military. Meanwhile, my mother was busy "explaining" to us children why our father was unable to continue his career as an officer. According to my mother, the Army had an oversupply of captains. Therefore they were discharging those captains who didn't have their high school diplomas.

My mother possibly had a vindictive motive for concocting such a spurious explanation. Surely, this explanation — that the Army was getting rid of my father because he was just too ignorant or uneducated to function as an officer — was much more demeaning than the real explanation: namely, that he had lost his commission as a result of his having made many enemies who used his appearing in court while drunk as a pretext for getting rid of him.

For as long as my father was alive, my mother never forgave him for losing his status as an officer. She may even have suspected that he did this deliberately. If so, then her suspicions were well founded.

I have three reasons for believing that my father might have deliberately sabotaged his own career. First, when my father was an officer his drinking problem wasn't that serious: in those years I can hardly remember him ever being drunk. Second, a year after my father lost his commission, he confided in me that he felt much happier as an enlisted man than he had been as an officer because he had far fewer duties and responsibilities to cope with. Third, he probably had no further motivation to continue serving as an officer since he had already served as a captain long enough to qualify for a captain's pension even if he were to retire as a private. The suspicion that my father's sudden bout of drunkenness was a calculated act is bolstered when one considers that had he staged a similar act a mere ten days earlier he would not have been eligible to retire as a captain.

Still, this is only speculation. It is wholly uncertain just what my father's intentions really were.

My father's fateful bout of drunkenness occurred in June 1957, shortly after I had graduated from the sixth grade. That summer we spent a lot of time camping near a beach on Washington's Olympic Peninsula. For this purpose, my father had just purchased an old eight by twenty-five foot trailer.

On our first such outing, while my father hobnobbed with one of his GI buddies, my mother developed a sudden urge to become a writer. "If Betty MacDonald could publish a book with a ridiculous and uninteresting title like *The Egg and I*," she bitterly declared, "then certainly I should be able to publish a much more interesting book about my family." With this, she set up a card table in a secluded nook in the gloomy, moss-laden rain forest not far from the trailer, and began clacking away at her typewriter. As she worked on her book, my mother seemed highly perturbed. She would lose her temper whenever anyone came near her, or got close enough to peek at her manuscript.

After about a week or two, my mother abandoned her literary project. Nevertheless, her dream of becoming a writer had served its purpose: it helped her cope with her sudden loss of status.

At the end of July, my father received his severance pay from the Army. During the month of August we traveled extensively throughout the western part of the United States with the trailer hitched to the car.

While staying briefly at a trailer court in northern California, I had a most unpleasant experience. This unpleasantness began when my father called me back after I had been absent-mindedly strolling through this trailer court. "You can't go wandering through the trailer park that way or people might think that you haven't got all your faculties." He smiled and continued, "Now I know you have all your faculties, but others might not think so if they see you walking like that."

Since I hadn't the slightest idea that I had been doing anything odd, my father's remarks threw me into a state of anguished self-appraisal. Was there something about me that suggested a demented or mentally retarded person? Did I look weird or abnormal? To simply say that my father's words made me feel self-conscious would be a gross understatement. Rather, I felt as if I were totally naked and vulnerable.

This experience wasn't much in and of itself, but it signaled the resumption of an insidious process. Although this process wouldn't really begin to gather momentum until at least a year later, still the experience at the trailer court could be considered a harbinger of things to come — as the first drip, so to speak, of an endless Chinese water torture.

We continued traveling down the West Coast until we reached Los Angeles and then headed east. We stayed with some friends of my parents on a farm in central Texas for almost a week. Then we headed north, stopping briefly at Yellowstone National Park before heading home.

"Home" this time meant a trailer court on North Broadway in Everett

— right next to the motel at which we had stayed four years previously. However, we didn't remain at this trailer park for more than a few weeks before we moved two miles down the road and stayed with my maternal grandmother who lived in a small house on Broadway. During the time we lived at grandmother's, my mother and brother slept in the trailer in the back yard, while my sister and *I* slept in the house.

Upon reaching Everett, my father became extremely worried and began a frantic search for work. But since the country was in the midst of a severe recession, there wasn't much work to be found. My father applied at Safeway for a stock clerk position, and was given a battery of personality tests but no job. Finally, after fruitlessly looking for work for about a month, he resigned himself to the necessity of re-entering the Army as a private first class.

My father was shipped to Lompoc, California, where he worked as a guard at a military prison. While manning a tower on the periphery of this prison with another guard as his partner, he alternated between reading a book and sleeping.

While my father was living in California, my mother was going through a great deal of emotional turmoil. She couldn't decide whether to move to California so she could live with my father, to stay where she was, or to give up on her marriage altogether and seek a divorce.

At this time, however, my mother wasn't the only member of our family who was undergoing emotional difficulties. While lying in bed my sister began experiencing vivid tactile hallucinations. She was absolutely convinced that people were piling television sets on top of her chest.

At night my sister always went to sleep in grandmother's bed while the rest of the family was watching television in the living room. Then, sometime during the night, my mother would pick my sister up while she was still asleep, and transfer her to the living room couch which would be made into a bed. Falling asleep in grandmother's bed and waking up on the living room couch always gave my sister a weird feeling of disorientation.

But this wasn't the cause of her hallucinations. Rather, she was an extremely sensitive girl who was acutely aware of the emotional distress our mother was going through — to such an extent that it began to affect her.

My sister — who was then eight years old — made repeated attempts to convince my mother that someone was piling television sets on top of her. "Ah, honey," my mother would say, "you're just imagining things." At this, my sister would grow indignant and blurt out, "But people really are trying to put television sets on top of me!"

My mother simply refused to take my sister's hallucinations and delusions seriously. Strangely enough, she seemed to show no concern at all. What a bizarre contrast to the way she had treated me! When I was seven years old, she was almost ready to have me committed for behavior which was rather typical of a boy my age — namely, my mixing up a batch of muck in a paint can. Obviously, she had the fixed idea that I was the sick one in the family, and simply overlooked the possibility that my sister might have a problem similar to mine.

Still, it was fortunate for my sister that my mother acted in the way she did. Had my mother taken her to see a psychiatrist, my sister could have been permanently damaged as a result of being labeled mentally sick. As things turned out, within a week my sister's hallucinations had cleared up completely. She has never had any similar problems since.

The eight months I spent at my grandmother's house were a relatively happy and tranquil period in my life. With a room of my own, I probably had more privacy than any other member of my household. I could pretty much come and go as I pleased with a minimum of supervision. Not only that, I was always able to find interesting things to do.

I used to love to wander through a neighborhood frequented by winos and tramps — an area along the railroad tracks cluttered with abandoned buildings, dilapidated warehouses, junkyards, and run-down saw mills not far from where I lived. Near the center of this area of picturesque squalor was the city dump where my father used to go to shoot rats when he was a boy. Just south of the city dump, there was a large hobo jungle of approximately twenty shanties sprawled along the edge of a swamp and along the west bank of the Snohomish River.

Two blocks north of the city dump, across the railroad tracks from a large junkyard, there was a horse stables where riding lessons were given. Occasionally my sister would come here with a friend of hers to sneak a ride on one of the horses. This was a matter of some concern to me since this area was literally swarming with tramps.

At that time Everett was something of a mecca for hobos and tramps, partly because the town offered them such a wide variety of attractive nooks and crannies where they could roost without being seriously harassed. But of far more importance was the fact that if one wished to hop a freight train headed east, Everett was the only town for many miles around where this could be done.

Although I didn't want my sister coming anywhere near these derelicts, I rather enjoyed their company myself. Since I halfway expected to become a bum myself, I was always eager to pick up a few pointers from the pros. Most of my more meaningful encounters with these people, however, usually occurred when I was with my friend David.

David was a heavyset and rather uncouth looking boy who had an unruly mop of black hair and eyes that seemed to glitter with a fanatical intensity. I met David through a cousin of mine while I was still living at the trailer court. At first, I merely tolerated David's presence because he was my cousin's friend. Later I found him to be a very pleasant person whose coarse exterior hid a sensitive and almost poetic nature.

In the weeks and months to come, David and I became inseparable companions who shared a number of interesting activities. We enjoyed hiking to inaccessible and out-of-the-way places and probably explored every wooded area within a five-mile radius of Everett. We went boating on the Deadwater Slough on Ebey Island. We also went rafting on the Port Gardner Bay, as well as on a couple of small ponds near the mouth of the Snohomish River. We once camped out beside a brook on the bottom of a heavily wooded ravine. We especially liked to stroll through the run-down and disreputable sections of Everett. One of our favorite places was Hewitt Avenue, which was somewhat notorious as a hangout for bums. We also liked to visit the winos who lived along the edge of the swamp near the city dump. Because these parts of town seemed to have an ambience of mystery and danger, our excursions to such places never failed to provide us with raw material for our fantasies.

David and I mutually appreciated each other's capacity to fantasize freely. We could never engage in any activity without creating the most elaborate fantasies. For instance, while rafting on a small pond, we would imagine there were vast cities situated along this pond, and we would tell vivid stories about the people who lived in these imaginary cities.

Sharing such fantasies lent an extra dimension to our activities, making them more meaningful and enjoyable.

# 6

## PARADISE LOST

In June 1958, my father returned to Everett and took our family back to California with him. We stayed at a number of ocean beaches throughout most of the summer. Then, sometime in late August, we pulled into a trailer park not more than a quarter of a mile from the prison where my father worked.

This trailer court consisted of approximately fifty trailers arranged in six straight rows. On each side of the trailer court there was a row of eucalyptus trees serving as a windbreak. Looking south through one row of trees, the prison itself was grimly visible. To the north, the other row of trees stretched along the edge of a ravine. Near the northwestern corner of the trailer court where we lived, a narrow gravel road wound down the side of the gulch past a sewage treatment plant; on the bottom of the ravine there were three settling ponds. Beyond the ravine to the north were the parched and desolate hills. Except for the two rows of eucalyptus, virtually no other trees were to be seen.

This is where we would live for the rest of our fifteen-month stay in California.

Like most trailer parks, ours certainly had its share of misfits and weirdos. Two of the most contentious weirdos in our trailer court were Mrs. Crinshaw* and Mrs. Bowers.* Mrs. Bowers was a fat, aggressively stupid woman who could be seen late at night or in the early hours of the morning peering into other people's windows with a flashlight, "just to see if everything was OK." Mrs. Crinshaw was a thin, mentally deranged woman who would periodically go berserk. Once, while standing in the middle of the street, she started to scream and fling garbage can lids at people who were passing by. More than once the military police had to drive into the trailer park in order to calm Mrs. Crinshaw down.

Mrs. Bowers and Mrs. Crinshaw hated each other. And, I was told that just before our arrival the trailer court had been split between the Crinshaw and Bowers factions who had been perpetually feuding with each other. This is wholly believable in view of the fact that as soon as

---

*Not their real names.

we arrived at the trailer park Mrs. Crinshaw contacted my mother and wanted her to take sides against Mrs. Bowers. My mother told Mrs. Crinshaw that she wasn't interested in fighting other peoples' battles.

For a couple of reasons, I found this trailer park an extremely difficult environment to cope with. First of all, I felt terribly isolated. The only person in this place who was my own age was a fat, homely girl. And this girl disliked me intensely. (Perhaps she derived her adverse attitude toward me from her father who disapproved of me due to my mischief making.) In addition to this girl, there were also two boys in the trailer court who were a year younger than myself. One of those boys did not socialize with anyone; the other was slightly retarded. As far as I was concerned, none of the children in the trailer court offered much in the way of companionship.

Nor was my social situation helped much by the fact that there were two boys my own age living just a half mile down the road. Those boys were inseparable companions, and although one of them liked me, the other one wouldn't tolerate my presence.

During the time we were in California, my brother was more fortunate than I in that he had just learned how to drive, had a car, and had friends outside the trailer park. However, my brother and I had never been very close. Since the time we had been living at our grandmother's house in Everett, we had, for the most part, simply ignored each other's existence.

Largely as a result of my near total isolation, I was horribly bored throughout my entire stay in California. There was virtually nowhere to go, nothing to do, and nobody to talk to. Because I found it so incredibly hard to find constructive things to do while living in such a squalid little hole as the trailer park, I was often getting into mischief. In a desperate attempt to relieve my boredom, I began, for instance, to knock down the picket fence which surrounded the playground in front of the trailer court. After I had knocked out and broken nearly half the pickets in the fence, a wrecking crew came and totally dismantled the fence. A few months later — not knowing what else to do — I used tree branches and other rubbish to barricade the road which led to the sewage treatment plant. Once, I was caught hanging a dead snake on the door handle of Mrs. Crinshaw's trailer.

I enjoyed tormenting Mrs. Crinshaw because I could always count on her to react like a perfect maniac whenever I teased her. My most enjoyable encounter with Mrs. Crinshaw occurred when I met a little urchin near her trailer who had warts on his hands. While inspecting his warts, I asked him: "Where did you get those warts, Jerry — from handling Mrs. Crinshaw?" "I heard that!" Mrs. Crinshaw shrieked. She rushed out of her trailer in an extremely disturbed state of mind and began pleading with Jerry. "You tell him, Jerry. You didn't get those warts from handling me!" Mrs. Crinshaw's embarrassed husband had to virtually drag her back into the trailer.

Another source of entertainment was a pudgy eight-year-old boy whom I had nicknamed Sarge. I called him that because he resembled Sergeant Garcia — the slob-like sergeant on *Zorro*, a television program that was then popular.

The other children in the trailer court found Sarge immensely amusing because he would always do whatever anyone told him to do. If, for instance, someone told Sarge to swallow a worm or to eat a handful of dirt, he would do it. Not only that, Sarge had the amazing ability to believe almost anything.

I first found out about Sarge from my sister who told me about his gullibility. She told me how one night she was able to convince Sarge that an eerie red light shining through the eucalyptus trees from the sewage treatment plant was really a demon. She had him absolutely terrified of her bogus demon.

Inspired by my sister's exploit, I conceived of a plan to convince Sarge that my sister and I were angels sent from heaven. My plan involved taking advantage of the fact that in a few days my father was going to buy a new trailer. On the day before our new trailer was due to arrive, my sister and I met Sarge on the street in front of our home and flatly told him that we were angels. I then produced a small sack of bogus gems — bits of colored glass which I had picked up along the railroad tracks while I was in Everett — and told him they were genuine emeralds, rubies, and sapphires which God had personally given to us as a gift. Finally, I told him we were going to use some of those gems to buy a new trailer.

When we told him that we were angels, Sarge seemed no more surprised or incredulous than had we just told him that we were American citizens. He just seemed to accept everything. After our new trailer arrived there was no longer any doubt in his mind that we were really angels.

However, a few days later Sarge's belief in our angelic nature was shattered when he came across us as we were wrecking the playground fence. Sarge just kept gaping at us and at the damage we had done with a stupid, bewildered look on his face. For a while he looked as though he couldn't believe his own eyes. Then a stern expression appeared on his face, and he said in a voice resonant with anger and disgust, "Hey, you're not really angels!"

We assured him that we were, but from then on Sarge no longer believed anything we told him. Nevertheless, others were still able to fill both his mind and stomach with complete rubbish. Those "others" who willfully misled Sarge included even my own father.

His encounter with Sarge occurred one Sunday morning as he sat at the kitchen table reading his newspaper. Suddenly, he flinched as a sharp *rat-a-tat-tat* rent the air. He looked out the window and saw Sarge standing near the trailer with a toy submachine gun cradled in his arms. "Well, I'll fix that" my father said as he walked out the door. "Hey kid, come here. Do you know what? There's *gold* inside that gun of yours! Why don't you go home and get a screwdriver or a hammer and see for yourself?"

Sarge looked at his toy gun with the eager expression of a boy who is about to open a Christmas present. He turned on his heels and headed home. The rat-a-tat-tat noise which irritated my father was never heard again.

Like Sarge, most of the people my father worked with weren't all that bright. At least that was my father's opinion. He was constantly talking about the "morons and imbeciles" he had to work with. He had special names for all of his coworkers — names like "Muddlehead" and "Zipperhead." According to my father, Zipperhead earned his name because he was so incredibly stupid that if he had a zipper on his head he would take out his brains and play with them.

It must have been humiliating for my father to have had to take orders from people like Zipperhead. Although my father had been promoted twice while he was in California and was paid as much as a buck sergeant, his rank of specialist 5 was still technically equivalent to that of a private first class. Zipperhead, on the other hand, was a corporal and therefore outranked my father. I don't think my father had ever fully reconciled himself to taking orders from anyone — certainly not from corporals or sergeants. Consequently, he was always looking for means — devious or otherwise — by which he could turn the tables and reassert his manhood.

Particularly during the period of time when he was separated from his family, my father was constantly playing practical jokes on his superiors. For instance, he began to harass a sergeant whom he especially disliked by sending him cards anonymously through the mail. On the outside of one such card was the question, "Want to lose ten ugly pounds?" On the inside was the reply. "Cut off your head." He also sent the sergeant several bon voyage cards in order to give him the impression that someone wanted to get rid of him. Because he always used a green ink pen in addressing the envelopes in which the cards were sent, my father was delighted when the sergeant began frisking people's pockets and searching through their desks, looking for a green ink pen in order to find the culprit responsible for sending him the cards.

Before we joined him in California, my father had been sharing a room in the barracks with a big husky man named Big Bob Neilson.* Unlike my father who merely manned a guard tower, Big Bob worked

---

*Not his real name.

inside the prison itself. It was his job to control especially violent or unruly prisoners. If, for example, a prisoner were to suddenly go crazy and start making noise or threatening others, Big Bob would walk into his cell and calm him down. Sometimes — if provoked — Big Bob would hurl himself at the prisoner, pin him against the wall, and crush his ribs. The mere sight of Big Bob always had a remarkably calming effect on the prisoners.

In addition to being roommates, Big Bob and my father were drinking buddies who often frequented the Lompoc bars together. Once, Big Bob was becoming increasingly rowdy as he sat getting drunk with my father in a tavern. The bartender was worried, and must have felt that it would only be a matter of time before Big Bob became violent. He therefore sneaked up behind Big Bob and hit him over the head with a blackjack as hard as he could. Big Bob didn't bat an eye. He continued drinking as if nothing had happened. A few minutes later, however, he scratched his head and exclaimed, "My head hurts." He turned and eyed the bartender suspiciously and asked, "Did somebody hit me?" The bartender flashed Big Bob an obsequious smile and unctuously reassured him that no one had hit him.

My father was so overawed by Neilsen's thick skull that the lack of brains inside never seemed to matter to him.

In the early months of our stay in California, Big Bob came to our home regularly. When he visited us, he and my father would always get drunk. When he was drunk, Big Bob would sometimes get a faraway look in his eyes and say in words so slurred as to be nearly unintelligible, "The Army is my life." Moreover, he would usually wet his pants when he was drunk, and after he left there would be a small puddle of urine under his chair.

Not only did my mother consider Big Bob a consummate slob, she also began to feel that way about my father. Soon after we had moved to the trailer court, she told me that my father was deteriorating — that day-by-day he was becoming more and more like a GI and less and less like the officer he had once been. Although her bitter feelings toward my father softened somewhat after he landed a second job driving an oil truck and started seeing less of Big Bob, her sense of estrangement only continued to grow more profound as time passed.

Like myself, my mother found the trailer park a social wasteland. Although she maintained some social ties both inside and outside the trailer court, these contacts were very superficial and unsatisfactory. She just couldn't bring herself to associate with such persons typified by the likes of a Mrs. Crinshaw or a Mrs. Bowers. Their world was an alien and hateful one for her. That my father seemed at home in such a world only served to intensify her frustration and rage.

While having a drink with his friends, my father loved to tell the following story.

When he was a second lieutenant, my father decided to retaliate against a captain who was constantly pulling rank and bragging about his special privileges. To that end, my father carefully scrutinized this captain's habits and found that he always sat alone in a latrine reading at a particular hour in the morning. After procuring a small quantity of plastic explosive, my father used a long pole to tamp the explosive down into the muck under the toilet seat where the captain usually sat. The next morning, a few minutes after the captain entered the latrine, my father detonated the explosive. Although my father had only meant to frighten the captain, the explosion was much greater than he had anticipated. In addition to blowing the roof off the latrine, it also blew the captain straight up into the air. He landed on the branch of a nearby tree. Yet, except for having singed buttocks and being spattered with sewage, the captain was unharmed.

As things turned out my father was incredibly lucky. When an investigation was launched to determine the cause of the explosion the captain told the authorities that he had flipped his cigarette butt under the toilet seat immediately before the explosion occurred. Logically enough, the authorities concluded that the explosion must have been caused by the cigarette butt igniting methane gas under the latrine, and the investigation went no further.

My father told this and other similar stories while he and my mother were visiting the Dawson's,* a couple who lived in a trailer directly across the street from us.

Mr. Dawson was a mildly eccentric man, whose bushy mustache made him look a little like his Scottish terrier. He lived in the extreme northwest corner of the trailer court, where in addition to cultivating a garden, he trapped sparrows and made stew out of them. He once told my brother and myself that he had heard strange noises and believed that his trailer was haunted. (We were unable to determine whether or not he was joking.)

Mrs. Dawson had been a captain in the army medical corps before she met her husband. She lost her army commission due to her romantic involvement with Mr. Dawson, who was only a corporal.

While visiting the Dawson's my father had too much to drink. Therefore it is not surprising that he revealed so many personal things about himself to people who were hardly intimate acquaintances.

Upon returning home with him after visiting the Dawsons, my mother threw a screaming tirade. "You horse's ass! How could you humiliate me in front of those people? Telling all those weird, far-out stories of yours to people you barely know. What will they think? They'll

---

*Not their real names.

think you're damn *crazy* — that's what they'll think!"

She kept yelling and banging things around. Although her tirade soon subsided, she refused to let the matter drop. A few days later with a roast cooking in the oven, she abruptly told my father that she was leaving him, packed a few of her belongings, and drove off in the car.

However, about an hour later, while we were eating, my mother drove up in the car. When she walked in the door she appeared a bit crazed. Ignoring everyone present, she started rearranging things in the kitchen. There seemed to be no purpose to what she was doing.

We watched her with a sense of mounting tension. No one said a word. Finally, my father ventured to compliment her on the roast she had cooked.

"Had it been cut from my own buttocks," she replied, "I would feel quite flattered."

Although no incident similar to the one above ever occurred again during the remainder of our stay in California, relations between my parents continued to deteriorate. Yet as their problems worsened, my parents became less and less able to use introspection or to view themselves and their situation with any degree of objectivity. Rather than locating their problems within themselves, they chose instead to worry about me as a way of taking their minds off their own inadequacies.

Admittedly, I gave my parents some cause for concern in that I seemed unhappy most of the time and was often getting into trouble. I recall one incident in particular that caused my parents to view me in a harsher light.

This incident began when Alice, Mrs. Crinshaw's eight-year-old daughter, accosted me on the street near her trailer and told me she had something to show me. Because she seemed friendly and sincere enough, I followed her to her trailer without considering what that devious little varmint had in store for me.

Alice scampered inside the trailer and bid me to follow her. However, as soon as I stuck my head inside her doorway, Dennis, Alice's younger brother, threw a glass of cold water in my face. Again, not thinking of what I was doing, I lunged through the door and grabbed Alice by her ankle. She fell and began to cry. I knew then that I had made a mistake.

Later in the day Mrs. Crinshaw paid my parents a visit. She appeared to be in an exceptionally good mood. She was very calm and rational as she explained to my parents what I had done. She was even a little apologetic when she told how her son had soaked me with a glass of cold water. "He just loves to torment people with water," she explained.

After Mrs. Crinshaw left, my father read me the riot act. First of all, he told me that I had just committed two felonies: breaking and entering, and assault. "If Mrs. Crinshaw decides to press charges against you, you could end up serving time in a reformatory. The only way I could prevent this would be to have you declared not responsible by reason of insanity, and have you committed to a mental institution."

My father paused and looked at me sternly. "What I can't understand, is what the hell were you doing in the first place fooling around with kids only half your age? You must have been out of your damn mind to have gone anywhere near those Crinshaw kids!"

I didn't see how I could argue with that last point. I felt utterly mortified.

The Crinshaw incident proved to be a watershed, for almost overnight my parents appeared to lose all confidence in me. They began relating to me in much the same way as they had when I was in the fifth grade. It was as if the clock had suddenly been turned back three years. Hereafter, even my most insignificant acts seemed to be a matter of grave concern to my parents.

This overconcern, or tendency to overreact, was especially characteristic of my mother. She had a gift for seeing catastrophe in situations where others would see only humor. For example, one afternoon when she saw me pedaling back and forth in front of our home on a ridiculously tiny tricycle, she became horribly upset and screamed at me to get off that tricycle immediately. Then, in an anguished voice, she started to denounce what she saw as my "grotesquely unnatural" act:

"Here you are nearly a man, riding a child's tricycle! Won't you ever grow up? I don't think so. If you haven't begun growing up by now, I don't think you ever will. I hate to say this, John, but I think there is something seriously wrong with you — in fact, I have known this for a long, long time."

Thereupon, in an effort to convince me what a hopelessly defective person I was, she began reciting a long catalogue of petty sins going back more than ten years. As she concluded her diatribe, tears were beginning to form in her eyes. "And now — with you riding down the street on that tricycle like some kind of deranged idiot — now everyone knows that I have an abnormal child — I'm so humiliated I could die! You have no idea how much pain you have caused me — you're only capable of thinking about yourself!"

I was so stunned by my mother's vicious outburst that I just couldn't think straight. Because of my intense dependence on my mother, I always had a tendency to see things her way. Therefore, throughout her entire tirade I couldn't help but empathize with her feelings. It seemed obvious to me that my mother was really suffering and that I was the cause of her suffering. Consequently, I walked away from her lecture reeling with shame and self-loathing. It seemed apparent to me that I actually was the defective person my mother made me out to be.

The incident involving the tricycle could be considered a kind of miniature conversion experience. Before my mother discovered me on the tricycle, I was fully aware of how ridiculous I looked: I viewed myself as a more or less normal person who was merely acting like a clown. However, after my mother's outburst, I actually believed that I had hopped onto that tricycle because I was the sort of person who was simply incapable of restraining himself from acting in an abnormally childish way.

As a result of repeated instances of this kind, I began to abandon my own point of view and adopt my mother's. Through the dual process of empathizing with her emotional suffering while I in turn suffered from her vicious tirades, I began to take upon myself the burden of my mother's own "pathology" or inner turmoil, which I introjected as an intangible yet real internal presence. Furthermore, this process was starting to have a clearly visible effect on me. During the last months of my stay in California, I could be seen wandering through the trailer park with a sad or worried expression perpetually on my face. Invariably, as I walked, I would be bent over looking at the ground in front of my feet with my hands either thrust deep into my pockets or clasped behind my back, where I would be wringing them as I clutched my shirttail.

After attending the public school at Lompoc for about two or three months, I was transferred to the school at Vandenberg Air Force Base which was somewhat closer to where I lived. While attending school at Vandenberg, I initially impressed my teachers as being an exceptionally quiet student. However, as soon as I felt more comfortable in my new surroundings, I started making wisecracks in class.

At first my teachers were delighted with my apparent change, and actually encouraged my witticisms, since they believed that I was coming out of my shell and participating more fully. However, in the months that followed, I became the school's most notorious eccentric.

Even before I had received a one-week suspension for passing around offensive limericks I had written about a teacher who was universally disliked, I had already become something of a celebrity among my fellow students. Yet my status was at best an ambiguous one, for although they loved me as an entertainer, most of the students preferred not to become too personally involved with me.

Jim, a student who admired me for my intelligence, told me that although my buffoonery had at first brought me a lot of favorable attention, it was becoming increasingly counterproductive as far as my acceptability was concerned. He advised me that if I were only to stop acting like such a clown, I would become one of the most popular boys in the school.

But I just couldn't stop. My compulsive buffoonery was the only means I had of keeping myself from being overwhelmed by my mounting anxieties and feelings of sadness.

Still, even if my classmates didn't wholly accept me, they didn't dislike me, either. I found most of the students friendly enough — especially the girls, many of whom considered me handsome.

One of the girls who found me attractive was Sandi. She was by common consent the sexiest and most beautiful girl in the school.

I first became aware of Sandi's existence after I had thrown a rock into a puddle and splashed her with water while she was walking in the schoolyard with some other girls some distance from me. As soon as the rock hit the water, she let out a blood-curdling scream and took out after me, declaring that she was going to pull my hair out by the roots because I had ruined her cashmere sweater. After chasing me for some time, she gave up, told my teacher what I had done, and stormed off madder than a wet hen.

I was unable to keep my eyes off Sandi in the days and weeks that followed. Although I didn't like her at first, I still couldn't remember ever seeing anyone so exquisitely beautiful. Of course, four years previously I had felt the same way about Carolyn. Sandi resembled Carolyn: both girls had black hair and blue eyes, were exceptionally beautiful, and looked markedly more mature than is usual for girls their age. At fourteen, Sandi already had a figure that very few women in their twenties could match.

Evidently, my numerous admiring glances had a favorable effect on Sandi. This became apparent one afternoon when I saw her talking to a friend, a few weeks after the mud puddle incident, as she was walking toward me down the hall. Her friend had just asked her about the ruined sweater. "Oh, that's no longer important," Sandi replied. "I have totally changed my mind about that boy. I now think he is just wonderful." As she uttered that last comment, she gazed lovingly into my eyes.

That look went straight through me like a bolt of lightning. I continued walking down the hall in a state of mind bordering on delirium. I felt deliriously happy — yet, I was confused. One thought, and one thought only, kept going through my mind: "How could anyone so gorgeous possibly love *me*?" I felt totally unworthy of Sandi's love.

A day or so later, while flanked by two other girls, Sandi sat down immediately across from me at my table as I was eating lunch in the cafeteria. After she had made repeated attempts to draw me into a conversation she was having with her friends, Sandi looked at me quizzically and asked, "Are you antisocial?"

I said nothing. I couldn't think of anything to say. I felt like a pauper in rags being visited by a magnificent queen. I just sat there chomping away at my bologna sandwiches, my mouth so dry I could hardly swallow. I felt utterly miserable and ashamed. After gagging down my sandwiches — not knowing what else to do — I made a paper airplane out of a sack, tossed it into the air, and watched it glide gracefully across the cafeteria.

Sandi looked at my airplane admiringly, and gave me a soft and tender look. She told her friends that the boy she liked was fond of making things with his hands.

Upon hearing that last remark, I became somewhat alarmed. I thought: "Does Sandi have a boyfriend? Why not? After all, a girl like that could have anyone she wants." Still, I felt that Sandi was probably referring to me which only made me feel more foolish and self-conscious.

I sat there contemplating Sandi wistfully, trying desperately to think of something to say. But it was useless, for my mind seemed totally paralyzed. Finally, I saw no other alternative but to admit defeat, and walk away from the table a complete failure.

Although she seldom pursued me as aggressively as she had then, Sandi nevertheless continued to let me know that she was completely available.

For my part, I continued to act just as idiotically as ever. Not once did I say a single word to that girl — not even a simple "hi". Every time that voluptuous little goddess appeared in my line of sight, my brain seemed to go into cold storage. However, although I acted stupidly, I can't say that I ignored her entirely. Once, when Sandi was standing on the edge of a porch about four or five feet above me, I started to look up her dress only to find that her skirt was obstructing my view. Therefore, after procuring a couple of sticks, I poked them up her dress and spread them apart in order to get a clearer view.

Sandi was tolerant of, if somewhat puzzled by, my aberrant behavior. Once, after I had been unable to control myself and had booted her in her large, shapely ass with my knee, Sandi whirled around and looked me over for a few seconds as if trying to decide what to do. Finally, she kicked me very lightly in the shin — just barely touching me — as if to show me that she was a lady, and therefore didn't quite approve of my conduct, but was nevertheless not really angry with me. As if to emphasize this latter point, the next day she walked entirely out of her way and up a flight of stairs just to park her opulent ass a few inches in front of me, deliberately tempting me to take another shot. When I declined the opportunity, she turned around and smiled at me.

Sometimes Sandi would become angry and impatient. When I snubbed her at a school dance — dancing is beneath my dignity — she communicated her displeasure afterward by giving me a rude shove as she stormed past me down the hall. She made me miserable by refusing to look at me for better than two weeks after that incident.

At the end of the school year, while accompanied by four of her closest friends, Sandi paid an unexpected visit to my classroom. She and the four other girls stood at the front of the class and sang "Dream Lover," a tune that was then popular:

Ev'ry night I hope and pray
A dream lover will come my way
A girl to hold in my arms
And know the magic of her charms
Because I want a girl to call my own
I want a dream lover so I don't have to
dream alone.

All the while she was serenading me, Sandi never looked at me once. Yet here she was, standing in the direct center of her group — the obvious instigator of what was now taking place. I felt immensely honored. It must have taken an enormous amount of courage for Sandi to have done such a thing, and I now knew that she cared for me deeply.

I interpreted her coming into my classroom and singing to me as an obvious invitation to visit her at her home so we wouldn't have to "dream alone" during the long, lonely summer months ahead. I therefore resolved to ask Sandi for her address and telephone number as soon as school let out.

At the end of the day as the students were boarding the buses to go home, I searched frantically for Sandi. I was almost heartbroken since I feared that she might have already boarded one of the buses and that I would never see her again. Finally, I saw her standing on the sidewalk by the bus stop. She was standing alone, nearly obscured by the students rushing past her. She appeared to be waiting for someone.

I took a few steps toward her and froze. For about thirty seconds I just stood there helplessly unable to advance any further, utterly paralyzed by the overwhelming sense of my own inadequacy. "Perhaps these notions of mine of her serenading me and wanting me to visit her are nothing but wishful thinking. If I tried to talk to her I wouldn't know what to say. I'd only be making a fool out of myself." With these dismal thoughts, I turned away from her and walked toward the bus bound for the army disciplinary barracks.

While riding home on the bus I realized that I had made a mistake. Still I consoled myself with the thought that at least I knew two very essential facts: I knew Sandi's last name, and that she lived at the Vandenberg Air Force Base. I would walk to Vandenberg which was only five miles away, look her name up in the telephone book, and visit her.

However, as usual, I was only deceiving myself. If I hadn't the courage to talk to her while she was waiting for me at the bus stop — or at countless other times when she had made herself available — how would I find the courage to visit her at her home?

Even while I was still going to school I had made several trips into Vandenberg in order to find out where Sandi lived. I would walk down a quiet road which wound through the hills, past an abandoned firing range. This was always an uncomfortable walk for me since one of my shoes pinched me, and caused an immense blood blister to form under my right heel.

Nevertheless, I persisted. I desperately longed to get a glimpse of Sandi and to find out where she lived. Upon searching through a telephone directory in a phone booth on my first trip into Vandenberg, I found there were four individuals whose last name was the same as Sandi's. I must have haunted that telephone booth for close to an hour trying to summon the courage to call one of those persons and ask for Sandi. Finally, with my heart pounding wildly, I made a call only to hang up the moment someone answered.

Yet my inability to locate Sandi by using the telephone didn't discourage me in the least. Because I believed Sandi had a picket fence around her house — picket fences were rare in Vandenberg — I thought I had a solid clue as to where she lived. I had received this "clue" upon overhearing Perry — a notorious lecher who was always grabbing at girls' breasts and buttocks — playfully teasing Sandi by threatening to "pull a picket" out of her fence. I took his remark literally, and concluded that Sandi must live in a house surrounded by a picket fence. However, in retrospect, it now seems obvious to me that Perry had other things on his mind besides clutching pickets.

Over a period of several weeks, I repeatedly visited each of the four addresses listed in the Vandenberg telephone directory and never saw a picket fence. Since the streets and houses in Vandenberg were so poorly marked, it never occurred to me that Sandi's picket fence just didn't exist.

One afternoon, immediately after the end of the school year, I was in Vandenberg still looking for that elusive house with the picket fence. Suddenly, I heard a young woman's voice calling, *Sandi! Sandi!* On hearing this, I scanned the horizon but saw no one. However, less than a minute later, I saw two girls in their late teens walking toward me. As they approached me, both girls scrutinized me carefully with severe expressions on their faces. One of those girls told her companion, "Ah, he doesn't look all that great to me."

I certainly didn't feel that way about the girl who had just made that remark. That girl bore such a striking resemblance to Sandi that for a while I just stood there a bit dazzled, unable to decide whether or not it was really her.

Upon contemplating that regal beauty as she walked down the street, it became apparent to me that she must be Sandi's older sister. Moreover, I had an intuition that Sandi must have seen me coming and had abruptly headed home with the expectation that her "dream lover" was finally coming to visit her. This would explain why her sister had been calling her, and why she had made that disparaging remark: she must have felt that Sandi had grossly overestimated my looks.

Therefore if (a) Sandi was at home that very moment waiting for me to visit her, (b) I had come to Vandenberg for the express purpose of visiting her, and (c) the only possible way I could accomplish this worthwhile goal would be to ask her sister — who now stood before me as if in answer to my prayers — where Sandi lived, then it follows that I should have done just that.

Instead, I began to follow Sandi's sister without any serious intention of even talking to her. I followed her to the Vandenberg Teen Club. There I sat alone in a corner for better than an hour and a half ardently admiring her beauty while I daydreamed about Sandi.

However, the stupidity of my actions finally dawned on me. I then asked myself, "What else have you accomplished by this long walk into Vandenberg other than to incur a horrible blister on the bottom of your foot?" As usual, I had a convenient rationalization for my appalling passivity. I was able to persuade myself that my hunch that Sandi must have hurried home in order to await my arrival was only another one of my wishful fantasies.

This pretty much sums up my relationship — if you can call it that — with Sandi. During the months I knew her, I was constantly day-dreaming about her. Yet I never once so much as considered making a realistic attempt to get to know her. The nature of this "relationship" was such that I might just as well have been in a coma, and Sandi might just as well have been nothing more than a beautiful dream.

About a week after I had sat ogling Sandi's sister in the Teen Club, I accompanied my mother to the Vandenberg post exchange. There I saw Joan standing by the cosmetics department examining a can of hair spray. Because Joan was Sandi's closest friend and had always been very friendly to me, I was glad to see her. I walked over to where she was standing and greeted her warmly.

At my salutation Joan stiffened, and looked as though she had just smelled a disagreeable odor. Then, with an air of contemptuous indifference, she nonchalantly put back the hair spray, and walked away from me without saying a word.

Since I had never antagonized Joan I understood that her unfriendly response was a direct reflection on how I had treated Sandi. It then became evident to me that my surmise that the last time I was in Vandenberg Sandi had been at home waiting for me to visit her, had been a correct one. I had failed her, and now Sandi despised me.

I was miserable throughout that entire summer. Indeed, I had been miserable throughout my entire stay in California. I hated the isolation and the boredom. I hated California itself with its monotonous sunshine and its scorched and barren countryside.

Once, while hiking up a lonely trail which led over and through the bleak and desolate hills, I was grieving my loss of Sandi's love. Yet along with sadness there was also a feeling of awe. I was wondering how a girl with Sandi's transcendent beauty could possibly have loved someone as insignificant as myself. That such a girl should love me seemed to me to be totally inexplicable — a miracle.

Then I thought about Carolyn. That a girl of Carolyn's caliber should like me, I also considered a miracle. Yet at the time I didn't consider it at all extraordinary that Carolyn should like me since I had regarded myself as being very handsome. Obviously, in the four years which had elapsed, my self-esteem had suffered considerably.

However, along with this loss of self-esteem, my thinking had also become increasingly distorted and divorced from reality. For instance, as I continued thinking about Sandi and Carolyn, the idea struck me that those two girls were in some significant sense *identical*. Not only did they physically resemble each other, but they also seemed to share a certain transcendental quality: they were unquestionably the most beautiful girls I had ever seen, and the fact that both of those girls had once cared for me seemed to me nothing less than a *literal* miracle.

Furthermore, the notion dawned upon me that such miracles must necessarily follow some sort of cosmic rhythm. Since Sandi had entered my life four years after Carolyn, I therefore concluded that such miracles must recur every four years. Hence I came to the comforting conclusion that in four more years another beautiful woman would enter my life and love me. This woman would be a sort of avatar of Sandi, just as I now regarded Sandi as an avatar of Carolyn.

Moreover, during this time my mind was becoming increasingly clouded with superstitious notions. For example, while walking or running beneath the eucalyptus trees, I couldn't trip and fall over a root or some similar obstacle without believing that God Himself had tripped me in order to punish me for my sins.

Once, while peering down into a gulch as I stood under the eucalyptus trees, my eyes lit upon a fissure in the side of the ravine. For just a second or two, I believed I saw gnomes entering and leaving that crevice, which was about four hundred feet from where I was standing. Filled with irrational hope, I hiked down into the gulch in order to get a closer look at that mysterious crack. To my dismay, I saw nothing in the crevice other than dirt. Yet for several more minutes I continued peering into it while filled with an incredibly intense sense of longing.

Above all else, I longed to go back to Washington state and resume my friendship with David. Sometimes that longing would become so intense that in desperation I would fall to the ground, bury my face in my hands, and pray to God to transport me back to Washington *immediately*. When at last I took my face from my hands, opened my eyes, and found myself still in my hated surroundings, I would curse God and tell Him that He was a damned fake.

While in California I began to have premonitions of my impending madness. Until I had moved to California, I never fully realized to what extent I lived in a world of fantasy. When I was in Everett I had had a very rich and satisfying fantasy life, which, to a large extent, grew out of my activities. I had shared both those activities and the accompanying fantasies with my friend David. However, in California I had no activities to speak of, and no one with whom to share my fantasies. Therefore, my fantasies tended more and more to serve as a substitute for any real activities and to isolate me more and more in a world all my own. At certain ominous moments, I feared that I was losing my ability to differentiate between what was real and what was imaginary. This "world all my own" would then seem like a prison from which someday I might not be able to escape.

# 7

# SCHIZO TRAINING TIME BEGINS
# WITH A VENGEANCE

In 1959 the Army relinquished control of the Lompoc penitentiary to the civilian branch of the federal government. Consequently, near the end of summer my father was transferred back to Fort Lewis, Washington. There he worked as a guard in the stockade guarding some of the same soldiers he used to defend — a situation he must have found extremely distasteful.

For the next two years we lived in Tillicum, a quiet village of approximately three or four hundred people situated just outside Fort Lewis. My first feeling upon arriving at Tillicum was one of joy, for I had finally got my wish and was back in Washington state! However, I was soon beset by a feeling of déjà vu — an oppressive feeling that here, as in Lompoc, there was nowhere to go, nothing to do, and no one to talk to.

While in Tillicum we stayed at a trailer court whose appearance and social atmosphere was suggestive of a shantytown. Immediately across the street from us in this trailer park lived a loudmouthed old woman who years ago had worked as a prostitute in Tacoma. She once told my mother that although she used to be a whore she still knew how to act like a lady because, to quote her exact words, "I wouldn't say the word 'shit' even if I had a mouthful." Living a few doors down from the ex-prostitute was a woman who regularly fed her watchdog gunpowder in order to "make him mean." These two women were typical trailer park specimens.

Somewhat less typical of the type of person who infested this trailer park was Mr. Morris,* our next door neighbor. To all appearances, Mr. Morris was a very solid and respectable man. Yet even he had his quirks. He was something of a necrophile who was always chasing ambulances so that he could get a titillating glimpse of a mangled body.

While I lived in Tillicum I didn't make a single friend. My closest companion during this time was a standard French poodle named Pepi whom we had acquired while we were in California.

---

*Not his real name.

That dog possessed a couple of strikingly human-like characteristics. For instance, Pepi was one of those rare dogs who express their affection by *smiling*. Pepi's other remarkable characteristic was his extraordinary intelligence, which is illustrated by the manner in which he solved the annoying problem of getting grass in his mouth whenever he chewed his bone. After picking the bone up in his mouth and walking across the lawn to where a crumpled rag lay, he then spread that rag out with his paws and dropped the bone on the rag — thereby solving his problem!

I never went anywhere in Tillicum without Pepi. I even took him boating with me on American Lake. He must have enjoyed this immensely, for a neighbor of ours once saw him wandering around down at Bill's Boathouse — a half mile from home — where he climbed into my rowboat and went to sleep.

Once every two weeks we would visit my paternal grandparents in Everett and stay at their house over the weekend. At such times, I often stayed with my friend David.

David had moved while I was in California to a rural area five miles south of Everett. At his new home he had a cabin all to himself about a hundred feet from the main house.

Upon seeing David again I found that he had undergone some sort of emotional crisis, and was now a guilt-ridden religious fanatic. While I was visiting him in his cabin, he kept going on and on about what a sinful life he had led. He mentioned the time when I had stopped him from committing a homosexual act with a man whom we had known for some time. This man wanted to pay each of us five dollars to take down our pants and sit on his lap. At that time David had been somewhat turned-on by the man's proposition. He urged me to comply with the man's wishes with the argument: "Just think of what we can buy with five dollars!" He now thanked me with heartfelt sincerity for persuading him to reject that "wicked temptation."

While continuing to express horror over his past sinful life, David quoted the following Bible verse: "The wages of sin are death." He then explained to me that death is caused by sin — that everyone must die because they have sinned.

However, since I viewed death as a natural process occurring in plants, animals, and humans alike, all this talk of sin causing death struck me as being utterly bizarre. I couldn't help but ask myself: "What dreadful sin must the wildflowers outside David's window have committed in order to make them wilt?"

Yet I was glad to see David despite his fanaticism. I found he had become an even more sensitive and considerate person since I had last knew him. Furthermore, in his own half-baked way, David was a rather intellectual boy who enjoyed having a serious conversation. In the months which followed, I spent many pleasurable hours with him discussing a wide variety of topics.

I also enjoyed talking to David's father. He was a very kind man who treated me like I was another one of his sons. (He had two other sons beside David, but they had already left home.) Although he was an unskilled laborer with very little formal education — he had even once been a hobo — David's father was nevertheless an amazingly well-read man with an extensive knowledge of history and philosophy.

As time passed by, I began to feel far more comfortable in David's house than I did in my own home.

I once overheard my father telling my mother about a problem he had encountered upon stopping off at the N.C.O. Club in Fort Lewis to buy a pack of cigarettes. He seemed nothing less than mortified when I heard him say, "They wouldn't let me in."

Since my father was paid as much as a sergeant, he might have been under the impression that this entitled him to enter the N.C.O. Club. However, if he believed that, he certainly had a brutal surprise. At an army post where not long ago he had once served as a captain, it suddenly became agonizingly clear to him that he now had fewer privileges and less prestige than even a lowly corporal.

Not long after the above incident, while my father was somewhat intoxicated, he had a man-to-man talk with me. At that time I was into body building, and my father tried to explain to me why intelligence was much more important than strength. "Because if you're not smart, someday you might want to enter an exclusive club and they will say, 'You can't come in here.'"

My father understood that I would never look down on him because he had lost his rank. Moreover, as my mother became less emotionally supportive toward him, he began to increasingly depend upon me for understanding and sympathy. I, of course, felt sorry for him. It was obvious to me that his self-esteem had been very badly shaken. It put a knot in my stomach whenever he made his pitiful boast to me that, for instance, he could have been a general, or that he had the expertise to lob an artillery shell through the roof of a particular building in Tacoma many miles away.

For better than a year I had often heard my father say that the Army was filled with stupid and incompetent men who were incapable of making it in civilian life. He would compare such men to a flock of sea gulls who had become so dependent on scavenging refuse at a city dump that when the dump was finally closed and covered over with dirt the sea gulls died from starvation. When I first heard my father talk this way, his voice was filled with scorn and reproach. But as time passed by, whenever he made this sea gull analogy, there was always a note of self-hate in his voice.

While we were living in Tillicum my father worked at three jobs simultaneously. In addition to working nights as a guard in the stockade, he also worked as a flight instructor and as a vacuum cleaner salesman during the day. He worked hard and incessantly, and this took a horrible physical and psychological toll on him. In just eighteen months he looked as though he had aged ten years.

Moreover, partly because he was under such stress at that time, my father would often go on drunken binges, usually lasting from two to four days. During this time my mother also drank excessively. But unlike my father, she could hold her liquor, so her alcoholism wasn't nearly as noticeable as his.

Whenever my father went on one of his drunken sprees, my mother would become very withdrawn. Other than making an occasional cutting remark, she seldom spoke to him when he was this way. Sometimes — particularly during the summer of 1960 — she would threaten to divorce him. She always backed up such threats by running away from home, taking us kids along with her.

During this time, however, my mother was never very supportive of my father even when he was completely sober. Instead she was constantly giving him subtle reminders that he was a nearly illiterate man without a high school diploma who had been unable to retain his rank as a captain.

My father loved my mother dearly. That she was on the verge of divorcing him must have hurt him terribly.

Nevertheless, even while we were living in Tillicum, my father's behavior toward my mother didn't change much. Although he was somewhat more withdrawn than he had been formerly, he never once raised his voice, uttered a harsh word, or looked at my mother with an angry expression on his face. For the most part, he simply ignored my sister's existence. But his behavior toward my brother and myself was something else entirely.

My father obviously had a great deal of pent-up rage inside him — rage at the way the Army, my mother, and life in general were treating him. Still, as far as I was concerned, even while we were living in Tillicum my father wasn't all that unpleasant to be around — just as long as he was drunk. When he was drunk, his behavior was that of a playful and affectionate child. As far as I can remember, he had never shown me any affection unless he had been drinking. While I was in Tillicum I began to wish that my father could stay drunk all of the time. Unfortunately, most of the time he was dead sober: he had to be in order to hold down three jobs.

Whenever my father wasn't working or drinking, he was persecuting my brother and me. Almost every day for several months he would lecture us on how totally worthless and selfish we were. With a hundred subtle variations, he would endlessly repeat the same old lecture about how he grew up in the Great Depression and was so virtuous while we were the scum of the earth for having such a soft life. Often he would relate various instances in which he had helped or bought things for his own father, and would ask accusingly, "What have you ever done for me?"

My father was constantly making the cruelest and the most cutting remarks. Sometimes when he was lecturing us he would be shouting at the top of his voice and threatening to break our bones. A physical beating would almost be a relief after such a psychological beating as this.

Although my brother merely thought my father was being unfair, I really took his lectures to heart. I thought about those lectures often and they poisoned my life. Because I felt sorry for my father and identified with his plight, his lectures caused me intense emotional anguish.

My brother was somewhat more fortunate than I in that he had a car, lots of friends, and was gone most of the time. In fact, he never came home except to eat and sleep. Not only that, my mother never harassed my brother. Instead she was openly critical of my father for being so harsh with him. However there seemed to be a tacit agreement between my parents that harassing me was a wholly legitimate activity.

I could never walk into my own home without feeling like I was under attack. For instance, whenever I went into the bathroom and sat down on the toilet, my father would always come barging in under the flimsy pretext that he needed to get something. When I complained that he was violating my privacy, he would explode: "What's the matter? Do you think your ass is made out of gold? Do you think that I come in here just to see your goddamned ass!?"

During this time I felt so tense that it seemed as if the air inside the trailer were charged with electricity and as if electrical currents were continually passing through my body. More than anything else, I felt trapped: even the smallest things such as the wrong sort of emotions or expression on my face could literally provoke a disaster. I remember, for instance, being approached by my father who started telling me how certain men will suddenly come home with an ax and smash everything in sight. "There are men who do this. It happens all the time." As my father spoke those words he seemed about ready to explode, and the only thing which held him back was that he had my complete and total sympathy!

My parents were ardent animal lovers. Besides a French poodle, we also had a Siamese cat, and a white rat named Kiki. Like my parents, Kiki was a confirmed alcoholic. Whenever my parents were drinking, they would fill Kiki's food tray with red wine and laugh as he avidly lapped it up.

One night my father stuck his hand inside the cage and began to pet his furry little drinking partner. However, because my father was drunk, he handled the rat a little too roughly and was bitten.

My father pulled his hand out of the cage and glumly inspected his bleeding finger. "Well, when he starts doing this, he will have to be put to sleep." With that announcement, my father grabbed a $CO_2$ fire extinguisher and emptied its contents out onto the cage until the entire cage was covered with a small mountain of dry ice.

I was glad my father had killed that rat. It had been my duty to clean its cage twice a week. To me it and its cage were nothing more than stinking eyesores.

However, I was careful not to betray my satisfaction at what my father had done. I could see that my mother was becoming increasingly upset over the rodent's untimely death, and I knew from experience that whenever she became angry with my father, I usually suffered for it. Therefore, I left the trailer because I felt that it was only a matter of time before my mother would punish me for my father's act.

I walked outside and sat down under the trailer's awning. I thought to myself: "What a relief! Well, at least I won't ever have to bother with that stinking rat again!" But I didn't have more than a moment's rest before my mother stormed out of the trailer and started lecturing me:

"Well, at last you finally got your wish: the rat's dead! Aren't you happy now?

"John, I hate to say this, but sometimes you make me ashamed to even call you my own son. You would rather see the entire world go to hell in a handbasket than help out a little. You resented that little animal's very existence merely because you had to spend ten minutes of your precious time cleaning out his cage.

"You really make me sick! You've got to be the most selfish and small-minded person who has ever lived! You're incapable of thinking about anyone but yourself!

"I just hope you're happy the rat's dead — that's all I got to say!"

With that, she stomped back into the trailer and slammed the door. Meanwhile, the effect of that speech was such that I felt as if I had been gloating over the death of my own brother!

My mother was a virtuoso in the art of inducing guilt. She was capable of making me feel guilty about nearly everything: for feeling sad, for feeling happy at inappropriate times, for a lack of enthusiasm in performing household chores, and so on ad nauseam, ad infinitum.

Not long after we had moved to Tillicum, my mother noticed that I was becoming increasingly self-absorbed. Consequently, she began to subject me to a constant barrage of criticism for being too "self-centered" and "introverted." (This, of course, only made me more self-absorbed.) Whenever she called me an introvert there was always an unmistakable note of hate in her voice. I think she must have expected me to fill a certain void in her life caused by her emotional distance from my father. This, together with the fact that I was unable to fulfill that expectation, was undoubtedly a major reason why I was the recipient of the rage she felt toward my father.

This being the case, it is easy to see how even the most ridiculously trivial transgressions on my part could trigger one of my mother's screaming tirades. But I hadn't the slightest suspicion that my mother was using me as a scapegoat. By the time I had moved to Tillicum, I was so emotionally off-balance most of the time that I was unable to maintain my own perspective. If either my mother or father stormed and raged at me, I automatically felt that I must be at fault. I therefore internalized all this psychological violence, and began to hate myself.

However, to the extent that I abandoned my own point of view and saw myself in a manner similar to the way my parents saw me, I became vulnerable to their suggestions that I was slowly going insane. It was therefore inevitable that some especially painful incident should arise and cause me to panic, and thereby bring about a course of events which would result in my psychosis.

One such incident occurred one afternoon in March 1960. On that day I was alone in the trailer and was ravenously picking at the leftovers of a roast in the refrigerator when suddenly my mother walked in the door. She gave me a sharp glance, and immediately walked over to the refrigerator and looked at the roast. "You filthy, stinking pig — you've eaten nearly half that roast! Has it ever occurred to you that there's other people in this world besides your own goddamned self!? We were going to have that roast for dinner tonight and now that's impossible!"

My mother was totally beside herself with rage. While screaming at the top of her voice, she assailed me as a worthless parasite who was utterly incapable of thinking about anyone but himself. For the longest time she continued yelling and screaming, and using the foulest and most violently abusive language. But as bad as this abuse was, my mother's real cruelty didn't even begin until after she had calmed down and was able to collect her thoughts. Then, like a prosecuting attorney, she reviewed certain selected events spanning my entire life in order to establish that I was an irredeemably defective person who was steadily getting worse. After citing instance after instance in which my behavior had been antisocial, selfish, crazy, or odd, she explained to me that because such behavior had been characteristic of me since my very earliest years, it must therefore have a genetic basis, and that it would only be a matter of time before I would end up in an insane asylum like my great-grandmother.

There was a hysterical note in my mother's voice as she concluded her lecture:

"When you were in the first grade, I had you examined by psychiatrists at the University of Washington. Those doctors advised me to have you committed to a mental institution. They told me if you didn't have immediate psychiatric care it would only be a matter of time before you would become completely insane.

"I now realize that I should have followed their advice. You have no idea of how much suffering you have caused me! You have always been cold and selfish — you would never let me love you!

"Year by year I've watched you become more selfish, introverted, and mentally deranged. Year by year you have become a bigger burden for me to bear. Yet I've always protected you, sheltered you under my roof, and loved you as best I could. But mark my words, John, the time is coming when I will no longer be able to do this. The time will come when you will have to be put away!"

Upon hearing this, I burst into tears and rushed out the door, overcome with intense grief and terror.

I wandered down the street in sort of a trance, howling in agony. As I walked through the village in this trance-like state, my entire life seemed to pass before me in review. In my mind's eye I saw the imposing buildings of the University of Washington campus, and then the gloomy, half-lit corridor in which I had been interrogated. I recalled the countless instances in which I had made my mother suffer. In my clouded, terror-stricken state of mind, the terrible verdict of the university psychiatrists had the ring of indisputable scientific authority, for I suddenly "realized" that at no time in my life had I ever been fully human — that I had always been a cold and selfish person who didn't even love his own mother.

Other thoughts equally lugubrious raced through my mind:

"And to think of all my mother has done for me. Year after year I have given her nothing but grief. Yet she always stood by me, loved me, and sheltered me in her home when by rights I should have been locked up in an insane asylum long ago!

"And now I've gotten so bad that even my dear mother can no longer bear the burden of my selfishness and depravity."

But what horrified me more than anything else was the thought that I had inherited my great-grandmother's insanity,* and had nothing to look forward to other than an inexorable descent into madness and a life behind bars in a mental institution!

In my unreasoning terror, I could see only one way out of spending the rest of my life in an asylum: *I must become good.* With this in mind, I rushed home in order to reassure my mother — and myself as well — that from now on I was going to be good. Upon entering the trailer, I told my mother with *heartfelt sincerity*:

"I realize that you were only saying those things for my own benefit. It was just like a surgeon lancing a wound in order to drain away all the

---

*That I had inherited my great-grandmother's madness is highly unlikely in view of the fact that she was neither schizophrenic nor psychotic but sociopathic.

pus. You said those things because you love me, and want to purge me of all the rottenness you see inside me."

When my mother heard this, she smiled and affectionately stroked my head. "I thought all I'd done was hurt your feelings. Well, it takes a very special person to feel that way."

Throughout the ninth grade I continued to act like a clown. I was constantly interrupting class discussions with my wisecracks and witticisms. My grades during this period were mostly D's — my worst academic performance to date. Even my performance as a buffoon was markedly inferior to what it had been a year ago: in the eighth grade the students had laughed mostly *with* rather than *at* me, while in the ninth grade things were pretty much the opposite.

Nevertheless, I was still in great demand as an entertainer. For instance, at the beginning of the second semester I overheard a couple of students bragging about their good fortune of having me in one of their classes. By that time I had perfected an impressive repertoire of weird gestures, mannerisms, noises, and facial expressions. Whenever I got up to sharpen one of my pencils in class and did my crazy walk, my classmates would give me a loud ovation.

My notoriety caused me some problems. Between classes students who were complete strangers to me would walk up to me and ask me to perform one of my weird acts. Some of my classmates thought there was something seriously wrong with me, and would attempt to assess my mental status by asking me to do various rudimentary mathematical calculations in my head or to spell certain words.

Strangely enough, I impressed many of my classmates as being a very warm and outgoing person. Unfortunately, my mother's view of me — that I was an introverted and emotionally aloof person — was probably much closer to the truth. During this period of my life there were only three persons in the entire world whom I could relate to: my friend, David; my dog, Pepi; and my younger sister, whom I had always been rather close to.

My introversion and emotional aloofness particularly irked my grandparents. At their invitation, I spent a week with them in their home in Everett over the Easter holiday. Throughout that entire time I avoided their company and seldom left the attic where I slept except to take a solitary walk. Whenever they spoke to me they were rarely able to get more out of me than a few mumbled monosyllables. This antisocial behavior greatly upset my grandparents — the more so since they had always felt especially fond of me. But at that time I was hardly capable of relating to anyone.

I even found my friend David difficult to relate to at times. I further irritated my grandparents by inviting him to stay with me in their house without first asking their permission. David was by then a hardcore religious fanatic, and when he was alone with me in my grandparents' house he tried to pressure me into making a decision for Christ. Had he made a homosexual pass at me I wouldn't have found his behavior much more distasteful than this clumsy attempt to convert me.

Notwithstanding his heavy-handed behavior, I still valued David as a friend and didn't want to hurt his feelings. When he implored me to accept Jesus Christ as my personal savior, I told him that I would think about it.

Not long after David had delivered his sales pitch for Christ and left, I stepped out for a walk. I strolled aimlessly along Hewitt Avenue looking at the old buildings. One particularly ornate brick building caught my eye. When I glanced up at the top of its facade, I noticed that it had been erected in 1896. "What an old building!" I thought.

When I returned from my walk I excitedly told my grandfather, "I've just seen the oldest building on Hewitt Avenue. It was built way back in 1896!"

My grandfather, who was born in 1895, didn't take kindly to that remark. As soon as his anger had subsided to the point where he could find coherent words, he told me:

"That building isn't old at all! Everett is a relatively modern city — you just don't find old buildings here. Even Marysville is older than Everett, and Snohomish is a far older town than either Marysville or Everett. If you want to see old buildings you should go to Europe. When I was in Germany, I stayed in buildings that were built back in the sixteenth century. In fact, I have seen buildings that are over a thousand years old!"

My grandfather began to speak warmly about the magnificent Gothic cathedrals that he and my grandmother had seen on their many trips to Europe. He probably loved those old buildings more than he loved people.

My grandmother fully shared my grandfather's peculiar values. In her eyes — as well as in his — the ultimate crime wasn't murder but the senseless destruction of property. Although my grandmother had been staunchly pro-American and anti-Hitler during World War II, she nevertheless did not regard the Nazis as being altogether evil men, since, to quote her words, "They never engaged in the wanton destruction of property."

To a limited extent, from my grandparents' point of view this made my father who had been a vandal when he was young even worse than a Nazi!

Therefore my remark about seeing the old building probably pleased my grandfather more than it angered him. That remark indicated to him that I shared his love for old buildings. Not only that, it must have been a considerable relief to him after trying fruitlessly for several days to draw me into a conversation, to discover at last a topic of mutual interest which we could discuss together.

That night my grandparents made one last heroic attempt to have a meaningful conversation with me. After we had eaten supper, my grandparents and I sat on the living room sofa together and thumbed through a giant book filled with color photographs of Europe's great medieval cathedrals. As I sat between them and turned the pages of this book, they recounted the history and unique beauties of each of the cathedrals. They emphasized the fact that it took hundreds of years to build those majestic edifices.

While we were looking at those pictures my grandparents made several attempts to elicit my comments. However, although I was impressed with the beauty and grandeur of those buildings, I was just too nonplused to do more than mumble a few noncommittal words by way of reply.

My grandparents were especially thrilled by the great rose window of the Chartres cathedral. When they excitedly asked me what I thought of that architectural wonder, I quipped, "Gee, I'd sure like to throw a rock through that window!"

While my grandmother gasped in horror, my grandfather reached over and slammed the book shut. Both my grandparents got up from the sofa. For better than fifteen seconds they were too stunned to say anything. My grandfather just stood there in the middle of the living room with a bewildered expression on his face. Finally, he pulled himself together and announced, "We're going to bed." He appeared haggard and forlorn as he walked slowly toward the hallway. There were tears running down my grandmother's cheeks as she followed him.

Feeling somewhat bewildered and alarmed, I decided to prepare for bed myself. After I had finished up in the bathroom, my grandmother met me in the hallway. She was still sobbing as she asked me, "Don't you love anyone or anything?" She then repeated some words which I had spoken — half in jest, half in earnest — several days previously, to the effect that I didn't trust my mother. After repeating those words, she admonished me:

"Everyone should trust their own mother! Your father did. When I was away on business in Minneapolis, Gram told your father that she was going to put him in an orphanage unless I came back to pick him up. He told her, 'She'll come back.' He wasn't at all worried because he had complete trust in me — that I'd come back and get him."

Her parting words to me were: "It's a tragedy you can't even trust your own mother! You don't love or trust anyone, do you?"

The next day when I found myself alone in the house with my grandfather, I could sense that a storm was brewing. As I was about to leave the house, my grandfather stopped me and asked sharply, "Where do you think you are going?"

"I am going to meet David — why?"

There was an ominous tone in my grandfather's voice as he said, "I want you to step into the kitchen for a minute — I have something to say to you."

Bracing myself for the worst, I followed him into the kitchen. When we were seated at the kitchen table, my grandfather gave vent to all the anger that had been building up inside him for the past several days:

"Now, John, we have invited you into our home with the understanding that you were going to visit with us. During the entire time that you have been here, you have totally ignored us! Each morning when you come down to have breakfast with us, you have never so much as said a single, 'Hello' or 'Good morning.' Yet if the breakfasts we fix for you aren't wholly to your liking, we certainly hear about it!

"You don't bother to observe even the most elementary rules of decency or politeness. When we talk to you we can hardly get a single word out of you. All you do is mumble something and look the other way. You treat us as if we didn't exist!

"And not only that — not only do you treat us as if we didn't exist, but you have the awful gall to invite your friend into our home without even as much as asking our permission! Now don't misunderstand me. I don't object to your friend staying with us. But you should have had the decency to ask our permission first!

"You don't ever consider anyone's feelings but your own. Here we invite you into our home and you totally ignore us and spend all your time with David!

"And not only that — a few days ago you said something that hurt your grandmother terribly. You've mentioned that you didn't trust your own mother. What that remark indicates to me is that you're incapable of loving anyone. You don't even love your own mother!

"And then there's your remark about wanting to throw a rock through the window of the Chartres cathedral. What kind of monster — what kind of subhuman are you to think of such a thing?! Do you have any idea of how much effort, how much patience, and how much *love* went into constructing such a building? I don't think you have the slightest idea of what love really is!"

Here my grandfather proceeded to deliver an eloquent and impassioned speech on the nature of love. At the climax of his speech he asked me rhetorically, "Do you want to know that love is?" He thereupon produced a picture of a house, flowers, and trees with a sea gull flying overhead, which my paraplegic cousin Ricky had very cleverly executed by means of a typewriter. Slapping that picture down in front of me, he declared:

"Now that is love. Ricky created that picture especially for me. He said, 'Grandpa, I want you to have this picture.' Do you realize how much effort — how much *love* — went into creating that picture? Ricky is nearly paralyzed from the neck down. He had to peck at the keys of the typewriter *with his nose!* Now that is what I call love, and that is exactly the quality which you utterly lack!"

My grandfather then looked at me earnestly and asked, "Have you ever loved anyone, John? Has there ever been a time in your life when you loved anyone?"

At my grandfather's question I burst into tears, for all at once the emotional barrenness of my life came back to haunt me, and I came to the panic-stricken realization that I had never loved anyone in my entire life. Overcome with grief, I staggered toward the back room and collapsed upon a sofa. While sitting slumped over in a fetal position I wept uncontrollably for nearly two hours. In my heartbroken despair, I kept telling myself that I was worse than an idiot or a criminal, since of all the people who had ever lived, I alone was incapable of love.

One of my parents' zaniest escapades occurred about one or two weeks after my visit to my grandparents. This memorable event occurred just as they were preparing to leave Tillicum and drive to Everett. My mother was making this trip in order to run away from my father. However, regardless of her wishes, my father was coming along for the ride. As my parents were preparing to embark on their meaningless journey, they were both beside themselves with rage. But what did they do? Did they talk things over? Did they argue or fight? Nothing of the sort! They began shouting questions *at me.*

The questions they shouted at me served no more purpose than their pointless trip. They weren't trying to elicit information from me. Nor had I done anything wrong. It is now obvious to me that those questions weren't even addressed to me. Rather it was as if I were a telephone receiver, and my parents were merely utilizing me in order to shout at each other.

As I walked out the door and headed toward the car, my father shouted one set of questions in one ear, while my mother screamed a different set of questions in the other. I could hardly understand what they were saying much less answer their questions. However, my failure to answer their questions threw them into an ecstasy of rage, and they began to shout louder and louder and ask their questions at an ever faster rate.

As soon as I climbed into the back seat of the car, my parents leaned over the front seat and continued screaming their questions at me. They were absolutely insistent that I answer their questions immediately!

For the first time in my life I began to stutter. Evidently my parents must have considered this a grave provocation, for when they heard me stutter they literally went wild! My father showered me with curses and threatened to smash my face in. My mother bared her teeth and began shrieking like an utter madwoman. Her words by now were wholly unintelligible.

Finally my parents' fury reached a climax, and suddenly abated. They turned around and drove to Everett as if nothing had happened.

Meanwhile, they had totally cured me, for after that last outburst I never stuttered again!

Sometime in late May 1960, I began to notice an inner paralysis creeping over me. I felt weak and helpless — that I was on a downward course, headed for certain failure. Yet at the same time I didn't feel particularly concerned about what was happening to me. I was just too numb to be very concerned about anything. In fact, I felt strangely happy or euphoric. Nevertheless, under this euphoria I had a vague feeling that there must be something seriously wrong with me.

My vague feeling that there was something wrong with me became very acute right after my dog Pepi died. (Pepi died of leftis spirosis, a rare kidney disease.) Although I had loved that animal, I felt absolutely nothing when he died. Not only that, upon leaving the trailer after hearing of his death, a silly smile was on my face and I was singing, "Old Pep has a wonderful home" — a parody of the song "Old Shep."

My sister overheard me and was shocked by my inappropriate behavior.

However — despite my numbness — my inappropriate response to Pepi's death shocked even me. While alone in a secluded wooded area I pondered the significance of my total lack of grief over that animal's death. For some mysterious reason I was unable to feel sad no matter how hard I tried. I knew that that dog had loved me — yet somehow I felt strangely elated at his death. This inexplicable euphoria seemed horribly unnatural to me, and I began to suspect my parents and grandparents were right about me after all — that I was some kind of monster or subhuman incapable of caring about anyone.

A few days after those somber meditations, I saw a clump of Pepi's hair lying on the ground not far from our trailer. As soon as I felt sure no one was watching me, I picked up that last remnant of Pepi and stuffed it into a discarded aspirin battle. I then hid the bottle under the trailer. When a couple of days later my sister found the bottle, I became horribly upset for I felt she had desecrated a sacred shrine.

While harboring the deepest feelings for Pepi, I still had no conscious awareness of even caring for him!

My mind was split. The inner emotional core of my being no longer wanted any part of the pain and verbal abuse which was its daily lot, and had gone into hibernation, so to speak.

But my mind was split in more ways than one. At this time I viewed my parents as being nearly perfect people. Their negative or persecuting characteristics were totally split off from my conscious awareness and internalized as living presences within me. These parental introjects — or internal persecutors — were always on the lookout for appropriate times at which to leap out at me and cry, *monster! subhuman! lunatic!* Thanks to their assistance, I became my own harshest critic.

Although my emotional numbness lasted no more than a couple of weeks, my internal persecutors grew steadily more powerful and more godlike in the months which followed. During the summer of 1960, I did little more than brood over my faults and past sins going all the way back to my early childhood. However, to the extent that my feelings of guilt and inferiority increased, I became increasingly vulnerable to my friend David's attempts to convert me. In his campaign to win me over to Christianity, David had a most formidable ally in the person of Mr. William Raymond Waters.

Mr. Waters was a genial man in his mid-sixties who had been a nurturing influence on David's life ever since David had been a neighbor of his several years back. Mr. Waters had been a kind of teacher or father figure not only to David, but to his two older brothers as well. He was also a good friend of David's father.

Mr. Waters lived alone in a shack without running water or heat about two miles west of where David lived. To step inside Mr. Waters' cabin was an experience in and of itself. Hanging from the rafters of his cabin were numerous large calendars spanning the years from the 1930s to the 1950s on the back of which he had very neatly printed various Bible verses. Toward the front of his shack there were two or three old wind-up phonographs, and stacks of records — mostly of Irish folk ballads, spirituals, and classical music.

Everywhere one looked in Mr. Waters' cabin there were books — *thousands* of them! These books were stacked inside rows of upturned wooden boxes which served as makeshift bookshelves. There were row upon row of these makeshift bookshelves reaching nearly to the ceiling throughout almost the entire length and breadth of his cabin. The bulk of these volumes dealt with subjects dear to Mr. Waters' heart: history, astronomy, flying saucers, religion, and the occult. But these books also included a goodly amount of fiction — both of the serious and escapist varieties — as well as the usual reference books.

Mr. Waters' favorite tomes were all located either at or near the intersection of two towering walls of books. This is where he slept.

Whenever we visited Mr. Waters, he would usually be lying in bed fully clothed, huddled under an electric blanket reading a book. When he wasn't home we could always find him in the back room of the neighborhood grocery store playing checkers with the store's proprietor — a maimed World War I veteran and notorious shortchange artist whom the local residents called "the one-armed bandit."

Mr. Waters would always be glad to see us. While sitting on his bed surrounded by his favorite tomes, he would talk for hours on the mysteries of God and the mysteries of the universe.

Often his discourse would stray onto the topic of UFOs. Mr. Waters believed that nearly all the planets in our solar system were inhabited by intelligent beings, and that the earth was constantly being visited by aliens. He also believed that these aliens were in contact with several government agencies, and that the government was engaged in a gigantic conspiracy to keep this fact from being widely known.

Mr. Waters also believed there were human beings walking around who were nearly two thousand years old! He based his belief in the existence of such people on various texts in the New Testament such as Matthew 16:27-28, which states: "For the Son of man shall come in the glory of his Father with his angels; and then he shall reward every man according to his works. Verily I say unto you, *There be some standing here, which shall not taste of death till they see the Son of man coming in his kingdom.*" Because Christ hadn't yet returned to judge the world, Mr. Waters came to the logical conclusion that these people must still be standing around waiting for His return! For a similar reason, he also believed the high priest who condemned Christ had to still be alive, since Christ had told him: "Hereafter shall ye see the Son of man sitting on the right hand of power, and coming in the clouds of heaven" (Matthew 26:64). Moreover, according to Mr. Waters, the soldier who pierced Christ with his sword was also alive since Revelations 1:7 states: "Behold he cometh with the clouds; and every eye shall see him, and they also which pierced him." All of these people, according to Mr. Waters, were remnants of a generation which would not wholly pass away until all the prophecies concerning the end time were fulfilled (Matt 24:34). Although he wasn't sure, Mr. Waters thought there might be literally hundreds — possibly even thousands — of those ancient people still walking around.

Mr. Waters had an affinity for anything mysterious or esoteric. This being the case, it is only natural he would study such subjects as palmistry, phrenology, astrology, and numerology. However, except for numerology, which he utilized in his studies on Bible prophecy, Mr. Waters had a rather skeptical attitude toward these so-called "psychic sciences."

Above all else, Mr. Waters was an avid student of Bible prophecy. However, his studies in this area were motivated more out of a desire to be "in the know" so to speak, than out of any real sense of piety. In fact, when it came to studying prophecy Mr. Waters was a shameless eclectic, for he studied the prophecies of Nostradamus with almost as much zeal as he studied the Bible.

Although I was somewhat taken by Mr. Waters, I rarely socialized with him the first few times I came to his house. While he and David talked, I spent many pleasurable hours browsing through his immense library of occult books. These were the most otherworldly books I had ever seen! One of the most fascinating of these volumes was *The Sixth and Seventh Books of Moses.* This was a treatise on sorcery written in the fourth century A.D., which gave graphic instructions on how to summon demons. I would spend hours on end daydreaming about becoming a sorcerer while sitting in the dim corridors of Mr. Waters' library, contemplating that book's mystical diagrams and pentacles. I remember getting lost in the intricacies of such sublimely bizarre books as Madame Blavatsky's *The Secret Doctrine* and Dr. John Ballou Newbrough's *Oahspe: A New Bible in the Words of Jehovih and His Angel Embassadors a Sacred History of the Dominions of the Higher and Lower Heavens on the Earth.* I also remember thumbing through a book called *St. Germain and the Ascended Masters,* and being struck with awe and wonder upon seeing what appeared to be color photographs of saints or demigods with the most beautiful and radiant auras ascending into heaven. (The accompanying text claimed that those pictures were in fact photographs taken of real people!) I was especially impressed by the life and writings of Michel de Nostradamus, the mysterious sixteenth-century prophet. I was absolutely convinced of the authenticity of Nostradamus' prophetic powers. I believed he derived his prophetic powers from consorting with familiar spirits or demons, and I longed to follow in his footsteps.

Mr. Waters and his library opened up a whole new exciting world for me. I couldn't help but be impressed by the fact that Mr. Waters had read every book in his library. He struck me as being a very erudite and cultivated man. One of his most appealing traits was his total lack of dogmatism and fanaticism. He would never say to either David or myself, "This is the truth" or "You better believe that." Instead he would merely present his point of view for our consideration.

Mr. Waters never made a heavy-handed attempt to convert me to anything. Yet he was a most subtly persuasive man. His approach was to appeal to me through my *imagination.* He would first stimulate my imagination and curiosity, and then supply me with information. He was very generous both with his books and with his time.

By the summer of 1960, I began to regard Mr. Waters as something of a genius or saint. I would listen almost spellbound to his very long and scholarly lectures on Bible prophecy. I felt certain that the end of the world was at hand, and that Mr. Waters possessed detailed knowledge of what the future would bring.

I vividly remember one evening in late July listening to Mr. Waters read the awesome words of the Prophet Joel:

> And it shall come to pass afterward, that I will pour out my spirit upon all flesh; and your sons and daughters shall pro-phesy, your old men shall dream dreams, your young men shall see visions.... And I will show wonders in the heavens and in the earth, blood, and fire, and pillars of smoke. The sun shall be turned into darkness, and the moon into blood, before the great and terrible day of the Lord come.

Those words stirred something in my soul — something that was part longing, part a groping and unarticulated belief that some day God would choose me as one of His prophets.

# 8

# A PROPHET IS BORN

One hot day in the early part of August I was in Everett walking along the railroad tracks near the city dump when suddenly my attention became riveted upon a most interesting sight. From approximately seven or eight hundred feet ahead of me, I saw a tiny person walking toward me who looked like a visitor from another planet. His pointed head glistened in the sun and appeared to be made out of some kind of metallic substance. As I approached this person, I found that he was a man not much over four feet tall who appeared to be in his late sixties or early seventies. He was wearing a grayish-green tarp around his neck like a cape which covered a large backpack and made him look like a hunchback from a distance. On his head was an odd aluminum hat which came to a blunted point.

When this man saw me he hailed me warmly and asked me if I had time to talk to him. After I answered yes, he took off his backpack and we sat down facing each other near the railroad tracks. He reached into his backpack and pulled out a number of crumpled and faded brochures which he placed on the ground in front of him. After making a few perfunctory remarks to the effect that he made it his business to talk to as many boys and girls as he possibly could as he traveled around the country, he began to lecture me and to ask me questions in a very thorough and systematic way.

For the most part, his questions were based on the pamphlets which he had carefully arranged in front of him. While thumbing through his literature, he asked me questions such as whether I smoked or drank. He also asked me other questions relating to physical hygiene such as whether I ate the right kinds of food, got the proper amount of sleep and exercise, brushed my teeth at least twice a day, and so on. After asking each question he would deliver a short lecture.

The old man seemed genuinely concerned about my well-being. As he was putting on his backpack and getting ready to leave, he pleaded with me to get a good education so I wouldn't end up like himself — a poor wandering old man without a home or a family.

We continued to talk on increasingly friendly terms as we walked down the railroad tracks together. The old man continued to ask me questions and was pleased to hear that I believed in God and read my

Bible nearly every day. However he seemed rather upset when I told him that I didn't attend church and Sunday school on a regular basis. I tried to explain to him that attending church was totally unnecessary since I could study the Bible at home — and that besides, I found church and Sunday school intolerably boring. But the old man wouldn't accept my explanations. As we were about to part company, he was still insisting that attending church and Sunday school was an absolute necessity.

Since I had enjoyed talking to the old man, and because at that time I held the mystical notion that all good things recur in four-year cycles, my parting words to him were, "I'll see you again four years from now!" The old tramp responded to those words with a bewildered and hostile, "What...?!" He gazed at me for a few moments with an expression of astonishment mixed with alarm, then backed away from me.

The old man's frightened and hostile response left a bitter taste in my mouth. As I turned around and walked back down the railroad tracks from where I came, I was in a very troubled state of mind. Walking south I passed the city dump, where amidst the smoke and flames swarms of sea gulls were picking through the garbage. Upon reaching the old Sumner Iron Works, I left the railroad tracks and walked down a winding path to where I could see the wino shacks nestled along the edge of the swamp.

Feeling a sudden sadistic urge, I picked up a rock and flung it at the nearest shack. Although the rock struck the cabin's door with a resounding crash there was no response from within. I then began bellowing at the top of my voice, "*Hey winos! Hey winos! Hey winos!*" My voice echoed out over the swamp and died. There was absolutely no response. The wino community appeared totally deserted.

Peering down at the shacks, I spotted an ax on the chopping block beside a woodshed near the very edge of the swamp. Walking down a narrow pathway I cautiously approached the woodshed with the intention of using the ax to break into the cabins. As I was about to seize the ax, I heard a loud splash and whirled around in fright. Looking down at the green, stagnant water, I saw ripples fanning out near the shore.

With my heart pounding wildly, I turned around and grabbed the ax. I walked over to a dismal looking tarpaper shack whose front window was protected by a thick wire screen. After smashing the window and breaking the lock with the ax, I entered the shack.

Upon entering the shack I hastily surveyed its bleak and austere interior. Then, leaning the ax against a small round old-fashioned wood burning stove, I walked toward the back of the cabin. In the corner of the room I saw what I took to be an old set of encyclopedias on a bookshelf against the wall. On coming closer, I discovered that the encyclopedias were law books. I then glanced down at the bed which was covered with a drab, moth-eaten wool blanket and at the nightstand beside it. On top of the nightstand there were several old magazines and an antique alarm clock. Both the magazines and the clock looked like they had been salvaged from the city dump.

I picked up the alarm clock and wound it up. The clock worked. Upon putting the clock back on the table, it occurred to me that whoever lived in this shack had probably been gone for some time and most likely wouldn't be coming back soon.

After sitting down on the bed, I became aware of something that looked like an old shoe box lying on the lower shelf of the nightstand. My curiosity aroused, I picked up the box and opened it. I found the box to be full of old family photographs, which appeared to have been taken decades ago. The first photograph I looked at appeared to be that of a newly married couple. The man looked rather distinguished and prosperous, and was looking straight at the camera with a stern and somewhat frightened expression on his face. The woman was dark-haired, heavyset, and rather pretty. Her mouth was slightly open in a faint smile, and she was looking at her husband with a loving and trusting expression on her face. There were also photographs of children — of a boy and a girl. In the most recent photographs, the boy looked not much older than nine while the girl looked around twelve. The photographs were faded and dog-eared, and looked like they had been handled many times.

In looking at the man in those photographs I had a vague and disturbing impression that I had seen him somewhere before — an impression which I immediately dismissed. Feeling at once agitated and depressed, I put away the pictures and stood up. After pacing the room for a few seconds, I approached the front of the shack.

Near the front of the cabin I saw between twenty or thirty jars of preserves sitting on shelves in a small pantry. Beside the pantry there was a 1930s style blue pinstripe suit jacket hanging on a peg in immaculate condition. I reached up and grabbed a jar of apricot preserves and opened it. I poured half the jar of apricots into the left pocket of the jacket, then emptied the rest into the other pocket.

For close to a minute I just stood there with my mind completely blank, watching the apricot juice seep through the coat lining and drip onto the floor. Then, as if suddenly awakening from a dream, I realized the sadistic and cowardly nature of my actions and was overcome with shame. It occurred to me that had I broken into the house of a middle-class person, my actions though criminal would at least have taken a certain amount of courage. But here I was, vandalizing the home of an unfortunate and totally defenseless person — a person who had never harmed me — just minutes after telling someone how I believed in God and read the Bible nearly every day! The more I thought about what I had done the more ashamed I became. My shame was so great that I felt it as a palpable physical sensation throughout my entire body — as a nervous spasm coupled with an agonizing sense of inner defilement.

In my eyes my actions unmasked me as some kind of moral monster — as a vicious and cowardly lunatic whose actions were wholly inexplicable even to himself.

My security operations (defense mechanisms) were in a state of total collapse. I couldn't see how I could possibly justify, explain, or in any way minimize what I had done.

Trembling uncontrollably, I stumbled out of the shack. By the time I was outside the cabin, my shame and self-loathing had become so unbearable that I wanted to hide — to disappear forever from the face of the earth and be submerged a mile deep under the ocean. I visualized the waters of the ocean closing over me and suddenly everything around me grew a little dim. As I struggled back up through a steep and narrow pathway which led to the railroad tracks, I imagined myself being buffeted about by the currents of the ocean and that the bushes I was holding on to for support were seaweed.

Upon reaching the railroad tracks, I relinquished my fantasy of being on the bottom of the ocean — perhaps because I felt it wasn't making me feel any better. However, the very instant I shed this fantasy, I completely lost control of my mind. Thoughts began to race through my mind at a faster and faster rate, and to fragment and lose all meaning or coherence. I could actually *hear* my mind racing out of control and *see* my thoughts as swirling blue comets or sparks colliding against each other. As I walked down the railroad tracks, I was giggling uncontrollably while tears ran down my cheeks. My mind was one mad, racing kaleidoscope of totally random and fragmented thoughts. I remember during this time having but one coherent thought: *this is it; I'm going insane!*

While staring absent-mindedly at the ruined jacket, I suddenly realized that the cabin I was vandalizing belonged to old Ben — an individual whom I had first encountered when I was living at my grandmother's house back in 1958. I first saw Ben, I think, sometime in March of that year while walking alone down by the junkyard across the railroad tracks from the horse stables. I was walking around the scrap heap when suddenly I saw a tall, gaunt man who appeared to be in his early sixties about twenty feet in front of me. He was dressed in a 1930s style business suit which was much too big for his withered frame. He was walking slowly and hesitantly down a path which led through the waist-high grass and weeds, and appeared to be lost in thought. I scrutinized him carefully. His very being seemed to exude solitude and suffering. There was something almost otherworldly about that man — other-worldly in a very disturbing sense, which inspired my immediate compassion.

Two months later I saw Ben walk past me on Hewitt Avenue. At that time I was with David, and we were talking to an old man who knew nearly everyone who frequented the avenue. However, as soon as Ben approached us, we all stopped talking. After Ben passed us, the old man commented sadly, "Now there goes one of the most miserable men who has ever lived. He is absolutely convinced that he has committed blasphemy against the Holy Spirit — the unforgivable sin — and that he is going to be tortured in hell throughout all eternity."

I asked the old man what blasphemy against the Holy Spirit was, and why Ben believed he had committed this sin.

"Well, it's pretty complicated. Ben is an alcoholic who has been married twice. His first marriage was an absolute disaster and soon ended in divorce. But not long after meeting his second wife, Ben recovered from his alcoholism and never touched a drop. His second marriage was a happy one. However, after he had been married for several years, both he and his wife joined a screwball religious sect, and that's when his troubles began.

"Still, things went well enough the first few years after his joining the church. But then Ben's pastor found out that he had been married before and had divorced his first wife. Upon finding this out, this preacher told Ben and his wife that they had to separate because they were living in sin. Apparently it says somewhere in the Sermon on the Mount that one is committing adultery if one remarries after having been divorced — or something to that effect.

"Well, because Ben and his wife were such devout people they saw no other alternative but to separate — even though they loved each other. And even though they knew it would be hard on the children. But because Ben's wife wasn't considered properly married in the first place she was free to marry again — which she promptly did. She married one of the elders of Ben's church.

"This, of course, had a devastating effect on Ben. It completely destroyed him. He went right back to being an alcoholic. It's interesting to note that although Ben's church used wine in its Communion service, Ben did not become an alcoholic again until after his wife left him.

"Finally, things got so bad that Ben could no longer function in any capacity — and as devout as he was — Ben started staying away from church. The pastor and elders made repeated attempts to persuade him to come back to their church, but he refused. Finally, when it became obvious to them that Ben would never come back, the pastor and elders of the church told him that he had committed blasphemy against the Holy Spirit.

"Now in order to understand why these people told Ben that he had committed blasphemy against the Holy Spirit and what exactly they meant by telling him this, you have to first understand some of their beliefs. For instance, you must understand that the members of Ben's church believed that their church was the only true church and that all the other churches were false churches set up by Satan. You must also understand that these people believed that in becoming a member of their church you automatically received the Holy Spirit, and that you could not receive the Holy Spirit unless you first became a member. So to them becoming a member of their church and receiving the Holy Spirit were really the same thing. However, once you become a member of the church you are considered one of the enlightened; and as one of the enlightened you are held fully accountable. Therefore you cannot quit, or cease to be a member of the church without thereby committing blasphemy against the Holy Spirit.

"Although Ben had abandoned his church he never abandoned his belief in the truth of its doctrines. Moreover, from what I've been told, Ben already considered himself irredeemably lost even before the pastor and elders of his church officially condemned him — and so all they did was confirm his worst fears.

"I don't know Ben very well. He's kind of a hard person to get to know. But I have talked to a few people who know him well, including a man who has known him for close to forty years. They all tell me that Ben is a totally honest man who has never harmed anyone. In fact, he had helped lots of people when he was a lawyer. From what I under-stand, he was a darn good lawyer too. Now he's just another derelict without a family and hardly any friends to speak of."

As I continued walking down the railroad tracks, billows of smoke drifted toward me from the city dump, and with it the overpowering stench of rotting garbage. Though I could hear the shrill cries of sea gulls flying overhead I couldn't see them, for by that time the smoke had become so dense that my vision was almost totally obscured. As I walked, thoughts continued to race through my mind.

Fully aware of the seriousness of the condition I was in, I sought to calm myself as best I could. Finally, when my thoughts had become more intelligible to me, I recognized the words of King Solomon:

I have seen all the works that are done under the sun; and, behold, all is vanity and vexation of the spirit.... And I gave my heart to know wisdom, and to know madness and folly: I perceived that this also is vexation of the spirit. For in much wisdom is much grief: and he that increaseth knowledge increaseth sorrow.

I was overcome with grief, but there was something soothing — even exhilarating — about this feeling. But as this strange mixture of melan-cholia and elation faded, I was haunted by a certain indefinable sense of dread.

Feeling an immediate need to talk to someone, I hurried to my grandparents' house in order to call David. While using the wall telephone in the hallway of their house, I told David how I had just vandalized a wino shack. I neglected, however, to tell him that the cabin I had broken into was Ben's.

When I told him how I had found the shacks completely deserted, David expressed his opinion that all the winos were probably in eastern Washington picking apples in order to earn enough money to buy wine. In a very light way, he also scolded me for my mischief. "Now, John, you know how those people hate to work. Now you've forced that poor lazy slob to get off his duff and repair his shack. You shouldn't do that!"

Provoked by David's levity, I then told him that the cabin I had just vandalized belonged to old Ben. "You remember old Ben — the guy we saw on Hewitt Avenue a couple of years ago?"

"You mean the old man who believed he had committed blasphemy against the Holy Spirit?"

"Yes, that's the man."

"Well, you sure chose the right guy to pick on, didn't you? I suppose it never occurred to you that that man has enough problems without you breaking into his shack?"

"I didn't know it was his shack."

"Then why did you say it was?"

In an anguished and halting voice, I explained to him how I had found law books in his shack, and had recognized his face from old photos of him taken back in the 1920s and 1930s.

Sensing my state of mind, David tried to be reassuring. "I wouldn't worry about it too much if I were you. Just look at it this way: now you know better than to ever try anything like that again. Besides, from what you've told me, you really didn't do any major damage."

However, I found no comfort in David's words. As I stood in the hallway listening to him, I was still on the verge of panic. In my mind everything seemed irrevocably changed — I was no longer the person I once took myself to be, and the world itself no longer seemed such a hospitable place.

Soon after talking to David, I left my grandparents' house and headed back to my uncle's home where I was then staying. My uncle lived near Lake Stevens about four miles east of Everett.

That night at my uncle's house I felt restless and couldn't sleep at all. Yet when morning came I had so much energy that I went on a thirty mile hike. The temperature that day reached over ninety degrees. Nevertheless, after taking that long and torturous walk in the blazing sun, I still had enough energy left over to go for a swim in Lake Stevens.

On the night following my long hike, I was able to get about four hours of sleep. While this wasn't much sleep, it was still a considerable amount relative to what I would average over the next seven weeks.

Not more than a few days after my short stay at my uncle's house, my mother ran away from home again. She took us kids with her to Everett and stayed at the house of a woman who was a close friend of hers.

One night as I was lying awake in a room by myself in this woman's house, I was going through a great deal of emotional turmoil when suddenly I was overcome with a profound sense of resignation. At that moment I decided to turn to God and ask His forgiveness for my sins. This act of repentance had an immediate calming effect on me, and that night I slept soundly.

Upon awakening in the morning, I felt like a terrible burden had been lifted from my shoulders. My crushing sense of guilt was gone. It was like being reborn into a new world, a world of joy and peace.

However, the sleepless nights continued. For the first six weeks following my religious conversion I remember going night after night without getting any sleep at all. On those rare nights when I did sleep, I would usually sleep no more than two or three hours.

Yet curiously enough, I remember the early part of this period of prolonged wakefulness as being rather pleasant. In this early stage of my sleeplessness, my focus of attention was still relatively broad — broad enough at least to permit the existence of a rich and satisfying fantasy life.

Although my fantasies were of various kinds, they most often involved my identification with King Solomon and John the Baptist, two Biblical characters whom I deeply admired.

Since I considered wisdom the highest of all the virtues, it is only natural that I would admire King Solomon who was reputedly the wisest man who ever lived. I also felt a special affinity for Solomon due to my sharing his deeply pessimistic view of life.

I had begun to develop an obsessive interest in Solomon immediately after vandalizing Ben's shack. Understandably, I found it much more comforting and uplifting to contemplate the wisdom of Solomon than to be aware of my own viciousness and folly. For days and weeks on end after vandalizing Ben's shack, passages from Proverbs and Ecclesiastes — my two favorite books in the Bible — were continually running through my mind, producing a soothing and almost hypnotic effect.

While contemplating the wisdom of Solomon, I also began to become obsessed with John the Baptist. In some ways John seemed to me an even greater man than Jesus Christ. For instance, Luke 1:15 states that John the Baptist was filled with the Holy Spirit while he was still in his mother's womb, while Christ never received the Holy Spirit until after He was baptized by John in the river Jordon. In the accounts of all four of the Gospels, it appears that Christ derived His authority to preach from John the Baptist and could not have begun His ministry without him. Christ Himself implicitly admits His inferiority to John when He states, "Among them that are born of women there hath not risen a greater than John the Baptist."

I admired John the Baptist more than I did Christ. Because I considered John to be a person of tremendous spiritual grandeur, I longed to be just like him. This longing grew more and more intense, and as weeks of prolonged sleeplessness slipped by, I began to notice certain similarities between John the Baptist and myself. For instance, I felt that we both possessed the same type of personality: independent, forceful, uncompromising, and reclusive. Since I had always daydreamed about living out in the wilderness away from other people, it was easy for me to identify with a person like John the Baptist who actually lived that way. I believed, moreover, that it was a matter of some significance that we both shared the same name. Furthermore, at that time I believed the Second Coming of Christ was imminent; and just as John the Baptist had prepared the world for Christ's first arrival, so I longed to receive a mission from God to prepare the world for Christ's Second Coming. Finally, it began to dawn on me that I might actually be John the Baptist. "And why not?" I asked myself, "After all, Matthew 11:14 states that John the Baptist was Elijah, so why can't I be John the Baptist?"

Along with these fantasies of identification, I also had fantasies of *inviolability*. For instance, I remember having an extremely vivid fantasy of taking refuge from the world by walking into an ornate, neo-Gothic brick house and locking the door securely behind me. Entering this house was like entering a greenhouse. Everywhere I looked there were flowers, scrubs, and trees. In the living room of this magnificent house there was a small but deep pond. Directly above the house there was a tower which contained a room that only I knew how to reach.

Upon entering the house I would hastily disrobe and hide my clothes under a scrub. I would then dive headfirst into the pond. I would swim about twenty feet down under the water until I reached a narrow passageway which led directly under the tower. As I swam down this passageway, everything would be pitch-black. Finally, the passage broadened somewhat, and I would see dim light and swim up a column of water — a column of water which stood in the tower in utter defiance of the law of gravity* — into the secret room.

This room was a perfect octagon whose eight walls were lined with bookshelves containing occult and mystical lore. Facing north, south, east, and west in this room were four small stained-glass windows.

Upon entering this hidden room, the water would pour off my body onto the multicolored porcelain tile floor and down a small drain. Every time I entered this room I felt purified of all contact with the world. I

---

*At that time I was greatly impressed with the fact that water would not flow out of an open bottle if its neck was partially submerged under water. I forgot, however, that if the bottle had a hole in it air would enter the hole and equalize the pressure and allow the water to flow out of the bottle.

would climb out of the water and don a white flowing robe. Then I would slam a steel trap door over the entrance to the room and bolt it shut. As long as I stayed in this room I had the absolute assurance that no one could possibly find me or harm me.

During this early stage of my prolonged sleeplessness, my predominant mood was one of joy and inner peace. I was constantly rejoicing about my finding Jesus and being saved, and I wanted to share my joy with others. Yet I also felt profoundly helpless: that I was in the grips of a process over which I had no control. I conceived myself as being a human atom being swept along in the current of an onrushing Cosmic River — this River, of course, being God. As I walked around in a euphoric daze, I not only felt that God was in total control of my life, but also that He was controlling the world around me in accordance with my wishes as a special favor to me.

As my psychosis developed, my parents would often talk to each other about the "wonderful improvement" that had come over me. This alleged improvement consisted largely of my becoming a mere appendage of my parents — an improvement which began immediately after my mother had threatened to have me committed to a mental institution. This so-called improvement reached its consummation upon my becoming a Christian. By that time, I had repressed my own needs and individuality to such an extent that I came to view the world almost exclusively through my parents' eyes. Their moods, emotions, and attitudes toward me reverberated through my entire being, often bringing a strong visceral response.

At this time I was simply overflowing with love for my parents. They seemed to me to be wonderful, flawless people who could do no wrong. Whenever, for instance, my father would come barging into the bathroom when I was on the toilet, I would view his behavior as perfectly acceptable — a part of the natural order of the universe.

However, my change in attitude and behavior involved more than just passive acceptance. During this time I had a great deal of empathy for the people around me. On hearing, for instance, that my parents could not afford expensive dental work for my brother whose teeth were rotting, I was so overcome with dismay that I burst into tears.

Others besides my parents were also under the impression that I had improved. Upon returning to school in September, my serious and sober bearing made a very favorable impression on Mike, a student who knew me well while I was in the ninth grade. "You've certainly straightened out since I last saw you. I'm sure you're going to do very well this year."

However Mike's prediction proved far too optimistic to say the least. At school I was so tired and disoriented that I could barely find my way around. In fact, every time I entered my world history class I would find the class half over. I remember checking and rechecking my schedule.

Sure enough, my world history class was scheduled immediately after my lunch break. But on arriving at my history class just after having lunch, the class would always be half over. Yet I never complained or asked questions. I just accepted being late as part of my inescapable fate. Actually I felt that in just being able to find my history class I was doing extremely well.

Needless to say, due to the condition I was in, I couldn't concentrate at all, and I soon fell hopelessly behind in my school work. Moreover, my inability to keep up with my school work was extremely stressful: it greatly increased my sense of helplessness.

About a week after returning to school I found myself becoming a virtual sleepwalker. I remember one morning groggily plopping down in the seat of a school bus, closing my eyes, and having a strange vision which totally fascinated me. In this vision, I was in a profound hypnotic trance and was walking down the middle of a railroad track inside a dark tunnel which led under a great city. From far away, I could see the flickering light of an oncoming locomotive. However, this was no ordinary locomotive, but a living entity whose demonic searchlight eye was controlling my mind. I continued to walk toward this monstrous entity knowing that I was incapable of preventing my inevitable destruction.

In the days immediately following this vision, I was beset by attacks of anxiety which grew steadily worse. I felt constantly under pressure — pressure which I could almost feel as a tangible force bearing down on top of my head. The awareness that I was failing in school constantly oppressed me. Yet there were other fears as well — fears which are difficult to describe. I had a vague but ominous feeling that something terrible was about to happen to me: that somewhere in my mind there were demons waiting to burst forth from their cages.

As these fears grew, I became more obsessed than ever with the notion that the Second Coming of Christ was at hand, and that it was my mission to prepare the world for this impending event. As I lay awake nights contemplating the stupendous task which lay before me, I constantly sought guidance from the Almighty. Throughout entire nights for days on end, I prayed fervently to God that He grant me the wisdom of Solomon so that I could understand and faithfully carry out the divine mission which He had bestowed upon me.

After several nights spent in fervent prayer, I was certain that God had granted my request. I "knew" beyond a reasonable doubt that I possessed the wisdom of Solomon. How else could I possibly account for the fact that all at once I was having thoughts of such astonishing profundity? In all my life my mind had never worked so incredibly well!

After thanking my heavenly Father, I started utilizing the wonderful gift which He had so graciously bestowed upon me. First of all, I set about to solve a problem which had often puzzled me: why did Solomon toward the end of his life become an abject idolater? How could the wisest man who ever lived do such a blatantly *foolish* thing? As far as I was concerned the standard answer — that Solomon's pagan wives led him astray — merely begged the question, namely: why would a man of such transcendent wisdom as Solomon allow himself to be led astray on such a serious matter? Why would a man who was wiser than Jesus Christ or John the Baptist choose to spit in his Creator's face by worshipping idols?

I pondered this disturbing question day and night. Finally, one afternoon while I was alone in the trailer studying the Bible, the answer suddenly became starkly obvious: all at once it occurred to me that Solomon in his wisdom must have realized that God was worthy of nothing but contempt. I came to this horrifying conclusion upon reading the last chapter of the second book of Samuel. In this chapter of the Bible, God for no apparent reason was very angry and wanted to kill someone. However before He could begin His killing spree He needed a pretext. Therefore He moved King David — Solomon's father — to take a census of Israel and Judah. When following God's prompting, David ordered that a census be taken, God gave David his choice of three options: (1) seven years of famine, (2) three months of fleeing before their enemies, or (3) three days of pestilence. When David chose the pestilence, *God killed seventy thousand people for being counted in a census which He Himself had initiated!*

I was panic stricken. I was certain God knew my thoughts, and I could almost see Him furiously looking down at me ready to cast me into hell. I threw myself on the floor and began to whimper and beg for mercy. "Lord I know I am nothing but a piece of garbage who deserves to burn in hell. But please — please have mercy on me! I don't want to go to hell! I don't want to go to hell! I don't want to go to hell!" I started to scream and roll around on the floor in a paroxysm of terror. I stayed on the floor for close to an hour crying, pleading for mercy, and trying to flatter God by telling Him how powerful He was and how much I feared Him. Finally, I grew confident that my show of abject servility and fear had placated God's wrath, and so I got up from the floor in a much calmer frame of mind but still profoundly shaken.

That night as I lay in bed, I was thinking the darkest and grimmest thoughts that had ever passed through my mind. It was now obvious to me that God was a sadistic Monster who had created most of the human race for no other purpose than to torture them in hell. Furthermore, to make sure that most people would end up in hell, God created Satan, gave him almost unlimited power and authority, and turned him loose on the world. In His infinite and unfathomable viciousness, God even turned against His own Son and had Him humiliated, tortured, and murdered. One thought totally obsessed me: "If God did that to His own Son, what is He going to do to *me*?"

For the next few days I lived on the edge of the abyss: hating God and fearing the consequences.* In all my life God never seemed so terrifyingly real. Whenever I was alone I could sense His menacing Presence closing in on me. At such times I would cringe and cower, and would often thrust my arms up over my head as if to ward off a blow. Sometimes I would roll over on my back and whine like a frightened dog. By such measures I sought to pacify the fury of God, for I believed such fearful behavior was pleasing to Him. (After all, a proverb of Solomon states that the fear of God is the beginning of wisdom.)

But I was very much aware that mere abject fear by itself just wasn't enough: that in order to stand a decent chance of staying out of hell I had to learn to love the Monster. Therefore I was soon able to persuade myself that my perception of God's cruelty was nothing more than a symptom of my fallen and sinful nature.

However my newly reaffirmed faith in God's benevolence was repeatedly being shaken by my constant study of the Bible. For instance, I read how God met Moses at an inn and sought to kill him, and how He was appeased at the last moment by the offering of a foreskin (Exodus 4:24-26). Why God wanted to kill Moses in the first place was as inexplicable to me as His bizarre fondness for foreskins. I also read how God killed Uzza for his well-intentioned attempt to steady the Ark (1 Chron. 13:9-10). And I also read how God caused a couple of female bears to come out of the woods and rip apart forty-two small children for laughing at Elisha and calling him baldy (2 Kings 2:23-24).

Since I was so obsessed with religion and felt such a tremendous amount of guilt and self-loathing, it was easy for me to imagine that a vengeful God was closing in on me, and that this God was constantly reading my thoughts. Therefore every time I came across passages in the Bible such as the ones mentioned above, my old blasphemous thoughts would re-emerge and cause me to panic. I would then go racing out of the trailer and head straight toward a secluded clump of trees near the edge of the trailer park. Upon reaching this spot I would fling myself to the ground, bury my face in the mud, and pray as if my life depended on it:

"I'm nothing Lord. I'm nothing. I'm nothing but garbage — a rotting piece of garbage who deserves to burn in hell!

"Yet You in Your infinite greatness — You who made the universe — can still love a lowly and despicable sinner like myself! You've loved

---

*During this time I viewed my father as being a nearly perfect person. My father's negative characteristics were totally split off from my conscious awareness, internalized as a living presence within me, and then projected on to God. Hence it was no longer my earthly father, but my heavenly Father whom I perceived as my persecutor.

me so much that You sent Your Son to die for my sins. He endured horrible suffering so that I might have everlasting life.

"I am not worthy of such love! I am nothing, Lord. I am nothing. I am nothing but a depraved sinner who deserves to burn in hell. I know that my sins and wickedness are hateful to You — that in Your eyes my depravity makes me even more loathsome than an insect. Oh, I am nothing but filth! Rotten filth! I know I am rotten Lord! Totally rotten! Rotten to the core! I should be burning in hell right now if it weren't for Your infinite mercy!..."

I would keep this up until I felt a faint tingling sensation in my spine which I interpreted as the descent of the Holy Spirit. I would then experience a tremendous sense of relief. After I took my face from the mud and stood up, my mood would be one of great exaltation.

Soon such acts of self-abasement became an almost daily ritual.

However, in addition to these self-abusive prayers, I also practiced other — and much more pleasureful — forms of autohypnosis. For instance, as I walked the roads at night, I would gaze intently into the headlights of oncoming cars and tell myself that these headlights were the eyes of living beings who were looking into the very depths of my soul. This never failed to produce the most agreeably eerie effect. It felt as if I were actually encountering demons in the night. And these encounters seemed to be of the most intimate nature.

On the night of September 27, 1960, I sat down at my desk in the trailer and wrote the following letter to my friend, David. While writing this letter my mood was one of great exaltation, for I believed I was under the inspiration of the Holy Spirit:

Dear David,

I am Elijah! I am John the Baptist! I am Alpha and Omega — the Beginning and the End!

All the mysteries of heaven and earth have been revealed unto me!

For I have seen the Light — Reality!

For I have seen God!

For I have talked with God!

He hath given us a sacred mission!

We are the two witnesses foretold in the eleventh chapter of Revelations!

For we shall prophesy for one thousand two hundred threescore days while clothed in sackcloth!

For we shall make straight the path for the coming of our Lord who shall descend from the clouds with a shout!

For all the power of heaven and earth will rest upon our

shoulders!

For we will shut up the heavens and it shall not rain!

For we shall turn the waters into blood!

For we shall smite the earth with plagues!

For flames of fire shall issue from our mouths and we shall devour our enemies!

After one thousand two hundred threescore days Satan shall arise from the bottomless pit and shall kill us!

Then shall our enemies rejoice for three and a half days as our bodies lie uncovered in the cities of Sodom and Egypt!

Afterward the spirit of life from God shall enter our bodies and we shall stand upon our feet and the whole world will tremble with fear!

And then there shall be a great voice saying, come up hither!

And we shall ascend into heaven in a cloud of fire!

And there shall be thunder and lightning and earthquakes and continents crashing into the sea!

The sun shall be turned into darkness and the moon into blood!

Then shall our Lord return to rule the earth with a rod of iron!

Behold! All these things must shortly come to pass!

I am Alpha and Omega! I have the wisdom of Solomon and possess the keys to understanding all mysteries!

May the power of the Holy Spirit be upon you!

For you are my Aaron! For you are my Lot!

Be brave!

We must overcome!

Yours in Christ Jesus,

John

Not long after mailing this letter I went to bed, but my sleep was troubled by a strange dream. In this dream I felt myself to be a great evangelist leading a religious service in my high school auditorium. The students and faculty, many of whom I recognized, were swaying back and forth as if in a trance and were fervently singing the hymn, "Rock of Ages." As they sang this hymn, I stood before them in a state of religious ecstasy, literally basking in their love and adoration. However, as they continued to sing, their fervor reached the point of outright delirium, and I suddenly realized that they were not singing that hymn in praise of God, but in praise of me. With that realization I woke up in a cold sweat with an ominous feeling which soon escalated into stark terror.

I saw a huge pair of eyes staring at me from out of the darkness less than two feet in front of me. I felt certain that these eyes could only belong to the Rock of Ages Himself, for they seemed to radiate infinite power and fury, and had a certain primordial and almost reptilian quality to them. As soon as these eyes appeared they blinked, and I could see that the eyelids were extremely crinkled and lined with blood veins. In looking into those eyes, I received the awe-struck impression that those eyes had to be at least hundreds of millions of years old.

I felt the judgement of God upon me, for those wrathful eyes gazed into the very depths of my soul and saw all the rottenness concealed there. Never in my entire life had I experienced such excruciating terror!

Those eyes faded away.

A second and similar pair of eyes appeared and vanished. Although they looked very angry, they nevertheless seemed somewhat softer, more human, and less awesome than the first pair. I believed those eyes to have been the eyes of Jesus Christ.

A third pair of eyes appeared. These eyes were eyes of boiling blood which flashed with rage as flames of fire issued from them. I took this pair to be the eyes of a ferocious demon. But these eyes did not vanish. Instead they shot toward me and merged with my own eyes.

A fourth and very sinister pair of eyes appeared. These eyes were like diamonds; they sparkled as an eerie light radiated from them. These Satanic eyes lingered for some time before slowly fading away.

Near the doorway to my room to my right, a fifth pair of eyes appeared. These eyes seemed very mysterious and were gazing at me with a questioning look — as if expecting something from me, while at the same time appearing somewhat unsure of their own expectations. I took those eyes to have been those of John the Baptist. And I interpreted his questioning look as his sympathetic concern as to whether I would have the moral and spiritual stamina necessary to endure the trials of the special mission that my Creator had bestowed upon me.

When those eyes finally vanished I felt a sense of loss, for those were the only pair of eyes out of the five that seemed at all sympathetic toward me.

In a few moments, to my horror, the glittering searchlight eyes reappeared, and soon an entire face and figure materialized. It was Satan himself. Satan's body and face were human-like, but his mouth had fangs and a forked tongue which flickered like a snake's. His skeletal hands moved in an unnatural stroboscopic fashion. Light radiated from his entire figure, but was especially concentrated in his eyes.

Satan stretched forth his right arm, and I could almost feel his skeletal hand closing round my throat like cold steel. Then he withdrew his hand and looked deeply into my eyes. As I stared into those radiant glittering eyes, I felt myself begin to dissolve.

I found that I had become a disembodied spirit walking in the night through a desolate snow-covered terrain. Soon I was no longer walking, but gliding over the snow. I was traveling in the midst of a heavy blizzard and apparently I was carrying a flashlight, for as I moved over the snow my path was illuminated by a beam of light. I was clearly looking for something, but exactly what that "something" was was extremely unclear. Finally, I spotted a dark figure some distance ahead of me, standing under a black and withered looking tree. Upon my shining my light on that person, Satan turned his crystalline eyes upon me and at that very instant I saw my own reflection : *I was Satan!*

The next thing that I became aware of was that of lying in bed, looking up at the ceiling. It was pitch-black and thousands of stars were looking down upon me. I felt the eyes of the entire universe upon me. I had been given a sacred mission.

Morning came and I went into the bathroom and looked into the mirror. I half expected to see that my hair had turned completely white from the horrific visions I had seen the night before. But my hair was not white. It was the same color as usual. However, when I looked into my eyes, I saw a reddish glow. I therefore came to the conclusion that a demon dwelled inside my body.

I told my parents I would not be going to school that day and that I wanted to talk with them. Because of my serious demeanor, they asked no questions. In broken, half-finished sentences I told my parents that I had seen God and that God had conferred a mission upon me. Quoting from the words of the prophets, I proclaimed that the time was at hand when God was going to force the nations of the world to beat their swords into plowshares and their spears into pruning hooks, that the lion was going to lie down with the lamb, and there was going to be no more war.

And then — to my own astonishment — I asked my father to show me a one dollar bill. I took the dollar, looked at it, mumbled something about George Washington being the father of our country, and then proceeded to explain to my father the meaning of the symbolism on the back of that bill. The eagle holding the arrows in one talon and the olive branch in the other, symbolized our country. The eagle was looking toward the olive branch and away from the arrows because our country desires peace, not war. Then I fixed my eyes upon the all-seeing Eye of God at the top of the pyramid. I struggled to find words to explain what this meant, but I was reduced to incoherence and then to total silence as I remembered the horror of that night's encounter.

Thoughts raced through my mind helter-skelter as I sat talking to my parents. To my consternation, I strayed on to topics that were irrelevant — or at best only tangential — to what I wanted to say. An instance of such was when I was explaining to my father the symbolism of the dollar bill. While doing this I felt extremely frustrated because I was acutely conscious that what I was saying was a total non sequitur. Thoughts that I wanted to express either would not come or came only in fragments.

However, in order to understand my father's response to my rambling discourse on the symbolism of the dollar bill, one must first be aware of a few grim facts. For instance, a few months prior to the onset of my psychosis, I overheard my father bragging about how he had deliberately driven someone crazy for the sheer fun of it. Although I don't know exactly where or when this incident occurred, I do know that the person in question was a rather strange or eccentric soldier whom nobody seemed to like.

Before initiating his psychological campaign against this soldier, my father first marshaled the active and enthusiastic support of all the victim's closest associates. The first phase of this campaign was extremely subtle. Whenever this soldier entered his tent, my father's accomplices always made sure that he would find things just *slightly* out of order. Moreover, whenever this soldier complained about this state of affairs, everyone would act as if they were very concerned about what was happening. They would hint that he had been acting rather strange, and would seemed worried about his state of mind.

As time passed by, this harassment was very gradually escalated until the oddest and most inexplicable things started happening to this soldier. Meanwhile his companions were constantly giving him suggestions that he was losing his mind. Because this soldier was probably psychologically vulnerable in the first place, this sort of treatment couldn't help but affect his mind. And so one night as everyone was sitting around like vultures staring at this unfortunate soldier, the inevitable finally happened.

The men who witnessed the soldier's very sudden and dramatic crackup were absolutely ecstatic; and that night my father received lots of compliments. One of my father's fellow officers hailed him as a "master psychologist."

Now as I sat explaining my divine mission and the symbolism of the dollar bill to my father, that "master psychologist" seemed somewhat abashed. On seeing the Eye of God on top of the pyramid on the back of the dollar bill, I remember making an anguished and not very coherent attempt to tell my father about the terrifying and wrathful pair of eyes I had seen that night — the primordial looking eyes whose eyelids were lined with blood veins. In my utter madness, I told my father that those eyes were very much like his own. On hearing this my father appeared somewhat grief-stricken and ashamed. After a few moments spent in introspective silence, he told me defensively, "Now, John, one thing you're going to have to understand, is that there's a little bit of good, and a little bit of bad in everyone." He told me this repeatedly, and at the time I had no idea why he was telling me this.

I think my father probably had some awareness not only that I was mad, but also that his past behavior toward me had been a significant factor in causing my madness. His wanting me to understand the presence of good and evil in everyone now seems to me like some sort of veiled plea for my understanding and forgiveness.

I don't think my father had any deliberate or conscious intention of driving me crazy. Yet subconsciously, for my father, my madness was just as much a sought-after goal as the madness of the unfortunate soldier whom he had so methodically and wantonly persecuted. While he was in Tillicum my father was on the verge of cracking up, and it is likely that he harbored dark fears that he was going insane. Fearing madness in himself, my father looked for it in others, and sought to have others live out his own inner chaos. What he wanted above all else was the reassurance of being able to say: it is he and not I who is mad.

Yet madness in one of his sons was hardly a pleasant thing for my father to have to face — particularly if he felt responsible for causing this tragedy. Therefore, although my father must have had some awareness of my madness, he nevertheless chose to ignore its presence for as long as he possibly could. Consequently, for several days after I had announced my "divine mission," he and my mother were still talking about the "wonderful" and "miraculous" change that had come over me!

Moreover when I explained my special mission to my mother she appeared somewhat moved. She even made the initial suggestion that I might be a person similar to Joan of Arc. However as time passed by, she — like my father — became increasingly concerned.

After proclaiming my divine mission I went out for a walk. On exiting the trailer I felt immensely relieved not to have to go to school that morning. I also felt utterly exhilarated, for never before had the world appeared so exquisitely beautiful and alive! Although it wasn't yet October, the leaves of the scrub oak trees were already turning a brilliant red and gold. Everywhere I looked the colors were so intense that everything seemed to be in technicolor. While walking through the ankle-deep leaves beneath the trees, an autumn breeze came up and I felt myself being caressed by the spirit of God. I was radiant with joy for I was certain that God had claimed me as one of His own. I was His prophet — one of the most important persons ever to walk the face of the earth!

That afternoon I sat down and wrote another "inspired" letter to my friend David. In this bizarre and poetic letter, I claimed that I had walked down a flight of stairs into a tomb — into hell itself — where I had undergone first great suffering, then death and rebirth. Out of sheer love for me, my parents had crucified me — had torn me apart both physically and mentally in order to purify me of all my selfishness and moral depravity. The letter ended on a shrill note of praise for my parents' wisdom in forcing me to undergo this painful but necessary process of death and rebirth.

As I walked home from the post office, I suddenly became depressed and wished I hadn't mailed that letter. It occurred to me that David would find that letter wholly incomprehensible.

However, it is now apparent to me that David must have understood that letter — and its implications — quite well. He didn't share my belief that I was one of God's chosen prophets, and he dismissed my mystical visions as nothing more than a symptom of how my family had been treating me. He had a rather crude, reductionist theory that the mere fact that my family contained five members somehow explained my seeing five pairs of eyes — an explanation I found wholly unacceptable.

Still, David wasn't altogether convinced that I was crazy, either. In fact, he thought my mind worked extremely well — even to the point of halfway accepting my belief that God had given me the wisdom of Solomon. As a Christian who believed in a God who answered prayer, David could not dismiss the possibility that God might have granted me such a gift. Furthermore, it even seemed likely to him that I actually possessed such a gift in view of the fact that my madness had given me such a strikingly different perspective on things — a perspective he found totally fascinating.

David was especially impressed with my ability to see hidden meanings or special significance in nearly everything. He liked, for instance, my explanation of the spiritual significance of the forty-hour workweek. This explanation of mine was based upon my Bible studies. According to the Bible, as a result of Adam's fall, God cursed mankind with the necessity of having to earn a living by the sweat of one's brow. The necessity to work is therefore a punishment for Adam's sin. Furthermore, in the Bible, the number forty always signifies either punishment or self-mortification. Typical examples include the forty-day fasts of Moses, Christ, and Elijah; God punishing the world by making it rain for forty days and forty nights; God punishing the Israelites by making them wander in the wilderness for forty years; God stipulating that a slave could be given up to forty lashes as punishment, but no more; and so on. Hence the punitive significance of the forty-hour workweek.

David was well aware that there were people who considered me crazy. Yet for a number of reasons he himself was reluctant to seriously question my sanity. It is always painful to question the sanity of one's friends, and I was David's closest friend. Since David had been largely responsible for converting me to Christianity, I was also his special trophy. Due to the fact that I was the only person whom he had been able to proselytize, my conversion represented his greatest personal triumph — his only tangible proof that he was a successful practicing Christian. Needless to say, he wasn't about to dismiss me as a mere lunatic — especially when my delusions were largely derived from and wholly consistent with his own Christian beliefs.

My visual hallucinations confirmed my belief that I was one of God's chosen prophets — a latter-day John the Baptist. Moreover, the confirmation of this delusion had a calming effect on me, and made it possible for me to be able to get a full night's sleep. Although I still experienced some difficulty in going to sleep, I would no longer go night after night without getting any sleep at all.

As I became calmer and more rested, my thinking became increasingly more coherent until at last my delusions began to assume a strikingly logical nature. This logical aspect of my delusional system is best illustrated by the thoughts that were going through my mind one night as I was burning trash in an incinerator. As I lit the fire, I was meditating on the exact nature of my supernaturally acquired wisdom. Then suddenly the awesome truth dawned upon me: *I was demon possessed!* God had granted me supernatural wisdom by putting a demon inside me. Since a demon is a spiritual being and, as such, possesses far more wisdom than any mortal person, it seemed self-evident to me that my wisdom must be due to my being demon possessed.

As I gazed raptly into the fire, I felt that suddenly the secrets of heaven and hell were revealed to me. It occurred to me that Satan was actually a servant of God — a much maligned and abused servant, but a servant nonetheless. How could it be otherwise? Though immensely powerful by human standards, Satan is, after all, only a finite being. How could he offer any opposition to an omnipotent God? With his transcendent wisdom and knowledge, it is inconceivable that Satan could be so rash as to attempt such a thing. Obviously, God created Satan for the specific purpose of carrying out certain acts that are a part of His Cosmic Plan, but from which He wishes to distance Himself in order to protect His holy name.\* Satan serves God first as a faithful lackey, then as a convenient scapegoat. God could annihilate him anytime He wants, but has no wish to do so because He needs him desperately. Inasmuch as Satan was created by God and serves His purpose, Satan is good. Inasmuch as God created Satan and knew exactly what He was doing when He did so, God is evil. Every good contains an evil, and every evil contains a good. Judas' treacherous betrayal of Christ resulted in the spiritual redemption of mankind through Christ's death on the cross. Because God is all-powerful, everything that happens is a part of His plan. God is like a river that flows inexorably through time, a Current which nothing can resist. All of us, including Satan, must swim with the Current. Whether we end up safely on the other shore, or are smashed against the rocks and go down into perdition depends on His will, not

---

\*From my studies of the Bible I knew of several instances where God had sent evil spirits to do His bidding (Judges 9:23; 1 Samuel 16:14,23; 1 Kings 22:23). In 1 Chronicles 21:1, Satan provokes David to number Israel, while in 2 Samuel 24:1 God moved David to take a census of Israel and Judah. Since both passages refer to the same event, it was obvious to me that God had made use of Satan in order to furnish a pretext for killing seventy thousand people for having their census taken.

on our own.

As the fire dwindled into glowing embers, a feeling of peace settled over me. I felt I was one of the chosen Elect, one who was on intimate terms with the Most High. As such I no longer felt under any obligation to distort my thinking by believing pious absurdities and logical contradictions in order to placate Him and stay out of hell. I walked away from the incinerator with a feeling of gratitude toward God for revealing His precious truth to me through the intermediaries of His infernal demons.

For some time after experiencing my visions, I was in a state of mystical exaltation which lasted at a high level of intensity for several weeks. In this heightened state, everything appeared more beautiful and alive to me. It was my belief at that time that just by looking into people's eyes I could see inside their minds. And whenever I looked into people's eyes, I saw nothing but goodness and innocence. Nothing appeared unconditionally bad or evil to me — not even Satan. I remember one afternoon staring enraptured at the delicate beauty of a girl's hand while riding home on the school bus. However, this beauty, innocence, and aliveness seemed to gradually fade as I became my "normal" self again.

A few days after my visions, when I was feeling at the very peak of ecstasy, I sat in my health class listening to a discussion on water safety and life saving techniques. Without referring to God or the Bible, I launched into a description of my previous summer's experience, when I had swum down the Nisqually River, in the form of a highly symbolic parable. As I spoke, I felt something greater than myself guiding my speech. All that I can remember is exhorting the class in a grave and oracular manner not to try to swim against "the inexorable current." In my mind the river symbolized life, destiny, and God.

The reaction of the class to my speech was nothing less than utterly bizarre. Those students who sat close to me seemed deeply moved, while those who sat across the room from me seemed totally bewildered. When I had finished my parable, Carol, a beatifically lovely girl who sat immediately behind me, began a parable of her own. Her story concerned a boy who had shot at a bird with a BB gun, and as a consequence of his own foul deed, was hit in the eye by the ricochet of his own BB.

As if this little speech wasn't bizarre enough, as soon as she had finished, Ken, the boy who sat next to me, turned to me and asked, "Do you have a God?" Ken spoke with a thick British accent and at first I couldn't understand what he said, for his "God" sounded like "cod." However, when at last the meaning of his question became clear to me, I told him outright that I had seen God.

Ken didn't seem at all surprised by my reply. He then told me how he had once been a member of the Baptist church I was then attending, but had quit because he had felt like such a hypocrite. When I whispered in his ear that we were all hypocrites, he seemed immensely relieved.

The teacher, Mr. Talley, seemed at once deeply moved and utterly bewildered. Mr. Talley knew me well, for I had been in one of his health classes at Mann Junior High School the previous year. He remembered me as an especially irritating buffoon whom he had to constantly rebuke. Now he had to cope with something far weirder than a mere clown. After Carol and I finished speaking our parables, he could only stammer, "What you have witnessed here....What you have witnessed here..." However Mr. Talley didn't seem quite sure just what he had witnessed. Totally disconcerted, he simply changed the subject.

# 9

## I RECEIVE MY LABEL

There were certain days when I had a vague and uneasy feeling that something was drastically wrong. I was constantly rereading the eleventh chapter of the book of Revelations — a part of the Bible which I believed gave a graphic description of my special mission. Upon reading how I would be given the power to smite the earth with drought, famine, and plagues, and to turn lakes, rivers, and even oceans into blood, I felt simply overwhelmed. Somehow all this seemed so cruel and unnecessary. Moreover, I just couldn't see how I could possibly pull off such grandiose feats. After all, I couldn't even get passing grades in school. I was also discouraged by the fact that David wouldn't take my divine mission seriously. Where was my helper — the second of the two witnesses mentioned in Revelations?

One day while in the midst of an evergreen forest near the shore of American Lake, I flung myself to the ground and prayed for God to release me from the awesome responsibility and terrible burden of having to carry out the sacred mission He had bestowed upon me. While pleading with Him, I told Him that I felt totally unworthy of the trust He had placed in me. As I prayed, I felt certain there were others who were far more qualified to be a prophet of God than I. For instance, I remembered Mr. Waters showing me numerous passages in the New Testament proving there were two-thousand-year-old people walking around, many of whom had been among Christ's closest disciples. Moreover, I knew for certain that the Apostle John had to be one of those ancient people: in the last chapter of the gospel of John, immediately before Christ ascended into heaven, He told John to wait for Him until He returned.* I was sure that in some remote corner of the world John was still awaiting Christ's return; and it occurred to me that if there were any person who was qualified to prepare the world for Christ's imminent arrival, that person had to be the Apostle John. John's credentials were nothing less than awesome: in addition to being the author of the book of Revelations, and hence the foremost expert in matters pertaining to the End Time, he was also Christ's favorite disciple, and had had almost two thousand years of

---

*Hence the rumor went around that John would never die (John 21:23).

experience. "Surely Lord I am not nearly as worthy to act as Your prophet as the Apostle John. He is far wiser than I."

However, I knew darn well that I was the wisest person in the world. Therefore as soon as I uttered those last words I became painfully aware of the fact that I was lying through my teeth in order to wheedle my way out of fulfilling my God-given responsibility. Consequently, after imploring my Creator's forgiveness, I set about more grimly determined than ever to submit myself to carrying out His will.

In search of spiritual guidance, I began attending services at the Calvary Baptist Church on a regular basis. I was somewhat encouraged by the fact that my classmate Ken was now an enthusiastic member of this church. It was my hope that Reverend Hooper, the pastor, would somehow recognize who I was and would give me detailed instructions on how to properly fulfill my special mission.

Reverend Hooper was a genial man who treated me with kindness and respect. At my request, he preached a special sermon on the topic of the Second Coming of Christ. After services were over I would usually stay and chat with Reverend Hooper in his study. However I was careful not to divulge my delusions to this preacher. Nevertheless, one Saturday afternoon when I was in his study as he was preparing his sermon, I told him about how once Satan had once materialized in front of me. As I told him this I tried to seem as unemotional and detached as possible and was totally noncommittal as to whether or not the phenomenon I had experienced was actually real.

Interestingly enough, my confession of having seen Satan didn't seem to faze Reverend Hooper in the least. He merely told me that in his opinion my vision was probably due to my being a little overwrought from studying too much.

Still Reverend Hooper couldn't help but notice how withdrawn and solitary I was and this was a matter of some concern to him. More than once he admonished me that I shouldn't try to withdraw like a hermit or a medieval Catholic monk — that as a Christian I had a duty or moral obligation to live in this world amongst other people.

On two separate occasions I put a stone in the collection plate — a rock which I had ground down on both sides until it resembled a thick coin. I did this while under the inspiration of a cartoon I remembered seeing in *Mad* magazine some time back. This cartoon showed a devil with a sheepish grin on his face placing a button in the collection plate — a humorous illustration on how a typical preacher must view a typical member of his flock. However, no one saw any humor in my placing a rock in the collection plate.

At school during this time I was constantly jesting, talking weird, and playing games with other people's minds. I thought it absolutely hilarious when a girl in my history class told me she thought I had "gone off the deep end." I immediately agreed with her. I knew I was acting crazy. I was acting that way deliberately. Therefore my awareness that others considered me crazy didn't bother me in the least. I felt totally in control of myself and was perfectly aware of the effect I was having on others. Since I possessed this awareness and felt completely in control, I didn't see how I could possibly be crazy. In fact, I considered myself *supersane*.

In this "supersane" state I had a kind of hyperawareness of the fragility of other people's minds. I perceived everyone around me as tottering on the brink of madness.

I remember conducting psychological experiments on both my teachers and classmates in order to drive them crazy. It was my belief that everyone had a split mind consisting of a very tender and vulnerable inner personality protected by a somewhat harder but still very fragile outer personality. By utilizing my own split mind, I would attempt to drive other people crazy by simultaneously communicating with both their inner and outer personalities in an attempt to further split their minds by setting each personality against the other. I called this my "divide-and-conquer" technique.

A recipient of my divide-and-conquer treatment was a classmate of mine, a big football jock named Pee Wee. One morning before class started, I saw Pee Wee playfully wrestling with another student who was almost a foot shorter than him. As Pee Wee was pushing this student into a corner and twisting his arm behind his back, I walked over to Pee Wee and started talking to him. In a soothing and reassuring tone of voice which would have been appropriate in speaking to a very small and frightened child, I told Pee Wee what a strong person he was, and how much I deeply admired and respected him. I felt intuitively that behind Pee Wee's macho exterior there lurked an inner personality which felt weak, frightened, and inferior. A part of me felt a great deal of empathy for Pee Wee's inner personality. As I talked to him, my voice quavered with sincere admiration — and concern. Yet I said all of this with a sardonic look on my face as the other part of me gleefully watched Pee Wee's growing discomposure. Pee Wee blanched, released his opponent, and backed away from me, his eyes wide with fear. I walked away with a rather warm feeling toward Pee Wee, totally assured of my mysterious powers.

Needless to say, such morbid behavior didn't make me very popular with my fellow students. I could scarcely walk down the hall without having someone mock me or attempt to knock my books out of my arms. However, I took some solace from the fact that I had achieved a certain amount of fame. Everyone seemed to know who I was, and many students feared me. Even to this day I don't think I was imagining things when one morning I saw a student staring at me with a terror-stricken expression on his face as he exclaimed to his companion, "That's Satan!"

Nor was I especially popular with any of my teachers. It is highly likely that at least one of them (probably Mr. Talley) went to the appropriate authorities and lodged a complaint against me.

Consequently, one afternoon as I came home from school, I saw a mysterious stranger standing in the trailer browbeating my father. "Look, we're not just playing games. This has to be done whether any of us likes it or not!" My father meekly assented. "I'm not playing games, either. It will be done. I'll promise you that." As my father spoke those words he accompanied the stranger to the door, who brusquely exited the trailer without so much as giving me a glance.

That evening I found myself alone in the trailer with my father. He was in a cold rage. He brutally informed me that there were certain people who were planning to have me locked up. "You've been *preaching*, haven't you?* You have no right to be doing a thing like that — you're not even an ordained minister. That's like practicing medicine without a license or any medical training. You could be put away for doing a thing like that!

"Now I want you to answer just one question — and I'll admit it's a loaded question: *have you been preaching?*"

Since my father admitted he was trying to trap me, I didn't even try to respond to his question. Instead I became totally absorbed in watching *The Flintstones* — a new television series I had never seen before — and tried to tune him out.

But my father was persistent. He kept hammering away at me with his question: *have you been preaching? have you been preaching? have you been preaching?* While still repeating his question he followed me into my bedroom after I had finished watching *The Flintstones*. Then he exploded. "What kind of a stupid, illiterate fool do you take me for!? Don't you think I am able to see through all the games you have been playing with me and everyone else?

"Okay, maybe you have the makings of being a great preacher someday. If so, then I will help you. I'll put you through college so you can be a legitimate minister and not like one of those bums who stand on street corners passing out tracts. If you do things my way I can make you a greater preacher than Billy Graham. If Graham can save five million people, then you can save ten million.

"But first you're going to have to pass a few tests. There are people who want to know whether or not you're a madman. And believe me they're going to find out whether you like it or not! And so help me, if I find out that you are a madman, I'm going to make sure you spend the rest of your life rotting behind bars!"

My father's speech meshed very nicely with my delusional system.

---

*My father disliked preachers in general and was especially contemptuous of street preachers. Several days previously I had irritated him when I told him how I had converted Ken to Christianity.

It was my belief that the entire world knew who I was, and was preparing to officially acknowledge my special mission. That was how I interpreted the presence of the mysterious visitor. I felt sure that he and my father were in the process of making arrangements so that I could go on television and proclaim my message to the entire world. Therefore I viewed my father's offer to make me a "greater preacher than Billy Graham" a solid confirmation of my exalted status.

However, I was also a realist. I was aware of the fact that before the world would acknowledge my special status I would have to prove that I was a worthy person. I knew therefore that there were trials and tribulations ahead. So I steeled myself. I could sense from my father's hostility that these trials would be very severe.

In the next few days my parents made a number of trips to the Madigan Army Hospital at Fort Lewis. On the first two or three of such trips I sat in the car while my parents consulted with the psychiatric staff. As I sat in the car waiting for my parents to return my attitude was one of utter detachment. In the back of my mind I understood well enough what my parents were doing and why they were bringing me here. My attitude was a fatalistic "whatever will be, will be."

My brother accompanied us on at least one of these trips and I remember him making a few comments about schizophrenics. "From what I understand, once someone becomes a schizophrenic, they are absolutely hopeless. For example, if a psychiatrist were to succeed in convincing one of them that he wasn't really Jesus Christ, he would immediately adopt another delusion equally as outlandish." As my brother spoke those words I felt that he no longer considered me his own brother. And the feeling was mutual. I felt so emotionally removed from him that his words didn't even touch me. It was as if he were an alien being speaking from another galaxy.

My delusions for the most part centered around my identification with King Solomon and John the Baptist. When I was in an elated, mystical mood I tended to identify with John the Baptist, but in a melancholy and pensive mood I tended more often to identify with Solomon.

When at last I walked into the psychiatric clinic at Madigan while accompanied by my parents, I was in my King Solomon frame of mind. I thoughtfully surveyed my surroundings and found that things hadn't changed much in the nearly four and a half years since I had last been here. While my parents seated themselves in the lobby, I walked over to one of the windows and put my hand on the heavy mesh-steel screen which covered the window and looked out. By now the horrible reality of my situation had fully dawned upon me.

After looking out the window for a few minutes I sat down in the lobby with my parents and waited. While waiting I thumbed through several of the magazines lying about the table in front of me. In each of the magazines I perceived cryptic references to myself. I also believed my father was aware of these veiled references, for he gave my mother a knowing look and exclaimed, "Pretty select reading material they have here, wouldn't you say?"

Finally Captain Kamm, an army psychologist, greeted me and led me into his office. Captain Kamm was a soft-spoken, scholarly looking man who appeared to be in his mid-thirties. With a calming smile, Captain Kamm asked me to interpret some proverbs. Since I possessed the wisdom of King Solomon, the author of the Biblical book of Proverbs, I thought to myself that this should be no problem at all.

His first question came my way. "Why does a rolling stone gather no moss?" In my mind's eye I began to envision a primeval forest where even the trees were covered with moss. As I tried to fathom the deep and hidden truth which this mysterious saying undoubtedly contained, I felt my reputation as a wise man was at stake. *I didn't know*!

Captain Kamm asked me to interpret several other proverbs, and I was unable to interpret any of them. "People who live in glass houses shouldn't throw stones?" Captain Kamm's manner was very grave as he asked this, and as he turned and looked at me, the light reflected from his glasses and flashed. For a second Kamm's eyes reminded me of those of Satan's. I was totally disconcerted. Kamm's severe manner and intense gaze made me feel guilty and ashamed. Since I had thrown many a literal and symbolic stone in my life, I took his question as a personal rebuke. I was unable to answer. By the time the examination ended I felt all washed up as a wise man. "How could a person with the wisdom of Solomon fail to interpret a single proverb?" I asked myself pointedly. I even began to doubt my own sanity.

Immediately after examining me, Captain Kamm told me to go down the hall and talk to Dr. Jones,* the psychiatrist. Dr. Jones was a somewhat corpulent man in his early fifties whose bearing was cool, objective, and authoritative. My initial meeting with Dr. Jones had all the trappings of a religious conversion, for I eventually walked away from that meeting viewing myself as a schizophrenic. I was obviously ripe for such a conversion. Even before meeting Dr. Jones I had already begun doubting my own sanity as a result of my examination. Moreover, despite the fact that I had always been very careful not to reveal my delusions to anyone except my friend David, upon meeting Dr. Jones I told him flat out that God had given me the wisdom of Solomon. Yet as I told him this I felt profoundly shaken. I didn't know what to believe.

Dr. Jones reacted to my talk of possessing the wisdom of Solomon with an icy and contemptuous silence. I could see by the look on his face that he regarded my words as merely one of the symptoms of a disease.

---

*A pseudonym. I am unable to remember Dr. Jones' real name.

At this point, as if a dam had burst inside me, I went into what I later came to understand as a "sick act." I began bawling that I was being tormented by visions.* Like a small child trying to placate an overbearing father, I had anticipated what this man expected of me, and I told him exactly what he wanted to hear.

Dr. Jones was apparently pleased by my performance, for the contempt immediately disappeared from his face and was replaced by a look of benevolent fatherly concern. He uttered a few comforting words to the effect that he had some wonderful medicine which would help me. He then wrote me a prescription for Stelazine. After tossing the prescription across the desk to me, he dismissed me with a wave of his hand.

I had come to the psychiatric clinic with the conviction that I was a very unique person with a sacred mission, but I walked away from the clinic miserably clutching a bottle of Stelazine with the vague and uneasy suspicion that I might not be anything more than an emotional cripple. This vague and uneasy suspicion grew more and more into a certainty each time I took one of my Stelazine tablets. More than words could ever have done, taking those pills indoctrinated me with the notion that I was a defective person whose only claim to uniqueness consisted of a biochemical defect, probably genetic in origin.[1]

However, as I will later show, not one shred of scientific evidence exists to substantiate the claim for a biochemical defect in schizophrenia. What I had been taking did not "cure" anything but was merely a chemical lobotomy or straitjacket whose sole virtue stemmed from the fact that it tranquilized the people around me, and thus kept them from locking me up. Moreover, I was lucky. I did not get tardive dyskinesia, or any of the other often irreversible brain diseases that frequently result from taking such toxic drugs.

Despite taking my medication, my condition improved rapidly. In fact, this improvement had begun taking place about a week after I had undergone my visionary experiences. After I had had this elaborate visual hallucination certain internal pressures that had been welling up inside me for several months suddenly dissipated. I became calmer. And as I regained my emotional equilibrium, my thinking became more coherent. And slowly, I started coming back to reality. It is important to realize that my psychosis contained within itself the seeds of its own cure. For example, as my psychosis developed, my parents initially thought that I had greatly improved. Consequently, they started treating me with more kindness and consideration. When at last they became fully aware of the condition I was in, they treated me with even more consideration. (One result of my psychosis was to bring my parents closer together, so they

---

*When I met Dr. Jones I had had only one hallucination — a hallucination whose main effect was to *calm* me by making me feel important.

also began treating each other with more consideration.) I was taken out of school for a couple of months and during this two-month period I spent a great deal of time lying in bed reading and taking things easy. These were the factors which aided my recovery. I certainly wasn't cured by some "wonder drug."

I returned to school sometime shortly after Christmas. While still living at home I attended school at Western State Hospital. By the time I went back to school my delusions had pretty much faded. But I still clung to one very comforting delusion: the delusion that not only had I been perfectly sane before the visions had temporarily unhinged my mind, but that I had possessed supernatural wisdom as well. For me the "proof" of this belief of mine was the letter I had written to my friend David on the night I had encountered the hallucinatory eyes. I believed that that letter was inspired by the Holy Spirit and that it was the greatest epistle written since the New Testament.

Sometime in late January, about three months after my first visit to the psychiatric clinic, even this last comforting delusion was totally shattered. This event happened when I was visiting my friend David. As I was in David's cabin waiting for him to return, I happened to see that "supernaturally inspired" letter lying on the dresser. With a joyful anticipation of being reassured of my transcendent wisdom, I picked that letter up and began reading it. It was an exquisitely painful experience. In reading my own letter I was confronted with the stark and undeniable reality of my own madness.

All of my remaining delusions began clearing up the instant I started reading that letter. Within two months my delusions were totally gone.

In concluding this account on how I became a schizophrenic, one question needs to be asked: are we doing someone a favor if we convince that person that he or she has a *sick mind*? I think from my own experience the answer would have to be a resounding *no*! I cannot think of anything more destructive to one's sense of worth as a human being than to believe that the inner core of one's being is sick — that one's thoughts, values, feelings, and beliefs are merely the meaningless symptoms of a sick mind. Undoubtedly the single most important causal factor behind my mental breakdown was a sense of worth so badly shaken that not even the most florid delusions of grandeur could save it. What the concept of mental illness seemed to offer me was "scientific proof" that I was utterly worthless and would always be worthless. It was just the nature of my genes, chemistry, and brain processes — something I could do nothing about.

Psychiatrists are fond of stressing how much suffering schizophrenia causes. However, I can truthfully say being labeled a schizophrenic has caused me a hundred times as much suffering as the so-called "illness" itself. Since recovering my sanity in 1961, I have spent decades struggling to gain some measure of self-understanding and self-esteem. In this regard, I never fully recovered from what psychiatry and my parents did to me until I finally realized I had never been ill in the first place.

# 10

## RECAPITULATION, ANALYSIS & CONCLUSION

I had been trained to become a schizophrenic almost from the day I was born. Both my parents contributed their fair share in preparing me for this unique calling. Although they undoubtedly loved me, neither of my parents was able to communicate this love. This emotional unresponsiveness on my parents' part struck directly at my self-esteem and thus helped predispose me toward having a schizophrenic episode. Furthermore, my parents' inability to adequately love and nurture me also had the effect of making me more dependent on them. Because neither of my parents were emotionally available to me, I needed them that much more. Therefore to an extent unusual even for a small child, how I viewed myself depended upon how my parents viewed me. But as I have already indicated, my parents viewed me as a virtual psychotic. My mother always viewed me that way, while my father came to view me that way sometime after the university psychiatrists had declared my eventual psychosis to be an absolute certainty. For many years I lived with the vague but horrible awareness that both my parents viewed and were treating me as if I were in the process of going insane. This was excellent training indeed!

Yet the full rigors of my training as a schizophrenic did not begin until after I had moved to California. At that time a noticeable rift began to form between my parents. As their problems worsened, they became less and less able to use introspection or to view themselves or their situation with any degree of objectivity. Yet instead of arguing or fighting with each other, they began to act as if all their problems stemmed from my alleged madness or badness.

I was, of course, very much aware that my parents were having problems. Due to my love and empathy for them, my parents' suffering caused me a considerable amount of emotional anguish. Through the dual process of empathizing with their suffering while I in turn suffered from their vicious tirades, I began to take upon myself the burden of my parents' own "pathology" which I introjected as an intangible yet real internal presence.

I identified with my parents' point of view to such an extent that I hadn't the slightest suspicion they were using me as a scapegoat. If either of my parents stormed and raged at me, I automatically felt that I was the one who was at fault. However, to the extent that I abandoned my own point of view and saw myself in a manner similar to the way I believed my parents saw me, I became vulnerable to their suggestions that I was slowly going insane. It was therefore inevitable that some especially painful incident should cause me to panic, and thereby bring about a course of events which would result in my psychosis.

Not one but three such incidences arose. The first such instance occurred when my mother threatened to have me committed to a mental institution when she caught me picking at the leftovers of a roast in the refrigerator. The second panic episode happened as a result of my grandfather subjecting me to a harsh tirade after I told him I wanted to throw a rock through the window of the Chartres cathedral. The third and final panic episode occurred immediately after my vandalizing a wino shack situated along the edge of a swamp near the city dump in Everett.

These three panic episodes had a cumulative effect.

After the last panic episode my security operations (defense mechanisms) were in a state of total collapse. I was constantly on the verge of panic and was unable to sleep. I felt threatened by:

A) *Panic-producing thoughts*: Thoughts that I had inherited my great-grandmother's madness and was slowly but inexorably going insane. Thoughts that I was a grossly defective person who was incapable of love. Thoughts that I was a vicious and cowardly lunatic who, for some unaccountable reason, had victimized an unfortunate and defenseless old man.

B) *Horribly unpleasant feelings*: Anxiety, fear, guilt, shame, self-hate, and an eerie, uncanny, indescribable feeling.

C) *Internal persecutors*: Monsters and demons welling up from my subconscious mind which were constantly threatening to break into my field of awareness.

Consequently, in the days and weeks following my third panic episode, I underwent a drastic narrowing of interests. I became a religious fanatic who was totally obsessed with the notion of Christ's Second Coming and with the personages of King Solomon and John the Baptist. For seven weeks I stayed up night after night thinking about such matters to the exclusion of all else.

Thinking about such matters to the exclusion of all else kept the types of threats mentioned above from entering my field of awareness. Furthermore, the more I thought about — and identified with — King Solomon and John the Baptist, the better I felt. Such meditations worked wonders in restoring my badly damaged self-esteem!

Moreover, this drastically narrowed focus of awareness shielded me not only from panic-producing thoughts, unpleasant feelings, and internal persecutors, but from reality itself. In thinking nonstop, twenty-four hours a day, about John the Baptist and King Solomon, the reasons why

it was highly unlikely that I was a latter-day John the Baptist or a supernaturally wise man were simply ignored or forgotten entirely.

I have briefly outlined the sequence of events which led to my psychotic
break with reality. At this point a question needs to be asked: what
contribution does the medical model or disease hypothesis make in
explaining this sequence of events? In my opinion, absolutely *none*.

Not only is the medical model totally superfluous in explaining how
I became psychotic, but it is also of no use at all in explaining the origin
and nature of my so-called "symptoms."

How, for example, could the medical model explain my elaborate
visual hallucinations: the five pairs of hallucinatory eyes, my encounter
with Satan, and my Satanic transfiguration? If the medical model is
correct, my visions were merely meaningless symptoms of my sick brain,
and as such had no social, psychological, or cultural significance
whatsoever.

However, to anyone whose mind is not totally warped by psychiatric
dogma, the psychological significance of hallucinating a pair of staring
eyes is obvious to the point of being self-evident: namely, *guilt*. This
obvious interpretation is confirmed by the simple fact of my feeling
under divine judgment when I saw the first pair of eyes staring at me.
Those awesome eyes seemed to see into the very depths of my soul and
see all the moral depravity concealed there. This was certainly a
meaningful or significant experience if ever there was one!

Moreover, this guilt-shame interpretation of the significance of a
staring pair of eyes is also confirmed by my earlier experience of being
stared at by an evil wizard just after my being reprimanded by my
mother for my nasty "sorcery" involving the befouled paint can.

However this simple guilt interpretation by itself does not fully
explain my hallucinatory experiences.

The first pair of eyes that materialized out of the darkness before me
appeared to belong to no less of a person than the Creator of the universe
Himself. Those awesome eyes appeared to be hundreds of millions of
years old. Certainly no human being who had ever existed could possibly
have had eyes even remotely like those. Yet in my madness I told my
father that those godlike eyes looked very much like his own. Why?

The answer to this question is the key to understanding the true
significance of those eyes, for in a very real psychological sense those
awesome eyes did not merely resemble my father's eyes, *they were my
father's eyes*. If this seems strange, it must be remembered that immediately prior to my having that overpowering hallucination I viewed my
father as being a nearly perfect person. His negative characteristics were
totally split off from my conscious awareness and internalized as a
persecuting presence within me. Moreover, after my third panic episode,
this internal persecutor began to loom as an ever more real and threaten-

151

ing presence. To the extent that I began to limit my focus of attention to a few religious concepts in order to keep this persecuting presence from breaking into my field of awareness, so this internal persecutor began to assume the aspect of an all-powerful and wrathful deity. So it was only a matter of time before this wrathful deity would materialize before my very eyes as a sort of weird montage of my earthly and heavenly fathers.

These first hallucinatory eyes then have two complementary interpretations: They can be viewed as the projected image of my own sense of guilt or as a parental introject or internal persecutor.

The hallucinations that followed can be explained in much the same way. I will not, however, go into an explanation of their meaning or significance here. This work is, after all, not a psychological treatise but a polemic. My purpose here is to establish that my hallucinations were due to psychological rather than medical causes, and that they can be explained wholly in terms of the events that preceded them.

My hallucinations were caused by a number of factors. These factors include: the splitting of my personality; seven weeks of prolonged sleep deprivation, which, by itself, can induce hallucinations in ostensibly normal people; my drastically narrowed focus of awareness; and my obsession with religion to the point to where God seemed almost as real to me as any member of my family. God seemed so real and threatening to me that I felt compelled to placate Him with my self-abusive prayers — a powerful form of self-hypnosis which only made matters worse. Still another factor was my nightly ritual of walking the streets and gazing into the headlights of oncoming cars while telling myself that those cars were living beings who were looking into the very depths of my soul. It was as if I were making a deliberate effort to induce hallucinations!

In fact, I remember one instance in which I was able to hallucinate by a sheer act of will. This singular event happened in March 1961, a few days after my father had died in a plane crash. At that time I was alone in a cabin in a rather agitated frame of mind. While making a conscious effort to visualize my father I noticed distinct images of him beginning to flicker before my eyes. By concentrating on one of those images, I was able to make my father materialize before me with a degree of vividness as if he were actually standing in the room!

That schizophrenics actively — if unconsciously — strive to hallucinate, and are able to exert a considerable amount of control over their hallucinations, is supported by the clinical work of Silvano Arieti and by the experimental findings of Peter Bick and Marcel Kinsbourne.

The findings of Silvano Arieti — like those of Bick and Kinsbourne

— relate exclusively to auditory hallucinations.* According to Arieti, the psychological process which leads to auditory hallucinations has three stages. First, the individual projects his own feelings of self-disparagement on to the external world. In this initial stage, this person can almost feel hostility in the air. Believing that others are talking about him, this individual then puts himself into what Arieti calls the *listening attitude*. Finally, he hallucinates. He hears voices because he *expects* to hear them.

Dr. Arieti has found that his schizophrenic patients stop hallucinating as soon as he is able to get them to understand this three-stage process and admit to themselves that they are the cause of their own hallucinations.[1] However, Arieti has also found that in depriving his schizophrenic patients of their hallucinations, he also increases their anxiety and emotional suffering.[2]

That schizophrenics are able to control their auditory hallucinations is also supported by the recent experimental findings of Peter Bick and Marcel Kinsbourne of Harvard.[3] These researchers are impressed with the fact that their experimental subjects show complete indifference to their ability to suppress their hallucinations. Like Arieti, Bick and Kinsbourne are of the opinion that the hallucinations of schizophrenics are "... a way to project troubling thoughts, used as a coping device;"[4] and that in depriving a schizophrenic of his dissonant voices, one might "...expose the patient to a more dissonant state."[5]

I don't see how my hallucinations can be viewed as a symptom of my "sick mind" when it has been known for a long time that a normal person can hallucinate without becoming psychotic.[6] Two recent surveys have indicated that between 13.2 and 15.4 percent of college freshmen and sophomores have had auditory hallucinations.[7] In a comparative study of hallucinations, it was shown that 35 percent of the relatives of psychiatric patients hallucinated, 34 percent of nonpsychotic medically ill patients hallucinated, and 58 percent of unselected medical students gave evidence of having hallucinated.[8] Finally, a study of normal persons who were widowed revealed that 50 percent of the women and 66 percent of the men hallucinated.[9]

To sum up: my hallucinations were a meaningful and purposive attempt on my part to cope with feelings of guilt and low self-esteem, and can be explained wholly in terms of the events which preceded them. Moreover, to a large extent, I myself was responsible for causing my hallucinations. Since normal people hallucinate, my hallucinations make

---

*It is commonly believed that the hallucinations of schizophrenics are predominantly auditory. However in a 1989 study, Bracha, Wolkowitz, Lohr, et al., found a very high (56 percent) prevalence of visual hallucinations in their chronic schizophrenic subjects.

me no different from any other normal person. In short, my hallucinations were an expression of my humanity and not a symptom of a disease.

If the medical model is correct, my delusions were caused by a brain disease which rendered me incapable of thinking realistically.

However, as I have already indicated, my delusions were largely derived from and wholly consistent with my Protestant fundamentalist beliefs — beliefs that are shared by tens of millions of people. If we grant that these beliefs might actually be true, then it follows logically that my delusions might also have been true. Take, for instance, my belief that I possessed the wisdom of Solomon. If a God who answers prayers actually exists, then it is wholly possible that He might have answered my prayers and granted me the wisdom of Solomon. Wisdom is, after all, a very admirable and godly thing to ask for! Or take, for example, my belief that I was a latter-day John the Baptist whose mission was to prepare the world for the Second Coming of Christ. Such a mission — that of the two witnesses — is explicitly mentioned in the eleventh chapter of the book of Revelations. If one accepts the Bible as the literal word of God and believes in the Second Coming of Christ, then one must be prepared to assent to the possibility of my being one of those two witnesses. Moreover, in view of my undergoing those mystical visions, how could a zealous fundamentalist such as myself be blamed for believing that he was a chosen prophet of God? How were my visions any different from those of an Isaiah or an Ezekiel? If Matthew 11:14 is correct and John the Baptist was Elijah, then why couldn't I have been John the Baptist? How is one belief any more absurd than the other? Finally, if I was really as important a person as I thought I was — which is logically possible if my religious beliefs were correct — then my belief that the media (newspapers, magazines, radio, and television) were constantly making covert references to me could quite possibly have been true.

The mere fact that my beliefs were utterly mistaken does not necessarily mean that I was afflicted with a brain disease or that I was incapable of thinking realistically. As deluded as I was, I was nevertheless sufficiently in contact with reality to realize that others did not share my beliefs; and I wisely chose not to reveal my delusions to anyone except my closest friend. I was also prudent enough not to act out my delusions. For instance, I didn't go around telling others that the end of the world was at hand or that I was a latter-day John the Baptist, for I knew exactly what the consequences would have been if I had done so. Like any normal person, I possessed both common sense and an ability to make sound judgments.

Except for a brief period of time immediately preceding and immediately following my visual hallucinations, my ability to think clearly and logically was completely unimpaired. My clarity of thought is typified by my meditations on the nature of God and His relationship with Satan. I was able to understand that if there was an all-powerful God who had created a finite being such as Satan, then it would follow as a matter of logical necessity that Satan would have to be subordinate to God. Furthermore, from my studies of the Bible I knew of numerous instances where God had either acted in a thoroughly Satanic manner, or had sent Satan and his demons to do His bidding. Consequently, I viewed God as nothing more than an omnipotent Demon. What could be more ruthlessly logical than this concept of God? In my madness my thinking was still more lucid than that of any orthodox Christian theologian who had ever lived!

In his book, *The Origin and Treatment of Schizophrenic Disorders*, Theodore Lidz makes this very interesting point:

> A scientist capable of highly abstract or conceptual thinking will only agree to play poker with his friends when he has a rabbit's foot talisman in his pocket, or drink only certain brand of beer lest his team lose.[10]

On considering the delusions of schizophrenics, it is well to keep in mind that human beings in general tend to be highly illogical creatures. Consequently, the mere fact that schizophrenic delusions are often illogical or bizarre is no proof that schizophrenics are incapable of rational thought.

Moreover, what is considered rational varies with time and place. For instance, in some cultures is not unusual to interpret the flight of birds as an omen, or to predict the future by looking at the entrails of animals.

It is also important to realize just how common delusions actually are. For instance, in our culture the most ordinary people have the most extraordinary delusions of grandeur: they believe that after they die they will become demigods and live forever in a beautiful mansion in the sky. There are also large and growing numbers of people, many of them well-educated and sophisticated, who believe that their lives are controlled by the stars, and who are incapable of making decisions without first consulting an astrologer. Moreover, with the advent of the so-called New Age movement, many delusions and superstitions once confined to schizophrenics, borderline schizophrenics and other marginal people, are now becoming almost the norm. There are millions of people who firmly believe that little green men from outer space are going to land en masse on this planet and usher in a New Age — just as tens of millions of other people firmly believe that Jesus Christ is going to return and usher in a thousand-year Reich. There are also hundreds of apparently normal and well-adjusted people who sincerely believe they have been kidnapped by alien creatures and taken aboard UFOs, where they have undergone complicated and often painful medical examinations. The ability of ordinary people to delude themselves is virtually limitless!

Delusions are so common that their absence rather than their presence should be taken as an indication of abnormality.

To sum up: my delusions were largely derived from and wholly consistent with my Protestant fundamentalist beliefs — beliefs which are shared by tens of millions of people. Deluded as I was, my ability to think clearly and logically, to use common sense, and to make rational decisions was totally unimpaired. Since normal people have delusions, my being deluded made me no different from any other normal person. Since I have already explained in great detail just how my delusions were caused, it should be obvious to anyone who isn't severely deluded that my delusions were not caused by a disease.

At this point I am reminded of a story which has often been told concerning the meeting of Napoleon and the great French scientist Pierre Laplace. Laplace was the physicist who brought the Newtonian system to the apex of its perfection. When Napoleon met Laplace, that scientist had just completed his life work, a many-volumed book that he was holding in his hands. Laplace explained to Napoleon in great detail how, with the mathematical formulas he had worked out, he could account for the motions of all the planets, the moon, and the tides here on earth. Napoleon turned to him and remarked, "Monsieur, you haven't even mentioned the Creator." To this remark Laplace disdainfully replied, "I have no need of that hypothesis."

Likewise in explaining the causes of my schizophrenic episode and all of my so-called symptoms, I have no need of the disease hypothesis. I cannot see how the notion of an "illness" taking possession of my mind and depriving me of my reason is any less irrational or superstitious than the idea of my being possessed by a demon. If my madness had been due to either a brain lesion or an inborn metabolic defect, then how could I have possibly recovered? How could my delusions have suddenly cleared up by my merely looking at a letter I had written to a friend? Upon reading that letter was my brain instantly healed or my genes miraculously altered? To me such a recovery clearly indicates that I must not have been ill in the first place.

Yet — and this is a crucial point — I don't think I have been mislabeled or misdiagnosed. If the diagnostic criteria set forth in the most recent edition of the *Diagnostic and Statistical Manual* (DSM-IV) of the American Psychiatric Association have any validity, then my status as a schizophrenic is entirely secure. The DSM-IV criteria for schizophrenia are as follows:

A. *Characteristic symptoms:* Two (or more) of the following, each present for a significant portion of time during a one-month period (or less if successfully treated):

(1) delusions
(2) hallucinations
(3) disorganized speech (e.g., frequent derailment or incoherence)
(4) grossly disorganized or catatonic behavior
(5) negative symptoms, i.e., affective flattening, alogia, or avolition.[11]

Special note should be taken of the fact that, according to DSM-IV diagnostic criteria, in many instances an individual can earn a schizophrenic label by merely exhibiting just *one* of the first two symptoms listed above: either by having delusions that are considered bizarre, or by having hallucinations in which a voice is keeping a running commentary on one's behavior or thoughts, or in which there are two or more voices talking to each other.

I think my delusions that I was John the Baptist and that the media were constantly making obscure references to me were sufficiently implausible and bizarre enough to justify my being classified as a schizophrenic. Indeed, there was a time when I was unable to pick up a comic book without seeing a profound Holy Spirit-inspired message put there exclusively for my benefit.* If that wasn't bizarre delusional thinking then I would like to know what is!

According to DSM-IV diagnostic criteria, my delusions *alone* should have been sufficient to qualify me to bear the noble title of schizophrenic. However, there were other symptoms which should more than qualify me for my schizophrenic label: my elaborate visual hallucinations, my flattened or inappropriate affect at the time of my dog Pepi's death, and my disorganized speech or incoherence upon my attempt to explain my divine mission to my father by expounding upon the symbolism on the back of a one dollar bill. This last symptom — my illogical thinking and loosening of associations — lasted for at least a week after I had had my vision. Indeed, this loosening of associations and fragmentation of thought must still have been evident at the time I received my schizo-

---

*If God could inspire the Holy Bible then why not comic books? In fact, a stronger case could be made for the divine inspiration of the comic books I had read than for the Bible. After all, those comic book stories were far more plausible than the stories found in the Bible, and, unlike the Bible, contained no self-contradictions.[12] Besides I only believed in the divine inspiration of the comic books for one day before putting them away in the drawer and forgetting about them, whereas millions upon millions of people go through their entire lives believing in the divine inspiration of the Bible.

phrenic label — about a month after my vision — for at that time Captain Kamm explained to me that I had been given Stelazine in order to increase my ability to concentrate and make my "thoughts come together."

The other DSM-IV credentials which validate my diagnosis as a schizophrenic include: the deterioration of my academic performance immediately prior to and during my schizophrenic episode; the fact that, if both my prodromal and residual symptoms are included, I was symptomatic on a continuous basis for a period of at least three years (1959-1962); the fact that during this entire three-year period I never underwent a single major depressive or manic episode; and the fact that my mental disturbance wasn't caused by my taking drugs or by any known medical condition.

So far, the American Psychiatric Association has put forward five different sets of diagnostic criteria for schizophrenia: DSM-I in 1952, DSM-II in 1968, DSM-III in 1980, DSM-III-R in 1987, and DSM-IV in 1994.* I am proud to say that I would have qualified as a schizophrenic under each and every one of those five different diagnostic criteria.

*That I could be both schizophrenic and not ill at the same time is the strongest possible proof that schizophrenia is not a disease.*

However, one cannot question the status of schizophrenia as a real disease without thereby calling into question the legitimacy of psychiatry as a medical specialty. For this reason most psychiatrists will angrily dismiss my claim that schizophrenia is nothing more than an emotional disorder with an environmental cause. In their view, schizophrenics are not victims of their environment, but biologically inferior persons made of intrinsically inferior material: poor brains, bad chemistry, defective genes.

I will now examine this very interesting notion that people like myself are intrinsically inferior to other human beings.

---

*Most psychiatrists and schizophrenia researchers appear to be under the delusion that the concept of schizophrenia has remained essentially unchanged since it was originated by Emil Kraepelin and Eugen Bleuler. However, as Boyle 1990 points out, both Bleuler and Kraepelin considered the symptoms of encephalitis (sleeping sickness) as essential defining characteristics of schizophrenia — a view that very few psychiatrists now hold.

# PART III

# THE MEDICAL MODEL REEXAMINED

# 1

## PSYCHIATRY'S GIANT STEP BACKWARDS

A few years back, while in a bookstore in Seattle's University District, I overheard a student discussing the topic of schizophrenia. This student was telling his friend how the belief that schizophrenics are able to recover their sanity has been wholly discredited due to a recent medical breakthrough which has firmly established that schizophrenia is a totally incurable disease.

The so-called "medical breakthrough" mentioned above refers to a recent trend in psychiatry: for the most part, psychiatrists have abandoned the idea that schizophrenia is a transitory emotional disorder in favor of the view that schizophrenia is an irreversible biological process. This new psychiatric pessimism in regard to schizophrenia is stated succinctly by Joseph Coyle, a Johns Hopkins University psychiatrist:

> The natural history of the disease is one of deterioration. That has been the case in every schizophrenic I have ever seen.[1]

However, the "deterioration" Dr. Coyle speaks of has not occurred in us schizophrenics but in psychiatry itself. Since the early 1980s, psychiatry has been in the process of reviving the long-discredited late nineteenth-century notion that schizophrenia is a brain disease, and is currently advertising this ignominious retreat from reality as a glamorous medical advance.

Three trends — one ideological, one economic, and one political — have prompted psychiatrists to rally around the medical model and proclaim its truth with all the fervor of born-again true believers.

### The Ideological Trend

During the 1960s and 1970s, a number of authors, including Thomas Szasz, R. D. Laing, Erving Goffman, Michel Foucault, Thomas J. Scheff, David L. Rosenhan, Ronald Leifer, Theodore R. Sarbin and James C. Mancuso, published scholarly books and essays giving solid reasons for rejecting the medical model. Thomas Szasz in particular has argued that the concepts of mental illness and schizophrenia have no more scientific validity than the earlier notions of witchcraft and demoniac possession. Dr. Szasz points to the undeniable fact that no one is diagnosed as schizophrenic because he is ill in the accepted medical sense, but rather because his behavior has violated certain social norms. Szasz also points out that there is obviously a vast difference between social deviance and disease. Unlike social deviance, disease is a *physical* concept: it refers to cellular pathology: to histopathological lesions and pathophysiological processes. Szasz also reminds us that despite claims to the contrary, no one has been able to demonstrate a physical basis for schizophrenia. (Indeed, if a physical basis for schizophrenia actually exists, psychiatrists would utilize objective laboratory tests to diagnose this so-called "illness" rather than relying on such vague subjective criteria as the presence of delusions and hallucinations!)

Furthermore, according to Dr. Szasz, the act of diagnosing a person as schizophrenic is nothing more than a pseudoscientific ritual in which a person is degraded to a less than human status so that his basic human rights need no longer be given any consideration. Moreover, since psychiatry's inception back in the seventeenth century, its function has *always* been to keep certain individuals from being a nuisance to society — and this remains true even to this day. Since psychiatrists are committed to controlling socially deviant behavior, and since they also see themselves as legitimate medical practitioners, they have adopted the comfortable and self-serving delusion that socially deviant behavior is somehow equivalent to disease.

In short, it is the view of Thomas Szasz — as well as a number of other authors — that schizophrenia is a fake disease and that psychiatry is fraudulent medicine.[2]

To some extent, psychiatry's recent return to the medical model must be understood as an inevitable backlash against the school of thought represented by Thomas Szasz. Due to the fact that the views of Dr. Szasz have won increasing acceptance in many circles, organized psychiatry has been compelled to launch a massive propaganda campaign to convince the general public that they are a wholly legitimate branch of medicine — that the "illnesses" they treat are every bit as real as diabetes or cancer.

However, to fully comprehend the reactionary mindset of contemporary psychiatry, it is first necessary to realize that the views of Thomas Szasz are not nearly as radical as they may at first seem. As far back as 1906, Adolph Meyer, the founder of modern American psychiatry, had expressed views similar to those of Szasz. Moreover, throughout most of the twentieth century many eminent psychiatrists, including Harry Stack Sullivan and Theodore Lidz, have built upon the foundations laid by Freud and Meyer, and have not only expressed the view that schizophrenia is an emotional disorder with an environmental cause, but have also shed a considerable amount of light on exactly what causes schizophrenia. If the findings of Lidz and Sullivan are correct, then the truth of Szasz's view, that schizophrenia is not a disease, is virtually self-evident. For this reason the ideas of Freud, Meyer, Sullivan, and Lidz are no more accepted in contemporary psychiatry than are the ideas of Thomas Szasz. In short, in reacting against Dr. Szasz — and against others who share his views — psychiatry has been forced by logical necessity to totally repudiate its entire psychological heritage — and in so doing it has revealed its complete moral and intellectual bankruptcy.

## The Economic Trend

The economic uncertainties and stagflation prevailing in the 1970s and early 1980s had a traumatizing effect on everyone — especially on psychiatrists. Psychiatry was being seriously hurt. While being assailed by its critics, psychiatry was encountering difficulties of an altogether different sort: it was being plagued by competitors. During the 1960s and 1970s, nonmedical psychotherapies were springing up like mushrooms: encounter therapy, reality therapy, existential therapy, gestalt therapy, client-centered therapy, family therapy, behavior modification, transactional analysis, primal scream therapy, rolfing, Lifespring, Scientology, and est. As different as these therapies were from one another, they all had one thing in common: they all took clients away from psychiatry. In addition to these new therapies, psychiatry was also facing competition from psychologists, clinical social workers, psychiatric nurses, and a variety of counselors, all who were entering the field of psychotherapy in droves.

Faced with competitors encroaching on its once exclusive domain, psychiatry fought back. It unleashed a massive advertising and propaganda campaign to convince the general public that *all* mental disorders — including schizophrenia — were of a biological nature and could only be properly treated by therapists who were medical doctors.

The mendacity of this psychiatric propaganda campaign was exceeded only by its effectiveness. In the repressive, anti-intellectual social climate of the 1980s and '90s — in this era of social and intellectual conformity — no one any longer questions the authority of psychiatry or the notion that all mental disorders stem from biological causes.

## The Political Trend

It was certainly no coincidence that psychiatry returned to the medical model just as the political climate in this country was becoming markedly more conservative, for political and psychiatric reactionaries share a common ideology: *biological determinism.*

Biological determinism has always been an attractive ideology for political reactionaries since it seems to justify both the inequality of races, sexes and social classes, and a do-nothing social policy. Indeed, if biological determinism is correct, and the poor are poor because they are inherently stupid or inferior, then why should the taxpayers' money be wasted in a futile effort to remedy their plight?

During the Reagan and Bush administrations — and especially during the Republican juggernaut during the Clinton administration — every social program that had been set up to help the poor, the elderly, the handicapped, and racial minorities has been drastically cut. As a result of this callous penny-pinching policy, more and more people have been tossed on the human scrap heap.

Schizophrenics are among those people who have been ruthlessly discarded by society. Since the early 1980s it has become an unquestioned dogma that until medical science discovers a cure for schizophrenia sometime in the future — in perhaps five, ten, or a thousand years — people afflicted with this disease are totally beyond help. Therefore psychotherapy, counseling, vocational training, and other social rehabilitation programs aimed at helping such people are a total waste of time and money. Schizophrenics should be drugged to the point of stupor and simply left to rot.

Those who cling to the medical model will of course deny that they do so out of motives of social expediency. They will claim that over the past few decades psychiatry has accumulated a massive amount of facts which prove beyond a reasonable doubt that schizophrenia is a real disease — and that such discoveries will ultimately be the salvation of such pitiful, biologically inferior specimens as myself.

I will now examine the so-called "facts" that purportedly prove that schizophrenia is a disease much like cancer or syphilis.

# 2

# SCHIZOPHRENIA AS A BRAIN DEFECT

"Know syphilis in all its manifestations and relations, and all things clinical will be added unto you." These often quoted words of Sir William Osler (1849-1919) graphically and succinctly sum up the late-nineteenth and early-twentieth-century view concerning the nature and cause of schizophrenia and other forms of madness.

Since the early 1980s views similar to those of Osler's have been becoming increasingly fashionable.

One of the most vociferous proponents of this germ theory of schizophrenia is Dr. E. Fuller Torrey, a psychiatrist who for four years was Special Assistant to the Director of the National Institute of Mental Health. Dr. Torrey's own research has led him to believe that schizophrenia is caused by the herpes simplex virus.[1] In 1983, Dr. Torrey appeared on the *Phil Donahue Show* where he gave a presentation of his views on schizophrenia. When Donahue remarked that Torrey's views would hardly earn him a standing ovation in every quarter of the psychiatric community, Dr. Torrey flippantly replied:

> I think the psychiatric community that are reading their medical journals are almost unanimous now that schizophrenia is a brain disease. Unfortunately there is a segment of the psychiatric community that reads only the *National Geographic*. They have not got the word yet.[2]

To lend substance to his claim that schizophrenia is a brain disease, Dr. Torrey displayed and described pictures taken by a computerized axial tomographic (CAT) scanner:*

> This is two pictures. The top row are CAT scans from the brain of a normal person. This is taken as showing the black is the fluid in the ventricles. That's what a normal brain looks like. The bottom row is the brain of a person with schizophrenia. You can

---

*More often referred to as computerized tomographic (CT) scanners.

see how much larger the ventricles are. That's fluid you're looking at. That means this loss of brain tissue. That's the brain disease you are looking at.[3]

To get some idea of the deceptiveness of Dr. Torrey's presentation, let's imagine the following: instead of Dr. Torrey, suppose the Rev. Pat Robertson appeared on the *Phil Donahue Show*. After lecturing the audience on the evils of secular humanism, Rev. Robertson shows two pictures. One of these pictures is a CAT scan taken of a brain of a born-again Christian. This picture reveals the utter flawlessness of that person's brain. Then Rev. Robertson shows a CAT scan taken of the brain of a secular humanist. This picture reveals that the brain of that godless individual has grossly enlarged ventricles: a clear sign of brain atrophy. From this, Rev. Robertson comes to the thundering conclusion that secular humanism is a brain disease.

However, had Robertson presented the above argument as "proof" that secular humanism is a brain disease, his claim would have been met with almost total disbelief — and for three very good reasons. First, it would have been obvious to nearly everyone that the vast majority of secular humanists would have normal brains. Second, it would have been equally obvious that those suffering from brain atrophy would include a proportionate number of born-again Christians. Third, it would seem highly unlikely that any correlation would exist between secular humanism and brain atrophy.

*But the same sorts of objections which can be brought against this purely hypothetical or imaginary claim that secular humanism is a brain disease can also be brought against a similar claim made by Torrey in regard to schizophrenia.* First of all, in *every* computerized tomographic (or magnetic resonance imaging) brain scan study which has been done using schizophrenic patients and normal controls, it has been found that a clear majority of the schizophrenics had normal-sized ventricles. For example, in a 1983 review of such studies, it was found that anywhere from 60 to 95 percent of the schizophrenics showed no sign of brain atrophy or enlarged ventricles.[4] In fact, *at least a dozen brain scan studies exist which reveal no differences at all between the ventricular size of schizophrenics and that of normal controls.*[5]

Among the twelve brain scan studies mentioned above is one done by Terry L. Jernigan and her associates at the Stanford University School of Medicine.[6] This study involved 30 schizophrenics and 33 normal volunteers. Jernigan's study is particularly noteworthy in that the methods used in calculating the ventricular-brain ratio (VBR) are far more sophisticated than those of any previous study.[7] Furthermore, Dr. Jernigan sent the brain scans from her study to two other research groups — groups led by Drs. Daniel R. Weinberger and Charles Golden. All three of these groups blindly measured the VBRs of the subjects' brain scans and could find no difference between the VBRs of the schizophrenics and those of the controls.[8]

Significantly enough, while none of the three groups could find any relative difference between the VBRs of the schizophrenics and the controls, the absolute values of the VBRs measured by Dr. Golden were, on the average, almost twice those measured by Drs. Jernigan and Weinberger.[9] *Such discrepant results clearly indicate the inherent subjectivity involved in interpreting data derived from CAT scans.*

Another brain scan study of special interest was done by William R. Yates and his coworkers at the University of Iowa College of Medicine. Yates' study is the largest study of its kind to date. His study involves 108 schizophrenic patients, 50 patients with affective disorder, and 74 age- and sex-matched controls. Yates and his group found that neither the schizophrenic patients nor the patients with affective disorder had ventricles larger than those of the control subjects.[10]

The twelve brain scan studies that have found no differences between schizophrenic subjects and normal controls include four studies utilizing magnetic resonance imaging (MRI) — a technique capable of producing far clearer and more detailed pictures of the brain than is possible with computerized tomography. The four MRI studies include two studies done by Robert C. Smith and his associates at the Texas Research Institute of Mental Sciences in Houston;[11] a study done by Roy C. Matthew and C. Leon Partain of the Vanderbilt University School of Medicine in Nashville, Tennessee;[12] and a study done by Eve C. Johnstone and her colleagues at the Clinical Research Centre in Harrow, Middlesex, England.[13]

Although the twelve studies mentioned above are contradicted by other studies showing that *some* schizophrenics do have enlarged ventricles, the contradiction is more apparent than real since all the studies that have ever been done support the conclusion that *the vast majority of schizophrenics have normal-sized ventricles and show no sign of brain atrophy whatsoever.*

Moreover, it is equally important to bear in mind that there are groups of people who have enlarged ventricles but who still have no psychiatric problems. For example, it is known that ventricular enlargement is much more common in left-handed people than in right-handed people.[14] This is due to the fact that left-handed people have a tendency to develop brain lesions as a result of their brains being organized differently from right-handed people.[15] Yet no sensible person would claim that left-handedness is a brain disease. On the contrary, left-handed people tend to be gifted and contribute a disproportionate number of professional athletes, artists, architects, engineers, and mathematicians.[16]

Finally, various attempts have been made to establish meaningful correlations between ventricular enlargement (VE) and schizophrenic symptomatology. For example, Andreasen and others have found that VE is associated with the presence of negative symptoms (blunted affect, incoherence) and the absence of positive symptoms (delusions, hallucinations).[17] Other authorities such as Farmer have found just the opposite: that VE is associated with the presence of positive symptoms and the absence of negative symptoms.[18] Yet there are also other authorities such as Nasrallah,[19] Pandurangi,[20] Owens,[21] Obiols,[22] and Bankier[23] who have found no correlation at all between VE and the presence or absence of positive and negative symptoms, or between VE and the degree of cognitive impairment or mental disorder in their schizophrenic subjects. For instance, Owens has found that "Some of the most handicapped schizophrenic patients had ventricles in the smallest range of ventricle size,"[24] while Obiols has found in some cases that the schizophrenic patients with the most VE have the least cognitive impairment.[25] Moreover, while Pandurangi has found significant correlations between VE and impairment on several parameters traditionally associated with brain damage, he — like Nasrallah and Owens — is unable to find any correlation between VE and clinical variables indicative of schizophrenia.[26] Finally, as a result of his own study which found a total lack of any significant differences between schizophrenics with and without VE, Bankier has come to the conclusion that VE must be totally unrelated to schizophrenia.[27]

To sum up: First, the vast majority of schizophrenics do not have VE. Second, there exists a group of people who have VE (left-handed people) but who have no psychiatric problems whatsoever. Third, there exists a total lack of any significant differences between schizophrenics with and without VE. Facts such as these support the conclusion that VE must be totally unrelated to schizophrenia. *Consequently, Dr. Torrey's claim that the mere fact that some schizophrenics have VE somehow proves that schizophrenia is brain disease is totally without any logical or factual basis.*

Some psychiatrists are not content with merely claiming that schizophrenia is a brain disease, but have attempted to locate the exact spot in the brain where schizophrenia does its sinister work. Schizophrenia has been described by various authorities as a frontal-lobe disease,[28] as a temporo-limbic disease,[29] as a left-hemisphere disease,[30] and as a right-hemisphere disease.[31]

One of the claims encountered most often in psychiatric journals these days is the notion that schizophrenia is a disease localized in the hippocampus.[32] This theory stems from the work of Sarnoff A. Mednick, now at the University of California at Los Angeles, who has hypothesized that a lack of oxygen occurring prior to birth causes hippocampal damage — a condition that ultimately leads to schizophrenia.[33] More recently, in 1987, Nestor A. Schmajuk of Boston University has suggested that the behavioral disorders of rats with hippocampal lesions are an adequate model for understanding humans suffering from schizophrenia.[34] More to the point are the findings of two UCLA medical researchers, Arnold Scheibel and Joyce A. Kovelman. These investigators have found gross cellular disarray in the hippocampi of some schizophrenic patients.[35]

However, in a study similar to that of Scheibel and Kovelman's, Daniel R. Weinberger of the National Institute of Mental Health found just as much cellular disarray in the hippocampi of normal controls as he did in the hippocampi of schizophrenics.[36] Furthermore, in a more recent study, Scheibel and Kovelman have themselves been unable to find significant differences between the hippocampi of schizophrenics and nonpsychotic controls.[37]

It is, moreover, highly speculative at best to use the behavioral disorders of hippocampal-lesioned rats as a model for understanding schizophrenia. Certainly it would seem self-evident to anyone that the behavior of hippocampal-lesioned human beings would be of far more relevance in assessing the truth or falsity of the hippocampal theory of schizophrenia than the behavior of brain-damaged rats. An ideal test of this theory would be to surgically remove the hippocampus of a human being and observe the results. If that person becomes schizophrenic as a result of this operation, then the hippocampal theory of schizophrenia stands confirmed. If not, then the theory has been decisively refuted.

According to Jonathan Winson, such an operation — resulting in the removal of nearly the entire hippocampus — was performed on a twenty-nine-year-old epileptic man by a psychosurgeon, Dr. William Scoville, on September 1, 1953, at the Hartford Hospital in Hartford, Connecticut. In referring to this patient, Winson writes:

His pleasant preoperative personality was not affected by the operation, nor were his capacity to understand and reason.[38]

In fact, that patient did not exhibit any psychotic or schizophrenic symptoms during the entire twenty-five year period following his operation in which he was under intense scientific scrutiny.[39] But if schizophrenia is caused by damage to the hippocampus, then this man should have become a schizophrenic. That he didn't is a clear refutation of the hippocampal theory of schizophrenia if ever there was one!

However, as a result of having his hippocampus removed, the above patient did have one prominent symptom: his memory was severely affected. Although this man's old memories were completely intact, he suffered from a complete inability to learn new things or to remember events in his immediate past.

From cases such as the one mentioned above it has been learned that the hippocampus is that portion of the brain where new memories are stored.[40]

Therefore if (a) the ability to remember depends upon having an intact functioning hippocampus, and (b) schizophrenia is the result of a damaged hippocampus, then it follows logically that schizophrenics must suffer from severe memory impairment. Yet it has been known for a long time that schizophrenia leaves one's ability to remember totally intact. (If this were not the case, it would have been impossible for me to have written this book.) The mere fact that schizophrenia does not affect the memory is another reason that the hippocampal theory of schizophrenia is totally without any scientific basis.

Finally, we are presented with the pitiful spectacle of reputable medical researchers damaging the brains of rats, and fantasizing about these animal's "schizophrenic symptoms," when it has been known for decades (since 1953) that damage to the hippocampus has no bearing upon whether or not a person becomes schizophrenic!

By no means is psychiatry content with pointing to *structural* defects in the brains of schizophrenics. Recently, psychiatry has acquired a wonderful new tool — positron emission tomography (PET) — which allows it to point with pride to brain defects of a wholly *functional* nature.

Just as it has been claimed that CAT scans have revealed that schizophrenics have atrophied brains, it has likewise been claimed that PET scans have demonstrated that the brains of schizophrenics function in a grossly abnormal way. It has been claimed, for example, that while the brains of normal people burn relatively more energy in the frontal cortex and relatively less energy in the posterior areas of the brain, the brains of schizophrenics exhibit the exact opposite pattern — the so-called *hypofrontal pattern* — and burn relatively less energy in the frontal and relatively more energy in the posterior regions of the brain.[41]

This hypofrontal metabolic pattern is by far the best documented functional brain abnormality that psychiatric researchers have found in schizophrenics while using the PET scanning technique. Moreover, as with the CAT scan studies, the results in these PET scan studies have been very widely publicized, and claims have been made that such studies offer conclusive proof that schizophrenia is a bona fide brain disease.

Despite these claims, however, all the available evidence seems to indicate that the diminished metabolism encountered in the frontal lobes of schizophrenic patients is totally unrelated to their psychiatric disorders. Among the studies that support this conclusion is one done by Drs. DeLisi, Buchsbaum, and Holcomb and their associates at the National Institute of Mental Health.[42] In this study involving 21 chronic schizophrenics and 21 age- and sex-matched controls, the investigators found that one of the controls and eight of the patients exhibited the hypofrontal pattern. *These researchers were unable to find any correlation at all between schizophrenic symptoms and hypofrontality, or between the presence of the hypofrontal pattern and the severity of the so-called "illness."*[43]

The NIMH investigators found that hypofrontality was correlated with symptoms more characteristic of depression than schizophrenia: emotional withdrawal, disorientation, distractibility, and feelings of hopelessness and helplessness.[44] This is consistent with the fact that the hypofrontal pattern is also found in cases of major depression.[45]

Furthermore, not only is hypofrontality nonspecific to schizophrenia, the hypofrontal pattern is totally absent in most cases of schizophrenia. In fact, many research teams utilizing PET scans have been unable to find hypofrontality in their schizophrenic subjects.[46] For example, a research team headed by G. Sheppard at the Charing Cross Hospital in London, England, was unable to find any evidence of hypofrontality in twelve acute schizophrenic patients — most of whom had never been treated with neuroleptic drugs.[47] Moreover, like Sheppard, Raquel E. Gur and her associates at the University of Pennsylvania in Philadelphia were also unable to detect hypofrontality in twelve schizophrenic subjects who were not under medication.[48]

Since the hypofrontal pattern has been found to be associated with depression, and since many of the drugs used in treating schizophrenia are depressants,[49] it is only reasonable to suspect that these drugs might be a contributing factor to the hypofrontality encountered in schizophrenia. This suspicion is supported by two lines of evidence. First, three independent research teams led by Widen,[50] Volkow,[51] and Wolkin,[52] have done PET scans on schizophrenics both before and after the administration of neuroleptic drugs and have found that these drugs contribute to the hypofrontal metabolic pattern. Second, G. Geraud and his coworkers at Chu Rangueil in Toulouse, France, found that they were able to reverse the hypofrontal pattern in their schizophrenic subjects by administering a weak dose of piribedil, a drug whose effects are the direct opposite of the drugs used in treating schizophrenia.[53] Dr. Geraud and his associates also found that they were able to effect a similar change in some of their schizophrenic patients by merely taking them off neuroleptic drugs for a prolonged period of time.[54]

However, at this point it must be stressed that no amount of evidence will ever convince the majority of psychiatrists that schizophrenics have normally functioning brains. Whenever a theory about the supposed defectiveness of schizophrenic brains is abandoned, another similar theory always immediately takes its place. For instance, recently Henry Szechtman and his colleagues at McMaster University at Hamilton, Ontario in Canada, have proposed replacing the hypofrontal with *hyper*frontal theory of schizophrenia. According to these investigators, schizophrenia is a pathological condition characterized by a hyperactive frontal cortex — a condition which can be corrected by prolonged medication with neuroleptic drugs.[55]

"It should be remembered that, except for their brains, schizophrenics are basically like other people."[56] This remarkable piece of doublethink is from a prize-winning essay by John S. Allen, a postdoctoral fellow in the Department of Psychiatry and Behavioral Sciences at Stanford University. The sole evidence cited by Dr. Allen in support of his claim that schizophrenics have brains basically different from those of normal people is the now widely publicized observation that schizophrenics exhibit jerky eye movements when tracking the movements of a swinging pendulum, instead of the smooth-pursuit movements that are considered normal. However, these eye tracking movements are known to be controlled by the pontine reticular formation which is part of the brain stem. Since no psychiatric researcher seriously believes that schizophrenia is a disease localized in the brain stem, it is therefore hard to imagine what possible relevance the poor eye tracking performance of schizophrenics could have in regard to their mental problems — unless, of course, one regards the *entire* brain of the schizophrenic as being defective. Furthermore, studies show that anywhere from 14 to 48 percent of schizophrenics do *not* exhibit these aberrant eye tracking movements,[57] while as much as 8 or 9 percent of normal people *do*.[58] Moreover, in an experimental study, Brezinova and Kendell have demonstrated that when normal people are bored or distracted, their eye tracking performance is indistinguishable from that of schizophrenics.[59]

Finally, we are confronted with the astonishing discovery that schizophrenics have smaller brains and smaller craniums than normal people — a finding which accounts for the feeble-mindedness of people such as myself.* This earth-shaking discovery was made by Nancy Andreasen and her colleagues both at the University of Iowa College of Medicine and at Ohio State University, and was published in the February 1986 issue of the *Archives of General Psychiatry*.

Upon reading Dr. Andreasen's report on how the cognitive impairment of her schizophrenic subjects is correlated with the smallness of their craniums, I am reminded of the work of Dr. Samuel George Morton. Dr. Morton was an eminent nineteenth century Philadelphia scientist and physician who "proved" that black men have smaller brains and craniums than white men. From his anatomical and anthropological studies, Dr. Morton came to the conclusion that black men were inferior to white men — a conclusion which no one disputed. When Morton died in 1851 his obituary in the *New York Tribune* noted that "probably no scientific man in America enjoyed a higher reputation among scholars throughout the world, than Dr. Morton."[60] Upon his death Morton was also eulogized in the pages of the *Charleston Medical Journal*: "We of the

---

*Robert M. Pirsig, a diagnosed schizophrenic and author of *Zen and the Art of Motorcycle Maintenance*, has an I.Q. of 170. Were Pirsig's I.Q. 30 points lower, he would still be classified as a genius.

South should consider him as our benefactor, for aiding most materially in giving to the negro his true position as an inferior race."[61]

Just as the work of Dr. Morton was used as a scientific justification for slavery, the results of a variety of psychiatric studies — including studies utilizing CAT and PET scanners — have been used as scientific justification for involuntary commitment. Here, for example, are the words of E. Fuller Torrey:

> Schizophrenia is a disease of the brain, the body organ charged with the responsibility of recognizing sickness and the need for treatment — the same organ which is sick. Out of this unfortunate coincidence arises the frequent need for schizophrenic persons to be committed to psychiatric treatment settings against their will.[62]

From Dr. Torrey's reference to "treatment settings" it is obvious that not only does he approve of involuntary commitment, he also believes in treating schizophrenic individuals against their will.

The therapy most commonly used in treating schizophrenic persons is the administration of neuroleptic drugs — drugs which are known to cause severe and often irreversible damage to the brain. The use of such drugs is in turn justified by the notion that schizophrenics suffer from a biochemical imbalance.

# 3

# SCHIZOPHRENIA AS A BIOCHEMICAL DEFECT

As George Fink* has astutely observed, this is "the age of chemical phrenology." Just as nineteenth-century phrenologists believed that a man's virtues, vices, and mental capacities were located in specific areas of the brain and could be discerned by feeling the bumps on that person's head, the phrenologists of the twentieth century believe, in Fink's words, that "each neurotic and psychotic symptom is due to the malfunction of one specific chemical neurotransmitter system."[1]

Due to the peculiar prejudices characteristic of the age in which we live, it seems self-evident to many people that schizophrenia must be caused by some kind of biochemical defect. Yet the hollowness of this belief is exposed whenever the question is asked: If a person's schizophrenic symptoms are caused by a biochemical imbalance, then why isn't a blood or urine sample taken in order to confirm that person's diagnosis?

Psychiatric researchers have been working on developing such a diagnostic test for schizophrenia for over a hundred years. Since 1884, when the neurochemist Johan Wilhelm Ludwig Thudichum first announced that schizophrenia (or "insanity" as it was then called) was caused by "poisons fermented within the body,"[2] literally thousands of papers have been published on the biochemistry of schizophrenia. To a skeptic such as myself, psychiatry's utter failure to identify the hypothetical biochemical culprit responsible for causing schizophrenia is strong *prima facie* evidence that a biochemical cause for schizophrenia simply doesn't exist.

However, most psychiatrists don't share my skepticism. They will point to the apparent fact that a biochemical marker for depression has recently been found — an alleged discovery which permits a procedure known as the Dexamethasone-Suppression Test (DST) to diagnose who is suffering from this psychiatric disorder. Moreover, most psychiatrists are confident that it is only a matter of time before a biochemical marker

---

*George Fink is an Honorary Professor and Director of the MRC Brain Metabolism Unit, University Department of Pharmacology, Edinburgh, Scotland.

for schizophrenia is likewise found, so that a diagnostic procedure similar to the DST can be instituted for schizophrenics.

But if psychiatrists are confident they can find a biochemical cause for schizophrenia due to the recent development of the DST as a diagnostic procedure for depression, then their confidence has no rational basis whatsoever. For example, while it has been claimed that nonsuppression of dexamethasone is a specific physiological marker for endogenous depression, many investigators have found nonsuppression rates comparable to those reported in depressed patients in a variety of other psychiatric disorders including mania,[3] schizoaffective disorder,[4] schizophrenia,[5] and generalized anxiety disorder.[6] Moreover, in a study involving 40 presurgical subjects and 20 controls, Drs. Ceulemans, Westenberg and Van Praag found 19 of the presurgical subjects to be nonsuppressors.[7] Consequently, these investigators concluded that the stress involved in anticipating physical danger can cause nonsuppression on the DST. This latter finding is consistent with the findings of Stephen R. Shuchter and his associates at the University of California School of Medicine at San Diego. These researchers found that non-suppression was related more to levels of anxiety than to depression.[8]

What all of this means is simply this: as a means of diagnosing depression the DST is virtually worthless, and psychiatrists have no basis at all for believing that any similar procedure for diagnosing schizophrenia will be any better.

This is not to suggest that significant biochemical changes do not occur in schizophrenia. Clearly they do. But what I am suggesting, however, is that these biochemical changes are an effect rather than the cause of schizophrenia.

Illustrative of how psychiatry confuses the effects of schizophrenia with its cause is the now obsolete theory that schizophrenia is caused by too much adrenaline. Certainly *if* schizophrenics actually do produce excessive amounts of adrenaline, common sense would dictate that this elevated adrenaline production is merely a consequence of their being emotionally upset — not the cause of their mental problems. Unfortunately, however, many psychiatric researchers exhibit a shocking lack of common sense. As Manfred Bleuler notes:

> As a result of the preconceived notion that schizophrenia had to be based on an adrenal malfunction, the adrenal glands of schizophrenics were removed. But that did not cure these patients; it merely converted them into schizophrenics with Addison's disease.[9]

As I will later show, even the most modern and sophisticated biochemical theories of schizophrenia — the endorphin and dopamine hypotheses — illustrate psychiatry's propensity to confuse the effects of schizophrenia with its cause. In such theories we are presented with the irony of psychiatrists attempting to deny that schizophrenia has an environmental cause by putting forward biochemical theories as alternative explanations when — as we will later see — *those theories logically imply an environmental cause!*

Psychiatrists as medical doctors are inescapably committed to finding *biological* causes for schizophrenia. Consequently, they totally ignore the environmental causes of schizophrenia — and even deny that such causes could possibly exist. And so with their medical (or ideological) blinders securely in place, they go charging down innumerable scientific blind alleys and dead ends searching for the biological basis for schizophrenia. As M. K. Horwitt, an observer of this sad spectacle, notes:

> Year after year, papers appear which purport to distinguish between the state of schizophrenia and that of normalcy. The sum total of the differences reported would make the schizophrenic patient a sorry physical specimen indeed: his liver, brain, kidney, and circulatory functions are impaired; he is deficient in practically every vitamin; his hormones are out of balance, and his enzymes are askew. Fortunately, many of these claims of metabolic abnormality are forgotten in time with a minimum of polemic but it seems that each new generation of biologists has to be indoctrinated — or disillusioned — without benefit of the experience of its predecessors.[10]

The above observations were made back in 1956. Since then more than a dozen biochemical theories of schizophrenia have been announced as wonderful scientific breakthroughs only to be quietly abandoned. I think it is appropriate to review a few of these now-discarded theories, for in my opinion, they reveal the unmistakable modus operandi of the pseudoscientists at work. However, I will not spend much time beating these dead horses. Fully three-quarters of this chapter will be devoted to examining the currently accepted biochemical theory of schizophrenia — the dopamine hypothesis — a theory that will ultimately be discarded just as the theories I am now going to review have been.

## The Taraxein Hypothesis

The originator of this hypothesis, Dr. Robert G. Heath of Tulane University, has had a most interesting career: he has performed lobotomies, been heavily involved with the military and the CIA in mind-manipulation research, and has "cured" homosexuals, frigid women, neurotics and schizophrenics by implanting electrodes in their brains.[11] In 1957, Dr. Heath isolated a substance in the blood of schizophrenics which he called taraxein. When this substance was injected into prisoner volunteers, it purportedly caused symptoms characteristic of schizophrenia: disorganization and fragmentation of thought, feelings of depersonalization, paranoid ideas, auditory hallucinations, and catatonic behavior.[12] However, every attempt made to replicate Dr. Heath's experiment has been a total failure. In the most thorough and rigorous attempt to replicate the Heath experiment, only five of the twenty subjects who received taraxein exhibited psychotic symptoms. More damning still was the fact that *an equal number of control subjects who had only received a placebo also developed psychotic symptoms.*[13]

## The Ceruloplasm Hypothesis

Just prior to Dr. Heath's discovery of taraxein, Stig Ackerfeldt, a Swedish biochemist, reported he had found an abnormal amount of ceruloplasmin, a copper-protein, in the blood of schizophrenics — a fact which he claimed could be used to diagnose schizophrenia.[14] This apparent discovery of a diagnostic test for schizophrenia caused a worldwide sensation, and Ackerfeldt became an instant hero. However, the so-called Ackerfeldt test was soon discredited. It was found that a positive response to the Ackerfeldt test occurred only at those institutions where the inmates received an inadequate amount of ascorbic acid in their diet, and could therefore be completely explained as a dietary insufficiency of vitamin C.[15]

## The Adrenaline-Adrenochrome Hypothesis

The foundation for this theory was laid in 1952 when two British psychiatrists, Humprey Osmond and John Smythies, noted two facts which they thought were interrelated. First, they noted some similarities between mescaline psychosis and schizophrenia. And second, they noted a striking similarity between the mescaline molecule and adrenaline — the hormone which causes the "fight or flight" reaction when the body is under stress. They speculated that some process in schizophrenics transforms adrenaline into a hallucinogenic agent similar to mescaline.

Some time after Drs. Osmond and Smythies had published their speculations, Abram Hoffer, a Canadian psychiatrist, reported he had found an adrenaline-like substance (adrenochrome) in the body fluids of schizophrenics. He also reported that when adrenochrome was injected into normal volunteers, they exhibited symptoms typical of schizophrenia.

However more carefully done studies were unable to detect adrenochrome in the bodies of schizophrenics — or in the bodies of anyone else for that matter. Furthermore, adrenochrome was found to have no psychotropic properties whatsoever. In essence, Dr. Hoffer's experimental subjects "went crazy" because they were told that that was exactly what was going to happen to them.[16]

## The Peculiar Odor Hypothesis

In 1960, Kathleen Smith and Jacob O. Sines, of the Washington University School of Medicine in St. Louis, reported that there is a peculiar odor in the sweat of schizophrenics which sets them apart from the rest of the human race. These investigators, in effect, claim they were able to train rats to diagnose schizophrenia by training them to accurately discriminate between the sweat of schizophrenics with its strange odor and the sweat of nonschizophrenic patients without the odor.[17] In 1969, the odoriferous substance in the sweat of schizophrenics was identified as *trans*-3-methyl-2-hexanoic acid (TMHA), and the prestige of Smith and Sines' theory skyrocketed.[18] However, their theory totally collapsed in 1973 when TMHA was found in the sweat of normal persons.[19] This should have come as no surprise. After all, in their original 1960 paper, Smith and Sines admitted that the skunk-like odor found in the sweat of schizophrenics was also to be found in the sweat of 43 percent of the patients who were not schizophrenic.[20]

## The Serotonin Hypothesis

Interest in the role that serotonin plays as a causal factor in schizophrenia was stimulated by a paper by D. W. Woolley and E. Shaw.[21] In noting that such hallucinogenic drugs as lysergic acid diethylamide (LSD) block the effects of serotonin, these authors came to the conclusion that schizophrenia is caused by a lack of serotonin. However, it has also been noted that while 2-bromo-lysergic acid diethylamide has 1.5 times the antiserotonin effect as LSD, even at high doses this drug has no mind altering effects.[22] Since it was first proposed, the serotonin hypothesis has undergone many changes. Some researchers believe that schizophrenia is caused by too much serotonin, while other researchers blame too little serotonin. Most studies, however, indicate no significant differences between schizophrenics and normal controls in regard to serotonin metabolism.[23]

## The Endorphin Hypothesis

Three lines of evidence support the notion that schizophrenia is caused by an excess amount of endorphin. First, some studies show that acute schizophrenics have ten times as much endorphin in their cerebrospinal fluid as do normal controls.[24] Secondly, it is claimed that when endorphin is injected into rats those animals exhibit catatonic-like behavior.[25] Thirdly, some studies seem to show that naloxone — a drug which blocks the effects of endorphin — also has the effect of reducing auditory hallucinations in some schizophrenic patients.[26]

However, at least three kinds of objections can be brought against the endorphin hypothesis. First, in regard to the antischizophrenic properties of naloxone, in a study done by Glenn C. Davis and his associates of the National Institute of Mental Health, it was found that naloxone was totally ineffective in reducing hallucinations or any of the other symptoms characteristic of schizophrenia.[27]

Secondly, it can be argued that the endorphin hypothesis is based upon the fallacy of confusing an effect with a cause. For example, I know not only from personal experience, but also from the experiences of people who have been very close to me, that the process which results in schizophrenia always involves a considerable amount of mental anguish or pain. Furthermore, whenever a person is in intense pain — whether mental or physical — the brain secretes a morphine-like substance known as *endorphin* which is a natural pain killer or tranquilizer. Therefore *if* it is actually the case that schizophrenics have an elevated amount of endorphin in their systems, then all this could possibly mean is that such individuals are experiencing a tremendous amount of emotional pain — pain which the brain is attempting to remedy. In brief, an elevated amount of endorphin is an effect and not the cause of schizophrenia.

Finally, it can be argued that the endorphin hypothesis is inherently implausible. For instance, if too much endorphin causes schizophrenia, then why doesn't addiction to such endorphin-like substances as morphine or heroin cause either schizophrenia or a similar psychosis?

## The Dopamine Hypothesis

Unlike the above biochemical theories, the dopamine hypothesis has *not* been abandoned. However, not only is the dopamine hypothesis the currently accepted biochemical theory, it is by far the most widely accepted biochemical theory in the entire history of schizophrenia research. For this reason the remainder of this chapter will be devoted to examining this theory.

According to the dopamine hypothesis, schizophrenia is caused by hyperactive transmission in certain neurons in the brain which use dopamine as its chemical messenger. The principal support for this theory lies in the fact that the drugs used to treat schizophrenia — i.e., neuroleptic drugs — achieve their effect by blocking the dopamine neurotransmission systems in the midbrain, limbic system, frontal lobes, and cortex. Since these drugs make schizophrenics more docile and easier to manage, psychiatrists have gradually adopted the belief that these drugs must be specific antischizophrenia agents, and that schizophrenia must be the result of overactive dopamine neurotransmission.

However, the same drugs which are used to control schizophrenia — or rather human beings whom psychiatrists call "schizophrenics" — are also used to control nursing home inmates,[28] the mentally retarded,[29] prisoners,[30] Soviet political dissidents,[31] rebellious children,[32] and animals.[33] In fact, some psychiatrists such as Peter R. Breggin[34] and Henry L. Lennard[35] contend that rather than being true antischizophrenia agents, neuroleptic drugs are nothing more than pharmaceutical lobotomies or chemical straightjackets which are used to control or suppress unwanted behavior.

Of course, most psychiatrists are reluctant to view themselves as totalitarian thought-police who drug people into submission. And this reluctance to view themselves in this way is exactly what makes the dopamine hypothesis so attractive in psychiatric circles: if that biochemical theory is correct, then neuroleptic drugs are not chemical lobotomies but specific antischizophrenia agents. Hence, psychiatrists deserve a pat on the back for drugging their patients.

Yet despite psychiatrist's ulterior motives in adopting this theory, the dopamine hypothesis does contain a certain amount of truth. In an effort to ascertain just how much truth the dopamine hypothesis actually contains, I will examine both the direct and indirect evidence which supports this theory.

The direct evidence supporting the dopamine hypothesis is as follows:

In its earliest and most forthright formulation, the dopamine hypothesis states that schizophrenia is caused by excessive dopamine production at the dopaminergic synapses. However, while a few recent studies have shown that the more disturbed schizophrenic patients do produce more dopamine relative to the less disturbed patients,[36] most studies show that schizophrenics do *not* produce more dopamine than normal controls.[37]

According to the current formulation of the dopamine hypothesis, schizophrenia is not caused by too much dopamine itself, but by an abnormally high number of dopamine receptors in the brain. This second version of the dopamine hypothesis is supported by several postmortem studies which show there are an increased number of dopamine receptors in the brains of schizophrenics relative to normal controls.

However, it is known that neuroleptic drugs, by depriving the brain of dopamine, cause an increased number of dopamine receptors to form in the brain to compensate for those dopamine receptors which have been blockaded.[38] Furthermore, there are studies which indicate that this elevated number of dopamine receptors exists only in the brains of schizophrenics who had taken neuroleptic drugs, but not in the brains of drug-naive schizophrenics.[39]

Nevertheless, all of the above studies were postmortem studies — studies which are now considered somewhat obsolete due to the development of positron emission tomography (PET) scanning, a technique which enables researchers to determine the number (or density) of dopamine receptors in the brains of *living* subjects.

So far, four major research teams — the first headed by Dean F. Wong at the Johns Hopkins Medical Institutions in Baltimore, Maryland; the second led by Lars Farde at the Karolinska Institute in Stockholm, Sweden; the third led by Jarmo Hietala at the University of Turku in Turku, Finland; the last headed by Jean-Luc Martinot at the Atomic Energy Commission in Orsay, France — have utilized PET scanning in order to determine whether or not drug-naive schizophrenics have an elevated number of dopamine receptors in their brains. In studying chronic schizophrenics who had never taken neuroleptic drugs, Wong and his colleagues reported that their subjects had an elevated number of dopamine receptors.[40] However, in studying drug-naive acute schizophrenics, the teams led by Farde and Hietala reported that their subjects did *not* have an elevated number of dopamine receptors relative to normal controls.[41] Finally, in studying drug-naive chronic and subchronic schizophrenics, Martinot and associates — like the groups led by Farde and Hietala — reported that their subjects did not have an elevated number of dopamine receptors.[42]

Perhaps the simplest explanation for the conflicting results of the above four studies is to assume that schizophrenics do not in fact have an abnormal number of dopamine receptors in their brains and that Wong's findings to the contrary are utterly mistaken. The suspicion that Wong's findings might be erroneous is somewhat strengthened when one considers that in a preliminary study, Wong's group was unable to find an increased number of dopamine receptors in the brains of their schizophrenic subjects.[43]

Still, I think it is possible (even probable) that Wong's findings might be correct — that *chronic* schizophrenics may in fact have an abnormally high number of dopamine receptors in their brains. But I don't believe such a fact would necessarily support the dopamine hypothesis.

I think the increased number of dopamine receptors in the brains of chronic schizophrenics could be nothing more than a reaction to *prolonged* (mostly internally generated) stress — a type of stress which might possibly be unique to schizophrenia. Since dopamine is a stress hormone like adrenaline, any stress will tend to cause an increase in dopamine utilization or turnover.[44] Furthermore, according to Hans Selye's triphasic general adaption syndrome, exposure to stress would trigger increased dopamine turnover (the alarm reaction), then continued high dopamine turnover (stage of resistance), and finally a marked decrease in dopamine utilization (stage of exhaustion).[45] In this regard, two very recent studies utilizing advanced techniques clearly show that chronic schizophrenics suffer from a dopamine deficiency, and produce markedly *less* dopamine than normal controls.[46] But if schizophrenics produce significantly less dopamine than normal, then we would expect their brains to have an elevated number of dopamine receptors as compensation for their dopamine deficiency.[47]

It is highly unlikely, however, that this dopamine deficiency causes schizophrenia: it is probably no more the cause of schizophrenia than cirrhosis of the liver is the cause of alcoholism.

The most important evidence supporting the dopamine hypothesis is of an indirect or pharmaceutical nature. This kind of evidence is based upon observations of the actions of two types of drugs. On one hand, it has been observed that drugs which block dopamine supposedly help people suffering from schizophrenia by controlling their symptoms; while on the other hand, drugs which release dopamine worsen schizophrenia. This latter class of drugs includes amphetamines — drugs which can cause a psychosis virtually indistinguishable from paranoid schizophrenia.

To recapitulate: the two most important lines of evidence supporting the dopamine hypothesis are: (a) the alleged effectiveness of neuroleptic drugs in treating schizophrenia, and (b) the striking similarity between amphetamine psychosis and paranoid schizophrenia. Due to their importance, these two lines of evidence merit detailed scrutiny.

## Amphetamine Psychosis and Schizophrenia

Some authorities, such as Solomon H. Snyder,* claim there are at least two distinct varieties of amphetamine psychosis.[48] Snyder views the first variety as a "toxic psychosis" similar to delirium tremens, a psychosis which can be caused by a single high dose of amphetamine. In this toxic psychosis, visual hallucinations and persecutory delusions predominate, and the afflicted person is often so confused and disoriented that he doesn't know who he is, where he is, or what time of day it is. According to Snyder, this first type of amphetamine psychosis bears no similarity at all to schizophrenia.

The "classic amphetamine psychosis," the second variety of amphetamine psychosis described by Snyder, develops slowly and gradually after several days to several months of amphetamine use. This second type of amphetamine psychosis is characterized by ideas of reference, delusions of persecution, and auditory hallucinations which take place in a setting of clear consciousness. The person manifesting this second type of

---

*Dr. Snyder is Professor of Psychiatry and Pharmacology at Johns Hopkins University, and one of the world's most respected proponents of the dopamine hypothesis.

amphetamine psychosis is usually well-oriented, knows who he is, where he is, and what time of day it is. This second type of amphetamine psychosis is often misdiagnosed as paranoid schizophrenia.

Since this latter type of amphetamine psychosis is clinically indistinguishable from paranoid schizophrenia, and since it is known that amphetamine increases dopamine activity, many schizophrenia researchers such as Snyder view these two facts as strong evidence that schizophrenia is caused by overactive dopamine neurotransmission.

However, there is a very pertinent question which Snyder, in his enthusiasm to promote the dopamine hypothesis, has neglected to ask, namely: why is only the second, but not the first type of amphetamine psychosis similar to schizophrenia? Snyder avoids asking this question with good reason, for one cannot ask — much less answer — this question without thereby undermining the dopamine hypothesis.

Snyder and other schizophrenia researchers are uncomfortably aware of the fact that amphetamines cause insomnia, and they are haunted by the possibility that amphetamine psychosis might be due to prolonged sleep deprivation rather than to any biochemical derangement of the dopamine system. Or rather they *were* haunted by that possibility. At present, most schizophrenia researchers are smugly confident that an experiment in which people were purportedly driven crazy by regularly administered doses of amphetamine has decisively discredited the notion that amphetamine psychosis is caused by sleep deprivation.

The experiment in question was conducted by Dr. John Griffith and his associates at Vanderbilt University.[49] Dr. Griffith's experiment involved nine male volunteers, all of whom had had a history of amphetamine abuse. Dr. Griffith chose these people rather than drug-naive subjects out of fear that one or more of the subjects might have a rare hypersensitivity to amphetamine. However, five of Dr. Griffith's subjects had had a history of drug-induced psychosis. Yet other than that, and certain mild sociopathic tendencies, Dr. Griffith assures us that all of his subjects were essentially mentally stable persons.

Dr. Griffith's experiment began with a one-week control period in which the subjects were given a liquid placebo. Then, following the one-week control period, the subjects were given 5 or 10 mg of dextroamphetamine sulfate intravenously at regular one-hour intervals 24 hours a day.

Within five days after receiving dextroamphetamine, eight of the nine subjects had developed a paranoid psychosis. For example, one of the subjects complained of a "giant oscillator" on the ceiling controlling his thoughts, while another subject voiced his concern that his ex-wife had hired an assassin to kill him. None of the subjects, however, experienced either visual or auditory hallucinations.

The most striking result of Griffith's experiment was the fact that four of the subjects developed paranoid reactions before losing as much as two nights of sleep. In fact, two subjects became paranoid within 24 hours of the time they started receiving dextroamphetamine. According to Dr. Griffith, facts such as these decisively refute the notion that amphetamine psychosis is caused by prolonged sleep deprivation.

However, the paranoid reactions of the above mentioned individuals probably resulted more from suggestion that from any action of the drug itself. In this respect I don't see how Dr. Griffith's experiment differs that much from the earlier studies of Drs. Hoffer and Heath in which people were purportedly driven crazy by adrenochrome and taraxein. Like the subjects of those earlier studies, the subjects of Dr. Griffith's experiment probably had some awareness of what was expected of them, and acted accordingly. For example, Dr. Griffith admits that his subjects were "fully informed as to the risks and discomforts of the study."[50] Moreover, the so-called "control period" in which the subjects received a liquid placebo, was nothing more than a sham in view of the fact that all of the subjects were experienced amphetamine users, and would therefore be capable of knowing whether or not they were receiving the drug. Consequently, when dextroamphetamine was finally administered to the subjects, the drug probably acted more as a cuing mechanism or signal for action than as a direct cause of their paranoid reaction.

But most damning of all is Dr. Griffith's bland admission:

> Four of the subjects became psychotic after less than two nights of sleep deprivation. *This period is not sufficient to elicit a florid paranoid psychosis.*[51] [italics added]

Here Dr. Griffith in effect admits that the four individuals whose "paranoid psychosis" had supposedly disproved the sleep deprivation hypothesis, did not really undergo a paranoid psychosis in the accepted clinical sense. In fact, upon reading Griffith's report, we are left without any indication that the paranoia of those four subjects amounted to anything more than their intense mistrust for the people who were trying to drive them crazy!

Owing to its essential unsoundness, Dr. Griffith's experiment does not discredit the notion that amphetamine psychosis might be due in part to prolonged sleep deprivation.

At this point, a question I asked earlier now needs answering, namely: why does only the classic but not the toxic variety of amphetamine psychosis resemble paranoid schizophrenia? The answer is simply that paranoid schizophrenia (or schizophrenia in general) cannot be explained solely in terms of overactive dopamine neurotransmission. If it could, then the toxic variety of amphetamine psychosis would closely mimic schizophrenia, since this toxic psychosis can be wholly explained by the direct action of the drug causing excessive dopamine (and noradrenaline) neurotransmission and a hyperaroused state. In sharp contrast to this toxic psychosis, the classic amphetamine psychosis necessarily involves a slow and gradual process — a process due not only to the direct (or biochemical) effect of the drug itself, but also to amphetamine's indirect effect in inducing a narrowed focus of awareness, insomnia and a self-hypnotic trance, leading ultimately to a paranoid delusional state. Not without good reason is the classic amphetamine psychosis clinically indistinguishable from paranoid schizophrenia: both of these syndromes are caused by pretty much the same process.

Having already set forth my views on how people become schizophrenic in part I and part II of this book, I will now review certain biochemical aspects of this process.

A number of authors including Kempf,[52] Sullivan,[53] and Arieti[54] have emphasized the fact that schizophrenic breakdowns are usually preceded by brief but very intense panic episodes. In my case there were three such episodes. In my third and final panic episode, I felt as though I had been given a massive dose of amphetamine: all at once, both my physical and mental processes seemed greatly speeded up: I started trembling all over, my heart started beating wildly, and my mind seemed to be racing out of control.

It is well known that whenever a person is placed in a situation involving either physical danger or mental stress — such as the situation described above — the body always responds by producing a superabundance of stress hormones known as catecholamines: adrenaline,* noradrenaline,† and dopamine. Adrenaline, secreted into the blood by the adrenal medulla, speeds up the vital processes and tones the muscles of the body. Noradrenaline, secreted at the nerve endings in the brain, causes increased mental alertness. Dopamine is likewise secreted at the nerve endings in the brain. When released in the brain in excessive amounts, dopamine causes the environment to take on a heightened emotional significance.

All of the biochemical changes I have just described must have occurred during each of my three panic episodes. Moreover, some of these biochemical changes — or possibly other biochemical changes brought about by these biochemical changes — must have continued to manifest themselves for several weeks following my third panic episode. I think this must have been the case: how else can I explain the fact that in the weeks following my final panic episode I could go night after night without getting any sleep without feeling tired? In fact, during the first few weeks following my last panic episode, I don't recall ever having had so much energy in my entire life!

---

*Also known as epinephrine.

†Also known as norepinephrine.

How does this relate to amphetamine psychosis? First of all, the biochemical changes which occur as a result of taking amphetamines are identical to those which occur during episodes of panic: in both instances the body releases excess amounts of adrenaline, noradrenaline, and dopamine. Moreover, because the action of amphetamine mimics the biochemical changes which occur during panic, it is hardly surprising that feelings of anxiety, fear, and even terror predominate in amphetamine psychosis, and that the delusions are *always* of a persecutory nature.[55]

Second — as I have pointed out in the first and second parts of this book — between a panic episode and the onset of a schizophrenic psychosis, a person will narrow his focus of awareness in order to remain unconscious of certain disturbing thoughts. Likewise, as Calloway has demonstrated, one of the effects of amphetamine is to narrow a person's focus of awareness.[56]

Third — as I have mentioned before — the onset of a schizophrenic psychosis is usually immediately preceded by a period of prolonged sleeplessness. Moreover, despite the Griffith experiment, it is highly likely that prolonged sleep deprivation is one of the most significant factors in causing amphetamine psychosis. After all, it is well known that taking amphetamines causes insomnia. In fact, insomnia is by far the most commonly reported effect which amphetamines are known to produce.[57]

Fourth — as I have also explained previously — the final pathway which leads to schizophrenia involves a self-hypnotic process in which the individual becomes so totally obsessed with a narrow circle of ideas that he thinks about these ideas nonstop 24 hours a day, and literally thinks himself crazy. However, this process is typical not only of schizophrenia, but of the classic amphetamine psychosis as well. In his excellent phenomenological description of the process which results in amphetamine psychosis, Dr. Everett H. Ellinwood notes that as individuals become increasingly psychotic, they become increasingly obsessed with religious and philosophical ideas, and that these ideas gradually develop into full-blown delusional systems.[58]

It should now be evident that the mere fact that the classic amphetamine psychosis is clinically indistinguishable from paranoid schizophrenia does not support the dopamine hypothesis, since overactive dopamine neurotransmission is by itself only a minor factor in the process which results in either amphetamine psychosis or paranoid schizophrenia.

Yet there is a significance to this striking similarity between amphetamine psychosis and paranoid schizophrenia which — owing to ideological reasons — has been totally missed. For example, it has been noticed by a number of authors, including Dr. Philip Henry Connell, that of those people who become psychotic as a result of abusing amphetamine, a significant number were found to be well-adjusted, mentally stable persons before their psychosis — that is to say, their psychosis could not be explained as a result of any latent schizophrenic tendencies.[59] What this means is simply this. The supposed biological differences between schizophrenics and normal persons is purely imaginary, because if a so-called "normal" person undergoes a process that is even superficially similar to a process which schizophrenics undergo — such as biochemical changes which either simulate panic or are a direct result of panic, a drastically narrowed focus of awareness, prolonged sleep deprivation, and a self-hypnotically induced trance-like state — the end result will be a person who is virtually indistinguishable from a schizophrenic.*

## The Alleged Effectiveness of Neuroleptic Drugs

There exist several distinct families of drugs known by such trade names as Thorazine, Mellaril, Stelazine, Taractan, Navane, Trilafon, Moban, Haldol, and Prolixin which are commonly used in treating schizophrenia. Some of the drugs (Thorazine, Mellaril, Taractan) have sedative effects, while others (Haldol, Prolixin) cause extreme jitteriness. What all these drugs have in common is their capacity to blockade (or disrupt) the dopamine neurotransmission system.

Since drugs that block dopamine seem effective in treating schizophrenia, the notion that schizophrenia is caused by too much dopamine neurotransmission has achieved the status of a major psychiatric dogma.

But do neuroleptic drugs really have specific antischizophrenia properties? Consider, for example, this glowing 1926 report on the spectacular effectiveness of bromides in treating schizophrenia:

> In a group of eighty-five patients treated, fifty percent showed decided improvement and seventy-five percent showed some. Patients who had been wantonly destructive became more placid and clean; those subject to violent outbursts became better adjusted with their environment, and their activities were more easily directed into useful channels following treatment. Patients who required tube feeding took food voluntarily after two or three days. The most lasting improvement was found in those cases previously regarded as having an unfavorable prognosis. When one considers the changes in the environment of the patients treated — lessened disorder, confusion, and untidiness and conservation of energy for the nurses and other employees, the results are still of greater value. There is marked reduction

---

*However, it must be borne in mind that the similarities between schizophrenia and the amphetamine psychosis are very superficial: they are clearly not the same thing.

in the waste of clothing and bedding through tearing and soiling. Fewer articles have to be repaired and laundered, and fewer nurses are required to care for the disturbed patients. One nurse explained: "Before these patients were treated, I had to struggle with them every morning to get them bathed and dressed. Fights were frequent occurrences. Now I can supervise the bathing of many of them alone!" Failures occur from the fact that when improvement does not take place in a few days, the drug is stopped when it should be continued.[60]

This is almost exactly the same kind of improvement that neuroleptic drugs have been known to produce. Yet bromides are no longer used in psychiatry. No one any longer believes those drugs are effective in curing mental disorders. Rather than having any curative properties, bromides were highly toxic chemicals which physically and mentally weakened the inmates of psychiatric institutions, and thereby made them easier to manage or control.

According to Dr. Peter R. Breggin, neuroleptic and other currently used psychiatric drugs are much like bromides in that they have a suppressive rather than a curative effect:

Brain damage and dysfunction produced by the major psychiatric drugs are the mechanisms by which the drugs achieve their supposedly beneficial results. The brain dysfunction is not a "side effect," but the primary, overriding effect. The apparent improvement that patients show is actually a disability, a loss of mental capacity inflicted by the drugs. By rendering the patients less able to think, to feel, or to determine the course of their conduct, these drugs make patients less troublesome to others, and sometimes less troublesome to themselves. The drugs produce their effects independently of the presence or absence of any biological or psychological disorder. They have the same pacifying, subduing effects on normal individuals and, indeed, on animals.[61]

Breggin's view that neuroleptic drugs have a suppressive rather than a specific antischizophrenic effect, is strongly supported by the clinical observations of the psychiatrists who pioneered the use of these drugs. Here, for example, are the words of Drs. Heinz E. Lehmann and G. E. Hanrahan of Montreal, Canada, the first psychiatrists on the North American continent to utilize chlorpromazine* as a psychiatric treatment:

---

*Chlorpromazine [Thorazine — or Largactil as it is called in England] is the first of the so-called antischizophrenia drugs.

The aim is to produce a state of motor retardation, emotional indifference, and somnolence, and the dose must be increased accordingly as tolerance develops.

Patients receiving the drug become lethargic. Manic patients often will not object to rest, and patients who present management problems become tractable. Assaultive and interfering behavior cease almost entirely. The patients under treatment display a lack of spontaneous interest in the environment . . . they tend to remain silent and immobile when left alone and reply to questions in a slow monotone. . . . Some patients dislike the treatment and complain of their drowsiness and weakness. Some state they feel "washed out," as after an exhausting illness, a complaint which is indeed in keeping with their appearance.[62]

Of equal significance to Lehmann and Hanrahan's are the clinical observations of Dr. D. Anton-Stephens, the first British psychiatrist to treat patients with chlorpromazine. Here is Anton-Stephens' revealing description of the lobotomy-like effect produced by the drug:

*Psychic indifference.* This is perhaps the characteristic psychiatric response to chlorpromazine. Patients responding well to the drug have developed an attitude of indifference both to their surroundings and their symptoms best summarized by the current phrase "couldn't care less." As a result one has observed a loss of subjective anxiety and of distress arising from tension feelings; a reduction in the abnormal behavior responses to hallucinatory experiences and a loss of interest in them; a lessening of conviction in delusional concepts; and a lessening of preoccupation with obsessional and hypochondrial ruminations.

In the presence of the fully developed response — even in the absence of any somnolence — the patient lies quietly in bed, staring ahead, unoccupied and showing little or no interest in what is going on around him. He answers questions readily and to the point, but offers little, if any, spontaneous conversation. Questioning reveals that he is fully aware of his circumstances but the distress they may formerly have caused him has gone.[63]

Having taken chlorpromazine myself[64], I can certify that both of the above descriptions of the effects of this drug are 100 percent accurate.

In Dr. Breggin's view, such psychiatric pioneers as Drs. Lehmann and Hanrahan and Dr. Anton-Stephens, write with an honesty characteristic of discoverers.[65] Those psychiatric innovators never claimed chlorpromazine had any antischizophrenic properties, but were content merely to describe the drugs' pacifying and lobotomizing effects.

Nowadays, due to the widespread use of these drugs, such honesty is extremely rare. For example, many psychiatrists make the extraordinary claim that it is just as necessary for schizophrenics to take neuroleptic drugs as it is for diabetics to take insulin. Moreover, most psychiatrists will flatly deny that the drugs they prescribe have any lobotomizing effects.

Yet despite a steady barrage of psychiatric disinformation, an increasing number of people are becoming aware of the harmful effects of neuroleptic drugs. Furthermore, there still exist a few honest and outspoken men like Dr. Peter Sterling, a brain research expert from the University of Pennsylvania School of Medicine. Dr. Sterling does not hesitate to call a spade a spade:

> The blunting of consciousness, motivation, and the inability to solve problems under the influence of chlorpromazine resembles nothing so much as the effect of frontal lobotomy. . . . Research has suggested that lobotomies and chemicals like chlorpromazine may cause their effects in the same way, by disrupting the neurochemical, dopamine. At any rate, a psychiatrist would be hard-put to distinguish a lobotomized patient from one treated with chlorpromazine.[66]

That neuroleptic drugs have a nonspecific brain-disabling or lobotomizing effect, is evident even from studies which supposedly prove just the opposite — that these drugs are in fact specific antischizophrenic agents. Here, for example, are the results of a study done at the National Institute of Mental Health by Dr. Gerald L. Klerman and associates — an often-cited study which purportedly proves that neuroleptic drugs selectively improve or reduce schizophrenic symptoms. A partial list of the "target symptoms" rated by Klerman as improved by drug therapy are as follows: combativeness, markedly or moderately reduced in patients by 74 percent; hyperactivity by 73 percent; tension, 71 percent; hostility, 67 percent; hallucinations, 58 percent; and delusions by only 48 percent.[67] Of the 24 items on Klerman's list, insight and judgement were shown to be the least affected by drug therapy. Insight was markedly or moderately improved by only 12 percent, and judgement by only 22.5 percent.[68] As Dr. Breggin points out, since Klerman's study was neither controlled nor double-blind, we can expect his data to be distorted or biased in favor of supporting his hypothesis that neuroleptic drugs have a specific antischizophrenic effect.[69] Yet — as Breggin notes — in spite of this bias, Klerman's data clearly shows that such schizophrenic symptoms as hallucinations and delusions (*markedly reduced* by only 30.5 and 21 percent respectively) are not nearly as affected by drug therapy as are such nonspecific symptoms as combativeness, hyperactivity, tension, and

190

hostility — "symptoms" which are indicative neither of schizophrenia nor of psychosis.[70]

Commenting on the results of Klerman's study, Dr. Breggin notes that neuroleptic drugs are little more than chemical straightjackets:

> It is misleading to claim as Klerman does that these data show "the more manifestly psychotic the patient's behavior, the more he will respond symptomatically and behaviorally to treatment with the phenothiazines." Instead, the data show that the more the patient *causes trouble* (combative, hyperactive, hostile) and the more the patient *looks upset* (hyperactive, tense), the more he will be rated as improved when subdued with the major tranquilizers [neuroleptics]. The alleged "target symptoms" turn out to be the same old "management problems" for which lobotomy and electro-shock were once so frequently employed in the state hospitals, and the alleged improvement in the psychosis reflects nothing more than the "taming effect" so well documented in veterinary medicine and animal research.[71]

Certainly no one denies that neuroleptic drugs can have a calming effect on agitated schizophrenic patients. Moreover it is even possible that in certain happy instances the numbing effect of these drugs can diminish the mental anguish of schizophrenics to such an extent that they are able to regain their emotional equilibrium and reestablish contact with reality.*

However, a variety of other chemical substances have been reported to have an antipsychotic effect.[72] Here, for example, are Harry Stack Sullivan's observations on the therapeutic effectiveness of ethyl alcohol in treating schizophrenia:

> In such cases, recourse is had to chemotherapeutic agencies, notably ethyl alcohol, which impair the highly discriminative action of the more lately acquired tendency systems, and permit the at least rudimentary functioning of the more primitive, without much stress. After from three to ten days of continuous mild intoxication, almost all such patients, in the writer's experience, have effected a considerable readjustment. The *modus operandi* may be indicated roughly by remarking that these patients discover by actual experience that the personal environment is not noxious, and, having discovered this, have great difficulty in subsequently elaborating convictions of menace, plots, fell purposes, etc.[73]

---

*For a fuller explanation of how neuroleptic drugs work see Appendix A: "A Note on How Neuroleptic Drugs Work."

If as a result of his success in treating his patients with alcoholic beverages, Sullivan had claimed that schizophrenia was caused by a deficit of ethyl alcohol in the brains of schizophrenics, I would totally fail to see how his theory would be any more preposterous than the dopamine hypothesis!

At least six research studies exist which clearly indicate that in the long run, schizophrenics are better off not taking neuroleptic drugs.* The therapeutic ineffectiveness of these drugs has been most decisively demonstrated by Dr. Maurice Rappaport and associates, in a study involving 80 hospitalized young male patients undergoing acute schizophrenic episodes.[74] The 80 patients were randomly divided into two groups: a group which received from 300 to 900 mg of chlorpromazine a day, and a group which received only a placebo. On admission, at discharge, and at regular intervals during the three-year period following their discharge from the hospital, the patients were interviewed and a variety of clinical rating scales were administered to judge their improvement. Dr. Rappaport found that the patients who had been given only a placebo while in the hospital and who were off drugs during the follow-up period showed ". . . greater clinical improvement and less pathology . . . fewer rehospitalizations and less overall functional disturbance in the community than the other groups of patients studied."[75] In regard to the crucial factor of rehospitalization, the group which was the least improved were the patients who had received medication *both* during and after hospitalization: 73 percent of these patients had to be rehospitalized — as opposed to only 8 percent of the patients who had *never* received drugs.[76] Other studies which establish the long-term clinical ineffectiveness of neuroleptics include: a study by Easton and Link[77] showing that medicated patients have a higher relapse rate than patients who aren't on drugs; a study by Gardos and Cole[78] showing that relapse during drug administration is more severe and more apt to lead to rehospitalization than relapse occurring when the patient is on a placebo; a study by Rifkin and Kane[79] showing that neuroleptics adversely affect social adjustment; a study by Dion and associates[80] showing that neuroleptics adversely affect vocational adjustment; and a study by Hartlage[81] showing that neuroleptics cause a decreased ability to learn.

It is claimed that neuroleptic drugs achieve their alleged beneficial effects by exerting a corrective or harmonizing influence on malfunctioning neurotransmitters. However, according to Dr. Breggin, such claims have no scientific basis at all, since rather than having a subtle harmoniz-

---

*Indeed, how could it be otherwise? After all, recent studies show that chronic schizophrenics suffer from a dopamine deficiency and produce markedly less dopamine than normal controls. So how could such patients possibly benefit from drugs which block dopamine and cause a dopamine deficiency?

ing effect, these drugs are potent *neurotoxins* which affect *all* brain cells.[82] In addition to causing a lobotomy-like effect by impairing the reticular activating system, limbic system, and frontal lobes,[83] these drugs have the following neurotoxic effects:

*Parkinsonism.* Since parkinsonism is a dopamine deficiency disease, and since neuroleptic drugs deprive the brain of dopamine, it is only to be expected that these drugs would induce parkinsonism. Typical symptoms of parkinsonism include a rigid, masklike face; a tremor of the extremities when at rest, and recurring rigidity or spasms when the limbs are moved; a stooped, shuffling gait; and a slowing of all motor or muscular activities. Sometimes psychiatrists will deliberately induce parkinsonism in order to subdue unruly patients.[84] Some psychiatrists actually believe that inducing parkinsonism has a therapeutic effect.[85]

*Encephalitis.* It has been observed since the time the neuroleptics were first introduced, that the effects of these drugs closely mimic the symptoms and neurologic sequelae of encephalitis or sleeping sickness. Both neuroleptic drugs and encephalitis cause somnolence, parkinsonism, and a variety of bizarre neurologic disorders known as "dyskinesias." Dr. Breggin sees a tragic irony in the fact that while viral encephalitis was extinct by the time the neuroleptic drugs were developed, due to the widespread use of these drugs, neurologic disorders characteristic of encephalitis are again reaching epidemic proportions.[86]

*Akathisia* is a neurological disorder characterized by extreme jitteriness, restlessness, and anxiety. It is beautifully described by Jack Henry Abbott, a prisoner at a federal penitentiary who was being tortured into submission by Prolixin, the most powerful neuroleptic drug now in use:

> These drugs, in this family, do not calm or sedate the nerves. They attack. They attack from so deep inside you, you cannot locate the source of the pain. The drugs turn your nerves in upon yourself. . . . The pain *grinds* into your *fiber* . . . You ache with restlessness, so you feel you have to walk, to pace. And then as soon as you start pacing, the opposite occurs to you; you must *sit* and *rest*. Back and forth, up and down you go in pain you cannot locate; in such wretched anxiety you are over-whelmed.[87]

Psychiatrists *deliberately* and *frequently* impose akathisia on their patients. They do this specifically with withdrawn or immobile patients in order to get them on their feet and involved with ward activities.[88] In the euphemistic language of Dr. Nancy Andreasen, such drugs as Prolixin have an "energizing"[89] effect.

*Tardive Dyskinesia.* This drug-induced, usually irreversible disease is characterized by slow, rhythmic involuntary movements of the facial muscles, lips, tongue, extremities, and trunk of the body — a grossly disfiguring condition that makes the affected person look very crazy. In severe cases, this disease is totally disabling.[90]

An official *Task Force Report* of the American Psychiatric Association admits that at least 20 to 40 percent of the patients who take neuroleptic drugs develop tardive dyskinesia.[91] According to one respected survey, most scientific studies of tardive dyskinesia report incidences ranging from 24 to 56 percent.[92]

*Supersensitivity Psychosis.* During neuroleptic drug treatment, the dopamine receptors in the brain adjust to the dopamine blockade by becoming supersensitive to whatever amount of dopamine is still available. Consequently, whenever some patients are taken off neuroleptics, they become psychotic as a result of rebound hyperactivity of supersensitive dopamine receptors.[93]

Although the symptoms of supersensitivity psychosis are similar to schizophrenia, nonschizophrenics have been known to develop this disorder as a result of taking neuroleptic drugs.[94]

Like tardive dyskinesia, the supersensitivity psychosis is usually irreversible. The ironic fact is that the only known treatment for this disorder is the agent that originally caused it. This means that once a person develops the supersensitivity psychosis, that person must stay on neuroleptic drugs for the rest of his or her life.

According to one study, 22 percent of the patients taking neuroleptic drugs eventually develop the supersensitivity psychosis.[95] Moreover, the percentage of patients developing the supersensitivity psychosis will undoubtedly increase as more and more of these patients take clozapine, a much touted and exorbitantly expensive drug — a drug more likely to produce this disease than any other neuroleptic.[96]

*Neuroleptic Malignant Syndrome.* The symptoms of this drug-induced disease include fever, muscular rigidity or tremor, high blood pressure, rapid pulse, sweating, incontinence, confusion, and an elevated number of white blood cells.[97] Estimates of the mortality rate of this disease range from 20 to 30 percent.[98] The most frequent causes of death are respiratory failure, cardiovascular collapse, and acute kidney failure.[99] Two recent studies estimate the prevalence of this disease at about 1 percent,[100] while one recent study estimates its prevalence as high as 2.4 percent.[101]

The existence of the neuroleptic malignant syndrome proves that the toxicity of neuroleptic drugs is not limited to the central nervous system. These drugs have been known to cause a bewildering variety of side effects including jaundice,[102] impotence,[103] blindness,[104] disturbances of the autonomic nervous system,[105] and cardiac arrest.[106] Sometimes long-term use of these drugs causes the skin to turn a gray-blue, and this disfiguring pigmentation is usually irreversible.[107] These drugs have also been known to cause a variety of blood disorders including — in rare cases — a decrease in white blood cells, making the patient vulnerable to a dangerous or even fatal infection.[108]

Many patients on neuroleptics have died as a result of being too drugged to recognize or report serious and painful illnesses.[109]

Finally, we must realize that taking neuroleptic drugs causes psychological harm totally independent of these drugs' physical effects. Here I can speak from personal experience. I was totally unable to take those drugs without constantly reminding myself that I was a *schizophrenic* — a pitiful, helpless *defective* human being. Moreover, I felt that way even while I was only taking 25 mg of chlorpromazine a day — a dose much too low to have any clinical effect whatsoever.

Taking neuroleptic drugs causes a loss of self-esteem, a sense of helplessness and hopelessness, and a total paralysis of will. While taking these drugs it is nearly impossible to view oneself as a free agent. In taking those drugs one is being conditioned to see oneself as a *defective object* subject to forces totally beyond one's control.

To recapitulate: The alleged effectiveness of neuroleptic drugs as antischizophrenic agents is the main support for the dopamine hypothesis — and also for the more general notion that schizophrenia has a biochemical cause. However, it has been shown that these drugs have no specific antischizophrenic properties, but are instead brain-disabling agents whose sole effect is to make patients more tractable and less troublesome to others. That these drugs modify or suppress schizophrenic symptoms is totally beside the point: so do a variety of other brain-disabling agents, including ethyl alcohol. In the long run, schizophrenics are better off not taking neuroleptic drugs — as studies such as Dr. Rappaport's have shown. Neuroleptic drugs do not correct biochemical imbalances. They *cause* them. These drugs cause irreversible brain diseases, psychosis, and even death!

Ironically, rather than their alleged therapeutic effect, it is the ability of neuroleptic drugs to cause psychosis that is the strongest evidence which supports the dopamine hypothesis. I am referring to the supersensitivity psychosis. Consider, for instance, the following two facts: (a) the supersensitivity psychosis is very similar to schizophrenia, and (b) this drug-induced psychosis involves hyperactive dopamine neurotransmission.

All I can say is simply this. It has been proven beyond a reasonable doubt by several long-term follow-up studies, that *in spite of being subjected to mind-destroying neurotoxic drugs*, a very large percentage of schizophrenics manage to recover and lead full and meaningful lives.[110] The mere fact that schizophrenics are able to do this is nothing less than an ironclad proof that such people cannot possibly be the victims of any inborn biochemical defect.

In their zeal to promote the dopamine hypothesis, contemporary psychiatric researchers totally ignore a very pertinent scientific fact: *Hans Selye's general adaption syndrome.* For a present-day medical scientist to ignore Selye's theory of stress while trying to account for the changes occurring in the dopaminergic system in schizophrenia is much like a modern astronomer rejecting the Copernican theory in favor of the Ptolemaic notion that the earth is the center of the universe. In addition to being universally accepted, Selye's theory of stress explains nearly every known fact pertaining to the dopaminergic system and schizophrenia. First, it explains the increased dopamine turnover observed in the more disturbed (or "symptomatic") acute schizophrenic patients: the so-called "alarm reaction" and stage of resistance — the first two stages of the general adaption syndrome. Second, it explains why chronic schizophrenics produce markedly less dopamine than normal controls. Due to their chronic emotional distress, those individuals have reached the third and final stage of the general adaption syndrome: the stage of exhaustion. Third, the fact that chronic schizophrenics have reached the stage of exhaustion in regard to dopaminergic function explains why these patients are relatively unresponsive to amphetamine, a drug which increases dopamine neurotransmission.[111] Fourth, the depressed dopamine production in chronic schizophrenics in turn explains why these patients have an elevated number of dopamine receptors in their brains: as compensation for their dopamine deficiency. Finally, Selye's theory explains why acute schizophrenics — unlike chronic schizophrenics — do not have an increased number of dopamine receptors relative to normal controls. Being in an early phase of schizophrenia, acute schizophrenics have not yet reached the stage of exhaustion, and therefore have no dopamine deficiency. Having no dopamine deficiency to compensate for, there is no need for acute schizophrenics to have an elevated number of dopamine receptors in their brains.*

Given the fact that Selye's theory beautifully explains the biochemistry of schizophrenia, and given the fact that his stress theory is a universally accepted part of medical science, the question that naturally presents itself is this: *Why is that theory totally ignored by psychiatry?* The answer to that question is as follows. If psychiatric researchers were to utilize Selye's theory to explain the biochemistry of schizophrenia, they would have to conclude that schizophrenia represents a fundamental abnormality not in how the brain works, but rather in how a normal brain reacts to certain types of stress. Schizophrenics would then be seen

---

*Regrettably, I find I am unable to account for the very recent findings of Martinot et al 1990 that some chronic and subchronic schizophrenics have no increased number of dopamine receptors — a finding which, of course, is also totally at odds with the dopamine hypothesis.

as emotionally or mentally disturbed, but not as ill in the accepted medical sense. The preconceived notion that schizophrenia is caused by hyperactive dopamine neurotransmission would have to be completely abandoned. The belief that drugs which block dopamine have a specific antischizophrenic effect would also have to be jettisoned. Psychiatry would then be deprived of its medical — or rather pseudomedical — rationale for prescribing and administering neuroleptic drugs.* Those drugs would then be seen for what they really are: as brain-disabling, lobotomizing agents — drugs which make people more docile and manageable. Psychiatry would then have to face the grim fact that for over forty years it has been inflicting irreversible brain damage on hundreds of thousands of people *for no medically justifiable reason whatsoever!*

When seen in this light the dopamine hypothesis may not be good science, but it certainly represents the absolute state of the art in psychiatric apologetics!†

---

*Of course the psychiatric community could always adopt E. Fuller Torrey's (1988) preposterous theory that neuroleptic drugs work by killing schizophrenia-causing viruses.

†It also represents state-of-the-art advertising for the drug companies — companies which heavily subsidize psychiatric journals and psychiatric research.

# 4

# SCHIZOPHRENIA AS A GENETIC DEFECT

On November 10, 1988, the British scientific magazine *Nature* published two articles concerning the purported discovery of a schizophrenia-causing gene. The first article was by a research team led by Dr. Robin Sherrington at the Middlesex School of Medicine in London, England. These researchers reported that in studying seven British and Icelandic families with schizophrenic members, they had found a dominant gene on the long arm of the fifth chromosome causing a susceptibility to schizophrenia. The second article was by a group led by Dr. James L. Kennedy — an international team of researchers at Yale University, Stanford University, and the Karolinska Institute in Stockholm, Sweden. This research group reported that in studying a Swedish family with 31 schizophrenic members, they were unable to find the gene described by Sherrington. Furthermore, Kennedy's group claimed they had strong evidence that the purported schizophrenia-causing gene described by Sherrington and associates could not possibly exist where those investigators claimed it was located — at least not in the Swedish family they had studied.*

Dr. Sherrington's group was guided in its search for the schizophrenia-susceptibility gene by a clue furnished by Dr. Anne S. Bassett and her colleagues at the University of British Columbia in Vancouver, Canada. This clue consisted of a case in which two Chinese schizophrenic men — a 20-year-old student and his 52-year-old maternal uncle — had exhibited some very striking similarities: in addition to being schizophrenic, both men had overfolded, protuberant ears; widely spaced eyes; defective, or nonexistent left kidneys; abnormally short fourth toes on each foot; and other physical defects. These physical abnormalities were caused by a partial trisomy — that is, the presence of three copies of a segment of the fifth chromosome.[1]

However, the fact that both men were schizophrenic and shared the

---

*Several recent studies, including those of Aschauer et al 1990, Crowe et al 1991, Detera-Wadleigh et al 1989, and St. Clair et al 1989 have confirmed Kennedy's negative findings.

same physical defects was probably nothing more than a coincidence. After all, what do things like short toes or protruding ears have to do with schizophrenia? Nevertheless, Dr. Bassett came to the conclusion that the schizophrenia of the two men — like their physical abnormalities — must be caused by a defect on their fifth chromosome.[2]

While under the spell of Dr. Bassett's "brilliant" reasoning, Dr. Sherrington and coworkers must have hastily prepared their findings with the expectation of winning a Nobel Prize.

Dr. Sherrington's group may not win the Nobel Prize, but it has certainly won the adulation of the press. In gushing platitudinous prose in newspapers throughout the world, Sherrington's group has been exalted as medical saviors whose wonderful discovery will ultimately rid the earth of the terrible scourge of schizophrenia.

In one newspaper article referring to Sherrington's bogus discovery, there was the following comment:

> The breakthrough means that family tests could be developed to predict whether individuals, including unborn babies, may be at risk.[3]

Consider the sinister possibilities of such a test: "I regret to have to tell you this Mrs. Smith, but your child is not quite normal: he's carrying a gene for schizophrenia on his fifth chromosome." If Mrs. Smith is anything like my mother, one can well imagine what the consequences would be of her hearing a thing like that!

In part II of this book, I have shown how such self-fulfilling prophecies can cause schizophrenia. I will now show how even the studies which supposedly prove that schizophrenia has a genetic cause — the twin and adoption studies — instead prove just the opposite: that schizophrenia has a psychogenic cause, and is, in many instances, the result of a self-fulfilling prophecy.

## The Twin Studies

Those who believe schizophrenia has a genetic cause are fond of stressing the difference in the rate of concordance for schizophrenia in identical and fraternal twins. For example, according to the respected psychiatric geneticists Gottesman and Shields, if one identical twin is schizophrenic, the probability of the other twin being schizophrenic is about 46 percent; whereas if one fraternal twin is schizophrenic, the probability of the other twin being affected is only about 14 percent.[4]

However, if schizophrenia is caused by a genetic defect, the concordance for this disorder in identical twins should be 100 percent — not 46 percent.

Moreover, since we would expect parents to view and treat identical twins more nearly alike than fraternal twins, the higher concordance for schizophrenia in identical twins relative to fraternal twins is hardly surprising. We would also expect parents to view and treat like-sexed fraternal twins more nearly alike than opposite-sexed fraternal twins. Therefore, it should come as no surprise that some studies show the concordance rates for schizophrenia in like-sexed fraternal twins can range anywhere from 17.6 percent to 56 percent, while concordance in opposite-sexed fraternal twins ranges from 5 to 11.5 percent.[5]

The above figures on concordance for schizophrenia in fraternal twins were taken from an old study done by Don Jackson. According to Jackson, concordance for schizophrenia in twins is also determined by their degree of emotional closeness to each other. Jackson has taken note of the fact that in our society there are fewer cultural restrictions on intimacy between women than between men, and has argued that a greater emotional closeness between women explains why the concordance for schizophrenia is much higher in female fraternal twins than in male fraternal twins.[6] Moreover, this higher rate of female concordance for schizophrenia has also been reported in studies of identical twins.[7] Finally, in regard to this higher rate of concordance for schizophrenia in female twins, Jackson has argued that it is a matter of great significance that *folie a deux* — a condition where two closely associated individuals share the same delusions — is four times more common in women than in men, and occurs most frequently in sister pairs.[8]

Needless to say, neither the higher rate of concordance for schizophrenia in female twins nor the higher rate of concordance for schizophrenia in like-sexed as opposed to opposite-sexed fraternal twins can be accounted for by genetics.

In light of the facts presented above, the 46 percent concordance for schizophrenia in identical twins no longer needs explaining. Rather it is *discordance* that is in need of explanation: why, despite their identical heredity, strikingly similar environment and mutual interaction, do 54 percent of the pairs of identical twins remain discordant for schizophrenia? Probably the best answer to this question has been supplied by William Pollin and his associates at the National Institute of Mental Health. In exhaustively studying entire families containing identical twins discordant for schizophrenia, these investigators have found a pattern that is depressingly familiar to me. They have found that each twin in these families had been assigned a markedly different role almost from the day he was born. The nonschizophrenic twin was seen as competent and capable, while the twin who later became schizophrenic was viewed as vulnerable and weak, and treated accordingly.[9] Moreover, not only Pollin's group but every group that has studied identical twins discordant for schizophrenia has found the more submissive and better behaved of the twins was almost invariably the twin who later became schizophrenic.[10] According to Pollin, this schizophrenic twin had been a focal point of parental anxiety almost from the moment of birth, and because of this greater parental anxiety there has been ". . . a great deal more focus upon and intrusion into his activities, less separation, and a reinforcement of dependency."[11] Owing to this dependency, and to a half-conscious awareness of being viewed and treated as a weak and vulnerable person by his parents, the twin comes to accept his parents' distorted image of himself — and so we have a self-fulfilling prophecy.[12]

Pollin and his group seem to be of two minds in regard to why the schizophrenic twin should arouse his parents' anxiety and concern. On one hand they are of the opinion that the parents' attitudes toward the twin — particularly the mother's — are derived from

> the establishment of an early mode of perceiving and relating to the . . . twin as helpless, based on projective identification (the mother's own feelings of inadequacy and helplessness being projected on the infant and then perceived by mother as further evidence of the infant's helplessness.)[13]

Yet, on the other hand, Pollin and his coworkers seem drawn to the hypothesis that those parents' anxieties might be based on "constitutional reality"[14] — that is, on their realistic appraisal of the schizophrenic twin as biologically inferior. In support of this hypothesis, they claim they have always found that the schizophrenic twin has a lower birth weight and is physically weaker than the normal twin.[15]

However, Pollin's claim that the schizophrenic twin has a lower birth weight and is physically weaker than his cotwin has been disconfirmed by other twin studies.[16] Moreover, the simple fact that schizophrenia occurs no more frequently in twins than in nontwins[17] is difficult to reconcile with Pollin's claim that adverse prenatal experience together with a situation of increased comparative and competitive pressure during development are significant factors in causing schizophrenia, since these factors are encountered far more often in twins than in nontwins.

Due to the high rate of discordance for schizophrenia in identical twins and the fact that such twins are generally raised together in similar environments, even those who are of the opinion that the causes of schizophrenia are primarily genetic are forced to admit that the twin studies offer at best only weak and inconclusive evidence in support of their thesis.

According to most psychiatric geneticists, the studies which offer the strongest evidence supporting the notion that schizophrenia has a genetic cause are the adoption studies since in these studies heredity and environment are thought to operate independently of each other. However, as we will soon see, it is precisely these adoption studies that offer the strongest evidence supporting my thesis that schizophrenia can be caused by a self-fulfilling prophecy.

## The Adoption Studies

In recent years, due largely to two important adoption studies — together with three unfortunate social trends discussed earlier in this book — the notion that schizophrenics are a genetically distinct group of inferior people has acquired a facade of scientific respectability. The first of these two major adoption studies was conducted by Leonard Heston in 1966. Heston studied 47 offspring of schizophrenic mothers born at an Oregon state mental hospital during the years 1915 to 1945. All of these children had been separated from their schizophrenic mothers within the first three days of life, and reared by their nonmaternal relatives. Heston's study also involved 50 matched controls born of normal mothers during the years 1915 to 1945. It was found on follow-up that 5 (10.6 percent) of the offspring of the schizophrenic mothers were schizophrenic, while none of the controls were schizophrenic.[18]

The second major adoption study was conducted in Denmark by the American psychiatrists David Rosenthal, Paul Wender, Seymour Kety and their Danish collaborators.[19] This latter adoption study — often touted as the most flawlessly executed study of its kind — differed from Heston's in a number of respects. First of all, unlike the schizophrenic mothers of Heston's study, fully 87 percent of the parents of this study did not succumb to schizophrenia until long after the child was born — an average of 11 years after.[20] A second and more significant difference between the two studies was the fact that unlike the nonmaternal relatives of Heston's study, in almost every instance all adopting families of the Danish study were unaware that the children they had adopted had schizophrenic parents.[21] Consequently, unlike those of Heston's study, the children in the Danish study were not burdened by their foster parents' adverse attitudes and expectations in regard to their being at risk for schizophrenia. Finally, a third and crucial difference between the studies is the much lower incidence of schizophrenia in the Danish adoptees. As Lowing and associates have shown, when strict DSM-III diagnostic procedures are applied to the Danish study, only 1 out of the 39 Danish adoptees could be considered schizophrenic — an incidence of about 2.5 percent.[22]

The potency of parental attitudes and expectations in causing schizophrenia is clearly shown by the difference between the incidences of schizophrenia in the adoptees of the two studies described above. In Heston's study where the foster parents knew the adopted child had a schizophrenic mother, the incidence was 10.6 percent; in the Danish study where the foster parents were unaware the adopted child had a schizo-phrenic parent, the incidence was only 2.5 percent. If these two adoption studies have any validity at all, they clearly demonstrate that *parental belief that the child is at risk for schizophrenia together with rearing practices stemming from this belief are at least four times more effective in causing a schizophrenic breakdown than the individual's unfavorable genetic heritage.*

But do these two adoption studies really have any validity? Possibly not.* Since the number of subjects in these studies is so small — 47 in Heston's study and 39 in the Danish study — no definite conclusions can be drawn.

However, if *any* conclusion can be drawn from the adoption (and twin) studies, it is simply this: If schizophrenia has a genetic component, then that genetic component must be extremely weak.

In part I of this book I argued that schizophrenia is a strictly learned response, originating in how the parents communicate and how the family interacts as a whole. In support of this thesis, I cited Margaret Thaler Singer's success in predicting the nature and severity of the mental disorders of a variety of patients — schizophrenic, borderline schizo-phrenic, and neurotic — from their parents' scores on a number of psychological tests.

The investigations of Dr. Singer and her associates have direct relevance to the adoption studies — especially to an adoption study conducted by Paul Wender. Wender's study involved thirty families: ten families with adopted schizophrenic children, ten families with adopted normal children, and ten families in which the parents had reared their own schizophrenic children.[23] By blindly analyzing the results of Rorschach tests administered to the parents in Wender's study, Dr. Singer was able to differentiate both the biological and adoptive parents of the schizophrenic patients from the adoptive parents of the normal children with 100 percent accuracy.[24] Moreover, Singer found no differences between the adoptive and biological parents of the schizophrenic patients: in both sets of parents the styles of communication were equally deviant.[25]

Here again, as in the other two adoption studies, Wender's study provides strong evidence that schizophrenia has an environmental cause.

However, at this point a question must be raised as to whether or not the thought disorder in the parents of schizophrenics is the *result* rather than the *cause* of their children being schizophrenic. According to Singer and Wynne, there are several reasons why it is highly unlikely that the deviant cognitive styles of these parents are caused by their having a

---

* The validity of the Danish adoption study is questionable. For example, two studies, one by Lewontin, Rose and Kamin 1984, the other by Lidz, Blatt and Cook 1981, have found no difference in the incidence of schizophrenia in the index and control groups in the Danish adoption study.

schizophrenic child. First of all, as these authors point out, the changes that take place in parents as a result of their child becoming schizophrenic have more to do with changes in attitudes, feelings and moods, than in forms of thinking or psychological defenses.[26] Furthermore, all the available evidence indicates that cognitive styles — unlike moods and feelings — are highly stable and resistant to change.[27] However, this stability of cognitive style and character structure is far less true of the child than of the adult, and because of the child's greater malleability, it will be he, rather than the adult, whose cognitive style will be more likely to change as a result of their mutual interaction.[28] Singer and Wynne also make the very interesting observation that, although the patient's schizophrenic breakdown often causes their parents considerable mental anguish, these same parents are usually even more disturbed when their child begins to clinically improve.[29] Finally, these authors note that parents typically describe their schizophrenic offspring prior to the onset of their psychosis as having been "normal," "very good," and as "less trouble" than their other children.[30] Rather than having been a disturbing influence, such children according to Singer and Wynne, had ". . . helped maintain a family equilibrium."[31]

The view that a child's schizophrenic breakdown helps maintain a family equilibrium was certainly true of my own family. For example, rather than quarrel with each other, my parents chose to use me as their emotional punching bag. That state of affairs definitely helped maintain a family equilibrium. From the way my parents acted toward me you would certainly think that I was the disturbing element in our family. But that was hardly the case. In fact, my parents openly welcomed my psychosis as something desirable. At the very onset of my psychosis, my parents were constantly talking about the "wonderful" and "miraculous" change that had come over me. Finally, the consequences of my becoming psychotic were anything but disruptive. Instead, the ultimate effect of my psychosis was to bring my parents closer together and restore peace and harmony in my family.

In brief, the notion that the thought disorder and deviant styles of communication in parents are caused by their having a schizophrenic child is totally without any factual basis.

It is a tenet of psychiatric orthodoxy that aberrant rearing practices cannot possibly cause schizophrenia. According to this orthodox view, the mere fact that almost from the day I was born I was treated as if I were a lunatic, subjected to a constant barrage of verbal abuse, and threatened with commitment for doing perfectly ordinary things had no relation at all to my suffering a schizophrenic breakdown. According to this orthodox view, my schizophrenia was caused by a biological defect — my poor brain, bad chemistry, and defective genes — and if it weren't for these underlying biological defects, I would have continued to function as a perfectly normal person.

Am I overstating my case? I don't think so. Consider, for example, the views of Gottesman and Shields:

> The principal conclusion that can be reached at this stage from the adoption work is that it disconfirms the widely held hypothesis that the high schizophrenia rate observed in the children of schizophrenics was due to an interaction between schizophrenogenic rearing and genetic predisposition, and ipso facto, the cruder hypothesis that rearing by a schizophrenic parent was sufficient cause.[32]

These words pretty much speak for themselves. However, in all fairness to Gottesman and Shields, I must mention that those authors have modified their views somewhat in light of Margaret Singer's findings in regard to the Wender adoption study.[33] Nevertheless, that such blatant nonsense could be written by such prominent authorities in the last quarter of the twentieth century should be more than enough to shake one's faith in the rationality of psychiatric researchers.

In recent years schizophrenia researchers and psychiatric apologists have had nothing but bad things to say about the concept of the schizophrenogenic parent. Aside from their firm belief that bad rearing cannot possibly cause schizophrenia, these true believers have two main reasons for rejecting the schizophrenogenic parent concept. First, there are studies which indicate that children reared by schizophrenic parents are no more apt to become schizophrenic than children reared by normal parents.[34] Second, it is claimed that most schizophrenics come from perfectly normal families — families which have given those poor lost souls all the love in the world.

In regard to the studies which purportedly show that schizophrenia is not caused by being raised by a schizophrenic parent, one must bear two things in mind. First, those who claim that bad parenting causes schizophrenia insist that *both* parents must be aberrant in their ways for the child to be adversely affected. However, in the studies in question, *only one* parent was schizophrenic while the other parent was relatively normal.[35] Secondly, we must realize that *schizophrenic* parent and *schizophrenogenic* parent are not synonymous terms. Indeed, I can see no reason why schizophrenics cannot be perfectly adequate parents — just as I can see no reason why schizophrenics cannot be competent scientists or brain surgeons.

The claim that most schizophrenics come from perfectly normal families deserves very careful consideration.

In part I of this book, I presented three case studies of families of schizophrenics, one of which was the Abbott family. Although the parents in this family appeared to be very ordinary and sensible people, they were later found to be playing with their daughter's mind, subjecting her to strange "telepathy experiments" without her knowledge — a condition that was causing that young woman severe psychological problems. The crucial point here is that *it took over a year of investigation to discover those parents' bizarre behavior.*

According to Manfred Bleuler, a world renowned schizophrenia researcher, the families of schizophrenics often give the impression of being completely normal and harmonious, but closer observation almost always reveals ". . . a shocking picture of previously concealed misery."[36] For example, consider my family. Had a psychiatrist examined my parents back in 1960 when I was undergoing my schizophrenic episode, he would have found that they were basically sane and decent people. In addition to finding nothing strange or odd about my parents, that psychiatrist would have been favorably impressed with the fact that my parents were obviously very concerned about me. Moreover, had that psychiatrist known my parents intimately for several years he probably would have retained his favorable opinion of them.

At this point I must confess that although the portrait I have drawn of my parents is 100 percent accurate, it nevertheless presents a highly distorted picture of them. This distortion arises from the fact that in trying to get to the bottom of my psychological problems, I have been forced to dwell almost exclusively on the negative aspects of my parents' personalities.

However, even though my parents were basically decent and relatively normal persons, there is no doubt in my mind that their behavior toward me was the major cause of my schizophrenic breakdown.

Considerable effort has been invested in proving that schizophrenics are born rather than made. Though such efforts have been scientifically barren, they have nevertheless paid huge propaganda dividends for the psychiatric community. Note, for example, Dr. Sherrington's sensational discovery of a schizophrenia-causing gene. Though Sherrington's findings were contradicted by those of Kennedy and his group, *only Sherrington's findings were reported by the press.* Therefore, although Sherrington's findings may be scientifically worthless, they have, nevertheless, greatly strengthened the authority and prestige of psychiatry.

Or consider the breathtaking title of the following newspaper article, "Scientists clone gene linked to schizophrenia, Parkinson's" released by the Newhouse News Service on December 22, 1988:

PORTLAND — Scientists at Oregon Health Sciences University have isolated and cloned a gene related to a brain protein implicated in schizophrenia, drug addiction and movement disorders such as Parkinson's disease.

The breakthrough could lead to the development of safer and more effective drugs to treat those and other disorders linked to brain protein.

Oliver Civelli, assistant staff scientist at OHSU's Vollum Institute for Biomedical Research, heads the team that was first to isolate and clone the gene that codes $D_2$ dopamine receptor, a brain protein that receives chemical messages from other cells.

"It was the result of a good idea, a lot of work and a little bit of luck," said Civelli, assistant professor of cell biology and anatomy in the OHSU School of Medicine.

"The importance of the OHSU team's work is that the cloned receptor will give researchers a direct way to look at the molecular biology of the receptor and its synthesis," said Professor Ian Creese of Rutgers University, who in 1975 was the first person to identify the $D_2$ receptor." The work gives us a new handle for studying the genetics of schizophrenia and a new possibility of drug development."

Understanding how the dopamine system operates can lead to safer and more effective drugs for schizophrenia, manic depressive disorders and possibly a variety of other diseases including Parkinson's and drug addiction.

For more than 30 years overactivity of the dopamine system has been linked to schizophrenia, which affects 3 million people in the United States.

While symptoms in some schizophrenia patients are treatable with drugs that block the $D_2$ dopamine receptor, side effects have limited use of such drugs.[37]

What this glowing account of the progress of modern medical science fails to mention, is the simple fact that this so-called schizophrenia-linked gene was isolated in a *rat*.[38] While the findings of the OHSU scientists may be praiseworthy, their discovery hardly represents any advance in understanding the problems of schizophrenics. However, like the findings of Sherrington, the findings of the OHSU scientists represent a wonderful propaganda coup for psychiatry.

And this is only the beginning. In the future, many more schizophrenia-linked and schizophrenia-causing genes will be discovered.[39]

At this point we must ponder the possibility of scientists actually discovering a schizophrenia-susceptibility gene. *If* this happens, won't this be a clear-cut vindication of the medical model, or of the notion that schizophrenia is a bona fide disease?

The answer to this question is plainly no, for the simple reason that a socially undesirable human difference is not a disease even if that particular trait happens to be heritable. Consider shyness, for example. Like schizophrenia, shyness is officially listed in the *Diagnostic and Statistical Manual* as a mental disorder or disease.[40] Furthermore, it has recently been shown that shyness has a genetic basis.[41] But do these two facts mean that shy persons are sick in the *literal* sense of the term? Obviously not, for the concept of disease refers neither to social undesirwomen ability nor to heritability, but to cellular pathology: histopathological lesions and pathophysiological processes.

Consequently, even if a schizophrenia-susceptibility gene is found, that, by itself, would not prove that schizophrenia is a disease.

It is quite possible that many schizophrenics possess an innate sensitivity which renders them vulnerable to having a schizophrenic breakdown.[42] But sensitivity is hardly a defect: for although sensitive people may be more capable of being hurt, they are also more capable of enjoying life to the fullest.

Having examined the evidence which supports the medical model, I will now present facts which I believe prove beyond a reasonable doubt that schizophrenia cannot possibly be a disease.

# 5

# FACTS THE MEDICAL MODEL CANNOT EXPLAIN

It is an unquestioned dogma in most psychiatric circles that schizophrenia is either a degenerative brain disease or the result of an inborn metabolic defect. Yet although destructive organic brain diseases or diseases caused by an inborn metabolic defect do not recede but only grow worse, the fact remains that schizophrenics *do* recover. In fact, there are well-authenticated cases of schizophrenics emerging from their psychosis with stronger and better integrated personalities than they had prior to their schizophrenic episodes.[1]

That schizophrenics often recover has been proven beyond a reasonable doubt by at least five recent long-term follow-up studies. One of these studies was conducted by Courtenay M. Harding of the University of Vermont.[2] Harding's study involved 82 individuals — 41 men and 41 women — who had been retrospectively diagnosed to meet strict DSM-III criteria for schizophrenia.[3] Due to their chronic disabilities and resistance to drug treatment, these schizophrenic patients had qualified for a comprehensive rehabilitation program prior to their being released from the back wards of the Vermont State Hospital during the years 1955 to 1960. On interviewing both these 82 individuals and their close associates twenty to twenty-five years after these 82 subjects had been released from the state hospital, Harding found 68 percent of these former patients were totally free of their schizophrenic symptoms, and that 45 percent of them had no psychiatric symptoms whatsoever.[4] Harding also found most of the subjects had one or more close friends, required little or no help in meeting basic needs, and led moderate to very full lives.[5]

What makes the results of Harding's study so especially decisive is the fact that her subjects were not only schizophrenics, but *profoundly disabled* schizophrenics. At the time they were chosen for the rehabilitation program they had been schizophrenic for an average of 16 years, and totally disabled for an average of 10 years.[6] They had given no indication at all that they were ever going to improve. The recovery of such a large percentage of hardcore schizophrenics is the strongest possible evidence that schizophrenia is not an irreversible organic disease but a reversible functional disorder.

Results somewhat similar to Harding's have also been obtained by four other long-term follow-up studies. These latter studies include: two investigations conducted in Switzerland, one by Manfred Bleuler at Zurich[7] and the other by Luc Ciompi at Lausanne[8]; a study conducted by Drs. Huber, Gross and Schüttler in Bonn, West Germany;[9] and a study conducted by Drs. Tsuang, Woolson and Fleming in Iowa City, Iowa.[10] The length of observation of these four studies ranged from 22 to 37 years. These studies generally report a rate of recovery and significant improvement in the schizophrenic subjects of slightly more than 50 percent.

While it can't be denied that many schizophrenics neither recover nor improve, this unfortunate fact does not necessarily mean that these people have an organic brain disease or are incapable of recovering. On the contrary, it is quite possible that many schizophrenics have a psychological need to remain psychotic.[11] Consider, for instance, this excerpt from a personal letter of one of Manfred Bleuler's schizophrenic patients:

> I'm enjoying so much wonderful freedom in my mental illness, that I would be ever so much worse off at liberty, at liberty and mentally well. Besides, it sometimes suits my purposes to have the privilege of being mad. It is so comfortable to be able to remain aloof from the need for exemplary conduct before one's own self. Since one must live according to one's own individual mentality, or be declared a fake, one must live in a healthy spirit, since one is declared mentally defective anyway. . . . The life of a mental patient means being a prince, with all its freedoms revolving around the obligations to one's fellowmen.[12]

Obviously, this is hardly the letter of a brain-damaged zombie.

Manfred Bleuler was one of those intellectually honest psychiatrists who draws a clear sharp distinction between organic psychoses and schizophrenia:

> In the organic psychoses, depletion, simplication, and the inability to distinguish detail — in the schizophrenic psychoses, an unbelievably disintegrated inner life, overabundant in the most incredible imaginings, experiences, and emotions. In the organic psychoses, in severe cases, the final breakdown of the primary functions of memory, perception, judgement, and the more delicated modulated emotions. In the schizophrenic psychoses, however, the old intellectual competence, warmth, and emotional depth are discernible behind every serious state of morbidity, time and time again.[13]

Moreover, Bleuler also notes:

> But once we realize that seriously "demented" schizophrenics have not lost touch with a healthy psychic life, that in their case, healthy perception, memory, recall, judgement, and feelings are merely concealed behind their pathological behavior; that such probands actually do recover, then one begins to doubt the validity of the qualification of "idiocy."[14]

In his own 23-year follow-up study, Dr. Bleuler describes several instances where seemingly hopeless schizophrenics had either recovered or improved significantly after having been psychotic for *more than thirty years*.[15] Such improvements and recoveries would not have been possible had those patients been suffering from psychoses caused by an organic brain disease or an inborn metabolic defect. On that point Bleuler is categorical: "A long-term, severe organic dementia does not recede."[16]

That schizophrenia is not an organic disease is clearly shown by the situational nature of schizophrenic symptomatology — that is, a person can be schizophrenic in one social situation and normal in another. For example, Laing and Esterson present a case in which a young schizophrenic woman had complete control over her catatonic symptoms. In one instance this woman's mother visited her while she was in the hospital in a catatonic stupor, and reminded her that she had promised to act as a bridesmaid at her sister's wedding. The patient subsequently left the hospital and functioned with complete normalcy at her sister's wedding. She then immediately returned to the hospital and resumed her catatonic stupor.[17]

Such dramatic instances of schizophrenics suddenly shedding their symptoms are not uncommon. In fact, even a staunch defender of the medical model like E. Fuller Torrey will readily admit that "most schizophrenic patients who act inappropriately on hospital wards usually act quite appropriately when taken out of the hospital on trips."[18] (Unfortunately, Dr. Torrey never explains how the symptoms of a "brain disease" could be nullified merely by taking the patient out of the hospital.)

In addition to clinical observations, the situational nature of schizophrenic symptomatology is supported by the autobiographical accounts of schizophrenic individuals. The following comments of a 26-year-old schizophrenic woman speak for themselves:

> Finally I decided I'd never trust anyone again. For two years I closed myself up and froze so I wouldn't feel anything. But no matter how mad I made you, you always came back and were always on time. You had to show me you cared enough so that,

if I went away, you would chase me and even beat me to make me come back.

Hate has to come first. The patient hates the doctor for opening the wound again and hates himself for allowing himself to be touched again. The patient is sure it will just lead to more hurt. He wants to be dead and hidden in a place where nothing can touch him and drag him back.

I had to die to keep from dying. I know that sounds crazy but one time a boy hurt my feelings very much and I wanted to jump in front of a subway. Instead I went a little catatonic so I wouldn't feel anything. . . .

Patients laugh and posture when they see through the doctor who says he will help but really won't or can't. . . . The patients try to divert and distract him. They try to please the doctor but also confuse him so he won't go into anything important. When you find people who will really help, you don't need to distract them. You can act in a normal way.[19]

Finally, the situational nature of schizophrenic symptomatology is supported by experimental research. Two experiments will be reviewed here. The first experiment was conducted by Stanley P. Zarlock at the Veterans Administration Hospital in Lexington, Kentucky. In this experiment Zarlock divided a psychiatric ward into four distinct social environments: recreational, occupational, social, and medical. Zarlock found that his 30 male schizophrenic subjects showed considerable social adaptability in adopting roles appropriate to each of the four environments. Zarlock also found that almost all his subjects' pathological behavior and verbal responses occurred in the medical setting. Of a total of 351 verbal responses judged (by two psychologists) to be pathological, 3 occurred in the recreational, 12 in the occupational, 12 in the social, and 324 in the medical environment.[20] Of a total of 41 behavioral responses judged (by the experimenter, a nurse, and an attendant) to have a bizarre quality, 2 occurred in the recreational, 2 in the occupational, 4 in the social, and 33 in the medical environment.[21] From this experiment Zarlock concluded that bizarre behavior and pathological verbal responses are to some extent an artifact of the medical environment.[22]

The second experiment — or series of experiments — was conducted by Benjamin M. Braginsky and his associates at a large state mental hospital in New England. From his observations of schizophrenics and other mental patients, Braginsky noticed that rather than being passive victims of an illness, those people were capable of manipulating their environment through "impression management" in order to achieve certain ends — that is, in certain social situations schizophrenics were capable of appearing very "ill" in order to gain certain benefits, and relatively normal in other situations in order to gain other advantages.

One of Braginsky's experiments involved 60 hospitalized mental patients — 41 of whom were diagnosed as schizophrenic, 12 as psychotic but not schizophrenic, and 7 as neurotic. These 60 subjects were split into two diagnostically similar groups: Old-timers, or those who had been hospitalized for over three months — most had been hospitalized for over three years — and Newcomers, or those who had been hospitalized for less than three months. It was predicted that the Newcomers would be motivated to present themselves as mentally healthy in order to gain an early release, while the Old-timers would be motivated to present themselves as mentally sick in order to continue the way of life to which they had become accustomed.

Both groups — the Old-timers and Newcomers — were then split into two additional groups: those who were given a "Mental Illness Test" and those who were given a "Self-Insight Test." Other than their titles, both tests were in fact identical and consisted of 30 items on the MMPI test which were judged relatively neutral in regard to social desirability. The patients were told to answer each question either true or false. Those who took the Mental Illness Test were told that a preponderance of items answered true on the test would be an indication of severe mental illness, and that such persons would need prolonged hospitalization. On the other hand, those who took the Self-Insight Test were told that a preponderance of items answered true on the test would be an indication of superior self-understanding, and that such a person would therefore be less ill and would hence need a shorter period of hospitalization. The patients were required to sign their tests and were given the impression that the staff were trying to find out how ill they were and therefore how long a period of hospitalization they would need.

The results of the experiment were exactly as predicted. The Newcomers presented themselves as not being very mentally ill by answering more items false on the Mental Illness Test and more items true of the Self-Insight Test, while the Old-timers presented themselves as being severely mentally ill by answering more items true on the Mental Illness Test and more items false on the Self-Insight Test.[23]

According to Braginsky, both the Newcomers and the Old-timers were utilizing impression management in order to secure certain benefits. The Newcomers presented themselves as being less ill in order to shorten their period of hospitalization, while the Old-timers presented themselves as being severely mentally ill in order to continue the way of life to which they had become accustomed.

A second experiment of Braginsky's required that the patient submit to a two minute face-to-face interview with a staff psychologist. This second experiment involved 30 chronic schizophrenics who had been hospitalized for an average of ten years. These 30 subjects were split into three groups of equal size: an *Open Ward* group who were told that the purpose of the interview was to find out whether the patient should be assigned to an open or closed ward; a *Discharge* group who were told that the staff were interested in finding out whether or not the patient should be discharged; and a *Mental Status* group who were merely told that the staff were interested in finding out how the patient was getting along in the hospital.

The 30 interviews were tape recorded and independently analyzed by three staff psychiatrists. These psychiatrists were both unaware of the true nature of the experiment and unfamiliar with the patients. They were told the patients represented a wide variety of diagnostic categories and were instructed to rate the patients on their degree of psychopathology and how much control they thought the patients needed — ranging from complete freedom to maximum control.

It was predicted that the patients in the Open Ward group would want to retain the freedoms and privileges of their open ward status and would therefore be motivated to present themselves as relatively mentally healthy at the interview. It was also predicted that the Discharge group would feel threatened by the possibility of being discharged from the hospital and would present themselves as being very sick. Finally, it was predicted that the way the Mental Status group would present themselves would not differ substantially from the way the Discharge group would present themselves.

Again the results of the experiment were exactly as predicted. Not one patient in the Open Ward group expressed a psychiatric symptom at the interview while nearly half of the patients in the other two groups (nine patients altogether) did so.[24]

Before psychiatry's recent return to the medical model it was universally recognized that there is a qualitative difference between organic psychoses and functional disorders such as schizophrenia. While organic psychoses always cause a marked deterioration in the patient's mental abilities, it has been known for a long time that schizophrenia leaves the patient's mental faculties totally intact.[25] In fact, even while floridly psychotic, some schizophrenics have been known to exhibit amazing intellectual abilities. For example, even while severely schizophrenic, Emil Dolfuss was still able to select a stock portfolio for his psychiatrist which he correctly predicted would increase 40 percent on the market within a period of one year.[26]

My friend Paul offers another dramatic example of how even a severely schizophrenic individual can nevertheless exhibit amazing intellectual abilities.

One summer evening, Paul showed up at his sister's house in a terror-stricken state, and demanded that she hide him from the "Forces of Evil" that he felt were closing in on him. While in his sister's home, Paul was observed staring at the wall utterly transfixed with terror, apparently hallucinating.

At that point in time Paul had been undeniably schizophrenic for well over a year. When he arrived at his sister's home, Paul was at his very worst and his family was seriously considering having him committed.

However, I advised Paul's family against having Paul committed for a number of reasons. First of all, I argued that what Paul needed more than anything else was the feeling that he could trust the people who were closest to him, and that having him committed would completely destroy what little trust Paul still had in his family, and would therefore do him irreparable harm. Secondly, I argued what they were then witnessing was merely a temporary flare-up: that Paul would calm down as soon as everyone around him began to relax and treat him as if he were a rational adult. Finally, I advised that as long as he was staying at his sister's house Paul should be given something to do that would occupy his mind, and that this would help bring him back to reality.

Paul's family took my advice. While Paul was staying at his sister's house, his brother-in-law, who was a graduate student in geology, asked him to write a term paper for him. Paul, who had never studied geology before, studied his brother-in-law's books and wrote the paper.

That paper earned Paul's brother-in-law a solid A. Not only that, Paul's brother-in-law was startled when his professor called him into his office and asked, "Would you consider doing your Ph.D. thesis on the paper you just wrote?"

A believer in the medical model would argue that the only thing the above two stories prove is that neither Paul nor Emil Dolfuss could possibly have been schizophrenic.

However, in order to argue that Paul wasn't a schizophrenic one would have to completely abandon the currently accepted definition of schizophrenia. Here, for instance, is a list of Paul's symptoms:

*Prominent hallucinations.* Paul would often hear voices commenting on his thoughts and behavior. These voices often had distinct personalities, and consisted of "evil spirits" who criticized and mocked him, and "good spirits" who gave him advice and guidance.

Once, for days on end as he was traveling around the country on railroad boxcars, Paul was accompanied by an ethereal, Athena-like personage who was his constant companion. Paul's companion was continually giving him advice and instruction in esoteric wisdom. Paul would treat his imaginary companion as if she were a real person. He would courteously open doors for her, and would compose and recite poetry for her benefit.

Once when he was in a railway station in Portland, Oregon, Paul's companion told him that if he would only put his arms around her and kiss her all his problems would be solved. In front of gaping onlookers at the railroad station, Paul hugged and kissed his imaginary companion. Unfortunately, however, his problems only grew worse. Paul told me that he eventually became so utterly dependent on his hallucinated voices that he was virtually incapable of making a single move without having those voices tell him he should make that move.

Paul's hallucinations continued on an off-and-on basis for several years. According to the most recent edition of the *Diagnostic and Statistical Manual* (DSM-IV), those hallucinations *alone* would justify Paul's classification as a schizophrenic.

*Bizarre delusions.* Paul once told me that he was able to control what songs the disc jockey played over the radio by using telekinesis. Paul's earliest delusion was his belief that nearly everyone was accusing him of being homosexual. However, his first really bizarre delusion was his belief that the "spirits of the White Brotherhood" had chosen him as some sort of messiah. He later came to believe that he was a reincarnation of the prophet Ezekiel. Once when a squirrel scampered up to him, Paul voiced his belief that he was St. Francis of Assisi. There was also a time when Paul believed his mother was a witch. He believed his mother had cast a spell on him and was reading his mind. (That was when he took refuge in his sister's home.)

According to current DSM-IV criteria, those delusions *alone* would be more than enough to earn Paul his schizophrenic label.

This is only a partial catalogue of Paul's symptoms, but I believe my point has been made. Still, in a certain sense, a believer in the medical model would have some justification for doubting that Paul was in fact schizophrenic; for, if Paul's mental problems stemmed from his having an organic brain disease, his writing that term paper for his brother-in-law would not have been possible. I think the mere fact that Paul could exhibit such intellectual abilities while severely schizophrenic is nothing less than an ironclad proof that schizophrenia could not possibly be an organic brain disease.

Most of the time, my schizophrenic friends give me the impression they are quite reasonable people — the only exception, is when they are discussing their delusional beliefs. Then they can be wildly illogical and are not to be reasoned with. But schizophrenics are hardly unique in that respect, for whenever normal people begin discussing either religion or politics, they too can be both illogical and unreasonable. Hence how are schizophrenics that different from normal people?

How schizophrenics differ from normal people has been the subject of an immense amount of psychological research. It has been postulated that schizophrenia is a disorder in which a loosening of associations is always present; that schizophrenia is a disorder characterized by prelogical or paleological thought processes; that the thinking of schizophrenics is excessively concrete and shows an inability to use abstractions; and that schizophrenics suffer from an attention deficit. However, each of these hypotheses has been decisively refuted.[27]

To date, no cognitive deficit differentiating schizophrenics from normal people has been found — a fact which by itself is more than enough to totally discredit the medical model.

A logical corollary of the medical model is the notion that schizophrenics are helpless, defective persons who are totally unable to function. However, in their long-term follow-up study, Courtenay M. Harding and her associates have found that even some of their schizophrenic subjects who still had hallucinations and delusions were able to hold jobs, have lots of friends, and maintain good family relationships.[28] In fact, it has been reported that there have been attorneys and physicians undergoing treatment for schizophrenia on outpatient basis who were still practicing their professions and doing excellent work.[29]

Moreover, there is evidence which indicates that in some respects schizophrenics are able to function better than normal people. For example, the ability to empathize with other people has been shown to be more highly developed in schizophrenics than in normal people. This was demonstrated by Isidore Helfand at the Teachers College at Columbia University, in an experimental study in which schizophrenics and normal individuals were tested in their ability to take roles. Empathy was determined by the ability of the subjects to simulate the test performance of an author whose autobiography they had read.[30]

The results of this experiment were so contrary to expectations that Helfand felt compelled to attempt to explain away the embarrassingly superior empathic abilities of the schizophrenic subjects by claiming that such abilities are a result of an *impairment* — of a lack of a "generalized other."[*31] Nevertheless, the experimental findings of Helfand are wholly consistent with the clinical observations of a number of psychodynamically oriented psychiatrists including Harold F. Searles, Helm Stierlin, and Frieda Fromm-Reichmann.

The views of Fromm-Reichmann are well known:

> The schizophrenic's ability to eavesdrop, as it were, on the doctor creates another special personal problem for some psychiatrists. The schizophrenic, since his childhood days, has been suspiciously aware of the fact that words are used not only to convey but also to veil actual communications. Consequently, he has learned to gather information about people in general, therefore also about the psychiatrist, from his inadvertent communications through changes in gesture, attitude and posture, inflections of

---

*That schizophrenics have no generalized other is highly unlikely in view of their ability to simulate normalcy on the MMPI test. See Grayson and Olinger 1957.

voice, or expressive movements. Observation of all these intangibles is one way of survival for the anxious schizophrenic in the presence of threatening malevolent interpersonal performances which he is always expecting. Therefore, the schizophrenic may sense and comment upon some of the psychotherapist's assets and — what is more frightening — his liabilities, which had been beyond the limit of the psychiatrist's own realization prior to his contact with the schizophrenic patient. An insecure psychiatrist will be made anxious by being exposed to the schizophrenic's empathic capacity for this type of eavesdropping and so become preoccupied with his own defenses.[32]

Writing in a similar vein, Stierlin notes:

Thus in the schizophrenic — perhaps because of the necessity to survive — the capacity for communication with another person's unconscious has in his early life been overdeveloped and has been maintained longer than in more 'normal' people. His characteristic sensitivity to unconscious processes is a kind of subtle emotional radar system that developed under the specific conditions of early dependency, and was devised to intercept the danger signals from the mother or other important persons. This warning made it possible to respond to the threats embodied in his mother with adaptive maneuvers that would lead to the best possible symbiotization of the relationship.[33]

However, a contrasting yet complementary view is provided by Searles:

He introjects her not primarily out of hatred or anxiety but out of genuine love and solicitude for his mother whom he has found, upon close inspection which this 'crush' phase entails, to be not a person admirably stronger than he, but a pathetically crippled one who desperately needs relief, from the burden of her own personality-difficulties. He introjects her primarily in an effort to save her by taking her difficulties, her cross, upon himself.[34]

Obviously, the schizophrenic's superior empathic abilities can be readily understood from a psychodynamic point of view. Moreover, as Searles makes clear, it is precisely these individuals' exceptional empathic capabilities which renders them vulnerable to having a schizophrenic breakdown. For example, I know for a fact that at those times when my parents viciously berated me, that their tirades wouldn't have affected me nearly as much if I wasn't so acutely aware of their mental anguish and didn't empathize so completely with their feelings and point of view.

However, once we adopt the distorted — and dehumanizing — perspective of the medical model, such superior abilities by the schizophrenic seem totally inexplicable if not downright impossible. Indeed, it is a tenet of psychiatric orthodoxy that schizophrenics are virtual subhumans incapable of empathizing with the feelings of others — a grotesque projection if ever there was one: a stark indication of psychiatry's utter inability to empathize with the schizophrenic.

On reading the autobiographies of schizophrenics, including such works as August Strindberg's *Inferno*, Daniel Paul Schreber's *Memoirs of My Nervous Illness*, Anton Boisen's *Out of the Depths*, Lara Jefferson's *These Are My Sisters*, Joanne Greenberg's *I Never Promised You a Rose Garden*, Morag Coate's *Beyond All Reason*, Mark Vonnegut's *Eden Express*, Robert M. Pirsig's *Zen and the Art of Motorcycle Maintenance*, and the narrative section of this book, one is immediately struck by the similarities between schizophrenic and religious or mystical experience. Here, for example, is Morag Coate's description of the onset of her schizophrenic psychosis:

> I got up from where I had been sitting and moved into another room. Suddenly my whole being was filled with light and loveliness and with the upsurge of deeply moving feeling from within myself to meet and reciprocate the influence that flowed into me. I was in a state of the most vivid awareness and illumination. What can I say of it? A cloudless, cerulean blue sky of the mind, shot through with shafts of exquisite, warm, dazzling sunlight. In its first and most intense state it lasted perhaps half an hour. It seemed that some force or impulse from without were acting on me, looking into me; that I was in touch with a reality beyond my own; that I had made direct contact with the secret, ultimate source of life. What I had read of the accounts of others acquired suddenly a new meaning. It flashed across my mind, "This is what the mystics mean by the direct experience of God."[35]

Here a 21-year-old college student describes a state of heightened or mystical awareness in the weeks just prior to his being hospitalized:

> Before last week, I was quite closed about my emotions; then finally I owned up to them with another person. I began to speak without thinking beforehand and what came out showed an awareness of human beings and God. I could feel deeply about other people. We felt connected. The side which had been suppressing emotions did not seem the real one. I was in a higher and higher state of exhilaration and awareness. Things

people said had hidden meaning. They said things that applied to life. Everything that was real seemed to make sense. I had a great awareness of life, truth, and God. I went to church and suddenly all parts of the service made sense. My senses were sharpened. I became fascinated by the little insignificant things around me. There was an additional awareness of the world that would do artists, architects, and painters good. I ended up being much too emotional, but I felt very much at home with myself, very much at ease.[36]

Finally, there are my own mystical experiences. First there were my awesome visions. Then my seeing the world suddenly transformed into a place of exquisite beauty, aliveness, and innocence. Of particular importance was that memorable time when I sat in my health class where water safety and life saving techniques were being discussed, and delivered my "inspired" speech in which I recounted my experience of swimming down the rapids of the Nisqually River the previous summer in the form of a highly symbolic parable. What makes that incident so especially significant was the class's reaction to my speech. Carol, a girl who sat behind me, began a parable of her own; while Ken, a boy who sat next to me, asked me if I "had a God." Even the teacher, Mr. Talley, seemed deeply moved. *If my speech was nothing more than a symptom of a disease, then how could it have had such a profound effect on my teacher and classmates?* I think it is nearly self-evident that the experiences I had during my schizophrenic episode had far more in common with the kinds of experiences recorded by history's great mystics, saints, and prophets than to the sorts of experiences that occur as a result of an individual having an organic brain disease.

In marked contrast to the utter confusion and disorientation brought about by and characteristic of organic psychoses, one often encounters a certain coherence in the inner world of schizophrenics — a coherence which belongs more to the realm of mythology than to the realm of disease. Take, for example, the hallucinatory experiences of my schizophrenic friend Paul. When Paul was 28 years old, he began to hear "voices" which he took to be spirits. Among these so-called spirits were seven "good spirits" whom Paul believed to be members of an organization known as the White Brotherhood.

The spirits of the White Brotherhood told Paul they had conferred upon him the lofty mission of his someday becoming a messiah. They also informed Paul that he was on probation: that he had to undergo a period of rigorous spiritual training in order to qualify for his messiah status. The Brotherhood therefore began to instruct Paul in the tenets of an esoteric philosophy — a philosophy which to me seemed like nothing more than a hodgepodge of every occult book Paul had ever read. The Brotherhood also taught Paul various spiritual exercises. The purpose of these spiritual exercises were to help Paul ward off evil spirits or demons.

While Paul was training to become a messiah, he was also doing some very unmessiah-like things. He would walk into a restaurant, order and eat an expensive meal, and then leave without paying his bill.

Paul's aberrant ways infuriated the Brotherhood. They finally told him that if he ever left a restaurant again without paying his bill they would totally repudiate him.

When Paul was rash enough to disregard the Brotherhood's warning and walk out of another restaurant without paying his bill, he found that those "spirits" meant exactly what they said. The spirits of the White Brotherhood never spoke to Paul again. Paul's career as a would-be messiah then came to an abrupt end.

Unfortunately, however, in marked contrast to the Brotherhood, the evil spirits took a renewed interest in Paul. They began to torment him day and night.

In desperation, Paul contacted a Roman Catholic priest and pleaded with the priest to perform an exorcism on him. The priest stared at Paul with a look of helpless dismay, and told him that he was sorry but he was unable to help him.

When Paul first told me he had been contacted by spirits and that those spirits had given him some kind of spiritual mission, it was immediately apparent to me that Paul had suffered a schizophrenic breakdown. In fact, it had been painfully evident to me for well over a year that there was something seriously wrong with Paul. Yet at the same time it was very clear to me that Paul was not the victim of some extraneous disease process. Instead I saw in my friend's delusions and hallucinatory experiences an expression of his intrinsic humanity: of the peculiar whimsical way he had always looked at the world, of his value system, of his innate sensitivity and vulnerability, and of the tragic events that had simply overwhelmed him.

The case against schizophrenia being a disease can be summarized as follows:

First, in part I and part II of this book, I have shown in great detail precisely what causes schizophrenia. Since schizophrenia can be adequately explained without invoking the medical model, the medical model is therefore superfluous and should be abandoned.

Secondly, by its mere existence the amphetamine psychosis dramatically demonstrates the utter superfluousness of the medical model since it shows that if any normal person undergoes a process that is even superficially similar to a process that schizophrenics undergo — such as biochemical changes which either simulate panic or are a direct result of panic, a drastically narrowed focus of awareness, prolonged sleep deprivation, and a self-hypnotically induced trance-like state — the end result will be a person who is virtually indistinguishable from a schizophrenic. The amphetamine psychosis therefore demonstrates the correctness of my view on how schizophrenia is caused.

Third, in the previous three chapters, I have shown that not one shred of scientific evidence exists to substantiate the notion that schizophrenia is caused by a brain defect, a biochemical defect, or a genetic defect.

Fourth, in this present chapter, I have shown that all the available evidence indicates that schizophrenia is not — and cannot possibly be — an actual organic disease.

Why this utterly false and scientifically worthless notion that schizophrenia is a disease is so universally accepted will be the subject of the concluding chapter of this book.*

---

*For the inherent absurdity of the medical model see Appendix B: "On the Notion that Schizophrenia is Not One But Several Different Diseases."

# 6

# THE ANATOMY OF A DOGMA

The fact there is no vast difference between schizophrenia and normalcy helps explain why the exact opposite view is so universally accepted: so-called "normal" people can be every bit as deluded as schizophrenics.

Psychiatrists generally draw a sharp distinction between delusions and shared beliefs. However, that distinction is totally unwarranted because it is well known that delusions can be shared. For example, in part I of this book there is the interesting case history of Mr. Dolfuss, the wealthy manufacturer, whose delusion that he was the reincarnation of the Buddha was shared by his entire family, his closest friend, and his domestic servant. Adolf Hitler and Nazi Germany provide an even more striking example of shared delusions.

The delusions of normal people sometimes take the form of socially useful beliefs or ideologies. Moreover, due to their social usefulness, these ideologies tend to be far more resistant to change than the delusions of schizophrenic individuals.

It is very easy to understand why the medical model is useful to the psychiatric community. Psychiatrists could no more retain their identities as legitimate medical practitioners while admitting that schizophrenia and other mental disorders are not real diseases than the clergy could retain their identities as representatives of God while adopting atheism as their official creed. Can we really expect psychiatrists to give up the social prestige, special privileges, and high pay associated with medicine merely because there exists strong evidence indicating that schizophrenia and other functional mental disorders are not actual organic diseases?

However we must be charitable. Psychiatrists are not being con-sciously dishonest when they claim that schizophrenia is a physical disease much like cancer or diabetes. Their ideological commitments are such that they are simply incapable of seeing any facts that would undermine the medical model.

According to the eminent sociologist, Karl Mannheim, the concept of ideology refers to the fact that individuals or groups may become so intensely interest-bound to a situation that they are simply unable to acknowledge certain facts which would undermine their interests.[1]

As I will now show, the situation in which psychiatrists find themselves is such that they simply cannot question the validity of the medical model without in effect committing suicide; for once the protective ideological veil of the medical model is torn away, they will be revealed as total incompetents incapable of managing such mental disorders as schizophrenia in even a halfway enlightened or effective or humane way.

Although psychiatrists are perceived as medical specialists, nowadays with fewer and fewer exceptions, their training is virtually identical to that of an ordinary general practitioner. What specialized training psychiatrists do receive is limited largely to diagnosing the various mental disorders so that the proper drug can be prescribed.

It is wholly inappropriate for psychiatrists to take pride in their supposed "medical expertise" when the problems they usually deal with are clearly not of a medical nature. As far as preparing them to understand and deal with the problems of emotionally disturbed individuals is concerned, psychiatrists could just as profitably have devoted their time to studying astrology as medicine.

In fact, as far as increasing their ability to understand and empathize with their patients is concerned, medicine is the very worst subject that the psychiatrist could possibly study. In medical school the psychiatrist is taught to dehumanize the patient: to regard the patient as nothing more than a complex physiochemical machine. Certainly that sort of training is wholly justified if one intends to become a surgeon where any emotional involvement with the patient would have a disruptive effect on one's performance. But that sort of training is not appropriate in psychiatry where the ability to empathize with the patient is absolutely essential!*

Most psychiatrists have no knowledge at all of the actual social and psychological causes of schizophrenia and other mental disorders for the very simple reason that they firmly believe that such causes do not exist. What little training most psychiatrists have in psychology is limited to some very superficial instruction in the obsolete theories of Sigmund Freud — information which they do not utilize in their day-to-day practice.

In view of their lack of any useful training and lack of any insight that their training is totally useless, it is hardly surprising that psychiatrists generally do more harm than good. The kind of harm psychiatrists inflict on their patients can be put into three categories: physical, psychological, and social.

*Physical harm.* Psychiatrists routinely inflict brain damage on their

---

*In a controlled two-year follow-up study, Loren Mosher (1980, 1982) found untrained laymen were more effective psychotherapists than conventional psychiatrists.

patients by prescribing or administering potent neurotoxic drugs, by electroshock therapy, by insulin coma therapy, and by various forms of psychosurgery. Probably some of the brain atrophy or ventricular enlargement which many brain scan studies have revealed in schizophrenic and other mental patients is the result of drug therapy and electroshock.[2]*

In addition to the "therapies" mentioned above, here are some other lesser known atrocities which have been perpetrated against schizophrenics by psychiatrists:

*Hypothermia or refrigeration therapy.* This form of therapy involves immersing the patient in freezing water or some other kind of refrigerant for as long as 72 hours per session and lowering the patient's body temperature as much as 20 degrees Fahrenheit. As a result of one such experiment conducted by Drs. Douglas Goldman and Maynard Murray at the Longview State Hospital in Cincinnati, Ohio, in 1943, two patients died of pneumonia, while several of the survivors suffered prolonged mental retardation and physical decay bordering on cachexia.[3] Such Nazi-like experiments were pioneered by Drs. John H. Talbott and Kenneth J. Tillotson of Harvard University[4] and were still being conducted as recently as 1960.[5]

*Anoxia therapy.* This oxygen deprivation therapy was originated in 1938 by Harold E. Himwich and his associates at the Albany Medical College in Albany, New York. Dr. Himwich's procedure consists of having his patient breathe into a tight fitting face mask filled with pure oxygen where the oxygen is gradually displaced by nitrogen until the resulting lack of oxygen sends the patient into convulsions — a procedure which, as Himwich points out, has much in common with both insulin coma therapy and metrazol shock therapy.[6]

*Starvation therapy.* This irrational therapy consists of depriving the patient of all food for a period of up to 30 days in the belief that the biochemical changes that take place as a result of starvation have a curative effect on schizophrenia. This therapy was employed both in the United States and in the Soviet Union during the 1970s.[7]

*Sodium cyanide poisoning therapy.* There are at least two reports of psychiatrists using sodium cyanide to treat schizophrenic patients. The first account is of Drs. Loevenhart and Lorentz utilizing sodium cyanide in an attempt to treat catatonic patients — first in 1916, and then again in 1928.[8] The second instance was in a 1952 discussion on the effects of shock therapy where one discussant, Dr. Warren S. McCulloch, briefly

---

*Other factors contributing to the brain atrophy encountered in schizophrenic patients include: the wretched living conditions prevailing in most mental institutions, an inadequate diet, repeated and prolonged sleep deprivation, and the effects of prolonged emotional stress.

mentioned "a series of over sixty patients whom we decerebrated ten times with sodium cyanide."[9] What McCulloch meant by "decerebrated" is explained by Peter R. Breggin as follows:

> *Decerebration* is literally removal of the brain from its functional relationship to the body, as by severing the nerve connections between body and brain. It is done for experimental purposes in animal research. That McCulloch decerebrated his patients probably means that he poisoned them until their obliterated cerebral function mimicked laboratory animals with nonfunctional brains.[10]

*Psychological harm.* The psychological harm which psychiatrists inflict on their patients is a subject which is not often discussed. One reason why this topic is so seldom discussed has to do with the fact that the people who are the most knowledgeable on this subject — namely, the people who have been psychologically damaged by psychiatry — are rarely listened to or taken seriously.

The entire narrative section of this book illustrates the kind of psychological harm which psychiatry can cause.

Due to their ideologically induced blindness and lack of skill, most psychiatrists are so monumentally inept that they appear to be doing everything they possibly can to drive their patients crazy and keep them that way. Note, for example, how a psychiatrist will handle a person whose self-esteem has been so incredibly damaged that he must adopt the most extravagant delusions of grandeur in order to feel he's a person of any value or worth. A psychiatrist will tell such a person that an intrinsic part of his personality, as manifested in his beliefs, attitudes, and behavior, is nothing more than a symptom of a disease — in short, that he has a *sick mind*. That psychiatrist is in effect telling this person: "*You are a disease.*" Now I submit this isn't a very helpful thing to tell anyone — certainly not if that person's problems stem from low self-esteem!

Moreover, psychiatrists also undermine the psychological well-being of their patients by indoctrinating them with the demoralizing notion that their problems stem from an inborn biochemical defect, a condition which — although treatable by drugs — is essentially *incurable*. The psychiatrist will typically tell the patient that just as long as he continues taking his medication, he will be *almost* normal. That sort of talk will tend to instill in the patient a state of chronic passivity and despair. Needless to say, just as long as the patient continues to believe his psychiatrist he will never be able to muster the inner strength needed to overcome his problems.

In order to fully understand just how much psychological damage the notion that one has an innate mental defect can do to a person, one must realize that if *any* person is deprived of all hope of his or her ever developing into a person of any value or worth, that person will inevitably undergo a psychological decline characteristic of schizophrenia.

The ability to understand oneself is generally regarded as a mark of sanity while the lack of such self-insight is viewed as a sign of craziness. By dogmatically insisting that the causes of schizophrenia and other mental disorders are strictly biological, psychiatrists make it virtually impossible for their patients to achieve psychological insight into their problems. Indeed, psychiatrists consistently teach their patients to misunderstand themselves: to view certain aspects of their personalities as the meaningless and totally inscrutable symptoms of a frightening disease.

*Social harm.* Aside from their authority to prescribe drugs, the only skill most psychiatrists possess is their ability to paste dehumanizing labels on their patients.

Those labels *never* rub off. As a result of an individual being diagnosed as a "schizophrenic," "manic-depressive," and so forth by a psychiatrist, that person will end up with a permanent psychiatric record. That record will in turn become part of a computerized data bank whose contents will be made available to various government agencies, insurance companies, and to the individual's prospective employers.

And what is even worse, the psychiatric community seems to be doing everything they possibly can to increase the power of their labels to do social harm. For decades they have been spewing forth a steady stream of pseudoscientific poison or disinformation, to the effect that schizophrenics and others bearing similar psychiatric labels suffer from a number of biological *defects* — defects which make them fundamentally different from and inferior to other people.

In view of the above facts it is easy to understand why most employers would rather hire a convicted felon than anyone who has ever been near a psychiatrist.

As physicians, psychiatrists are supposedly bound by the Hippocratic oath which stipulates "first do no harm." However it is nearly impossible to practice psychiatry without doing considerable harm. How, for example, can a psychiatrist validate his identity as a medical doctor without labeling others as mentally sick — that is to say, without dehumanizing others and thoroughly destroying their identities?

As a social institution, psychiatry can be compared to the Ku Klux Klan and other racist or white supremacist organizations. In the late 1970s, when Alex Haley's *Roots* — a story dealing with the black peoples' struggle for human dignity — was shown as a movie series on television, many white racists and neo-fascists were outraged because they felt the television series "unduly ennobled the Negro." Many psychiatrists feel much the same way about Joanne Greenberg's *I Never Promised You a Rose Garden* and Mark Vonnegut's *Eden Express* as the Ku Klux Klan and neo-Nazis felt about *Roots*. Just as *Roots* undermined white racism by presenting the blacks in a favorable light, *Eden Express* and *Rose Garden* undermine psychiatry's attempt to dehumanize the schizophrenic: in reading those books one gets the truly subversive idea that the way schizophrenics think and feel is not that different from the way anyone else thinks or feels. Therefore in order to defend the notion that schizophrenics are defective, biologically inferior specimens devoid of all human attributes, psychiatrists must claim that neither Greenberg nor Vonnegut could possibly have been schizophrenic. Here, for example, are the words of Solomon H. Snyder, a Johns Hopkins University psychiatrist who has won international renown for his advocacy of the dopamine hypothesis:

> Anyone who has ever worked with schizophrenics for even a few weeks knows that neither Vonnegut nor Deborah in *Rose Garden* was schizophrenic. There is nothing joyous, positive, romantic, or productively creative about this disease. It destroys lives. It represents a fundamental abnormality in how the brain works.[11]

Just as Klansmen must view blacks as doltish primitive niggers in order to bolster their belief that they are members of a superior race, psychiatrists must view schizophrenics as inhuman brain-damaged zombies in order to confirm their view of themselves as legitimate medical specialists treating actual organic diseases.

The notion that schizophrenia is an organic illness is a wonderfully cost-effective concept, for it is much easier and cheaper to treat schizophrenics like *defective objects* than it is to treat them like human beings. With mental clinics as crowded and understaffed as they are, most psychiatrists have neither the time nor the inclination to understand their patients' psychological problems. It is easy to understand why most psychiatrists are so infatuated with the medical model. It simplifies everything. It makes their job much easier. All they need do is write a prescription for Haldol or Thorazine, toss it at the patient, and say, "Take your pills, sickie." There is no need for them to try to understand the social and psychological causes of their patients' problems, for in their view such causes simply don't exist!

However, psychiatrists are not the only ones who benefit from the medical model. The medical model is also a great benefit and source of comfort to the schizophrenic's parents for it absolves them of all responsibility for causing their child's mental breakdown. What a relief it is for these parents to be able to believe their son or daughter's problems stem solely from a physical disease — an illness for which no one is responsible! Consequently, as soon as the child is diagnosed as schizophrenic, the parents usually conclude that all the family's problems can be localized exclusively within the patient. They are sane, he or she is sick, and the doctor will take care of everything. Those parents can therefore stop worrying about their own mental problems and start worrying about their son or daughter.*

The medical model also helps society in general by providing a disguised form of social control. For example, what do we do with people who walk down the street with paper sacks over their head, or who claim they are Jesus Christ, or who cower before imaginary enemies? While such behavior violates social norms and is disturbing to others, such actions are still not illegal. Therefore we cannot lawfully stop people from engaging in such socially deviant behavior. However, we can "help" these troublesome people by locking them behind bars in "mental hospitals" and by socially degrading them "for their own good" since these people being "mentally ill" cannot possibly know what's in their own best interest. Thus we can get rid of our social nuisances in much the same way Russia has been known to take care of its political dissidents. And we can feel very altruistic about doing so too. After all, we are fighting "mental illness."

Moreover, the medical model with its concepts of "mental health" and "mental illness" also helps stabilize society's norms by providing a cryptoethical standard for evaluating human moral conduct. What we have here is an uncritical validation of society's taboos and moral prejudices so absolute as to suggest they are one and the same with the laws of the universe.

Consider what happens when a young child is brutally raped and murdered. In such instances do people usually say in a detached clinical voice, "Someday a medicine will be found that will cure such sick individuals"? or do they say in a voice choked with rage and moral indignation, "That vicious animal is really *sick!*"?

"Mental illness" simply means sin. Since science and medicine now have much more prestige than do religion or theology, the concepts of mental health and mental illness are now much more effective in manipulating people than are the concepts of sin and righteousness.

Still another reason why the medical model is so universally accepted is that it is in perfect accord with the prevailing mechanical *Weltanschaung*. However, as numerous authors including Whitehead,[12] Burtt,[13] Marcuse,[14] and Mumford[15] have pointed out, the mechanical world view has its origins in prescientific sources and is totally at odds with every major scientific advance that has occurred since the mid-nineteenth century.

---

*These parents have formed an influential organization, the National Alliance for the Mentally Ill, which boycotts — and sometimes even harasses — psychiatrists who aren't strict medical model adherents.

Throughout all of recorded history powerless individuals and groups have been oppressed and dehumanizing myths (racist, sexist, etc.) have been constructed in order to justify this oppression.*

It is hard to imagine a more powerless group of persons than people who are schizophrenic. In view of their extreme powerlessness — and even helplessness — and in view of how *disturbing* these people are to others, is it any wonder that schizophrenics have been the victims of dehumanizing myths?

The notion that persons who have been labeled "schizophrenic" are somehow biologically different from or inferior to other people is nothing more than a dehumanizing myth — another sad example of man's inhumanity to man — a myth which the psychiatric community has a huge vested interest in perpetuating.

It is a very sad fact that people who have undergone schizophrenic episodes are often the most fanatical supporters of the medical model. The reasons why this is so are complex and need to be analyzed in some detail.

During the process of recovering from a schizophrenic episode, a person is in a state of hypersuggestibility, and is apt to accept the first plausible explanation that anyone gives him in regard to his recent mental problems. Moreover, as this person recovers from his psychotic episode, everyone around him (his family, psychiatrist, and psychiatric personnel) are constantly pressuring him to accept the notion that his problems stem from his having a diseased mind. This person is repeatedly told that it is a mark of sanity for him to be able to recognize that he has a sick mind. He is also told that his inability (or unwillingness) to do so indicates a lack of insight: an infallible proof that he is still crazy. Since most recovered schizophrenics have an overwhelming need to appear as sane as possible — both in their own eyes and in the eyes of others — they end up wholeheartedly accepting the medical model.

However, because "schizophrenia" is not an extraneous disease process but an intrinsic part of the individual's personality, no schizophrenic can accept the medical model without feeling devalued as a person.

Yet paradoxically, the fact that the schizophrenic feels devalued in accepting the medical model is one of the factors which causes him to cling to the medical model with such tenacity. In order to understand

---

*In this regard it should come as no surprise that a number of studies have shown that individuals from the lower classes and members of racial minorities are more frequently diagnosed schizophrenic than are upper- and middle-class white persons, while women are more likely than men to be labeled mentally ill. See Hill 1983, Chesler 1972.

why the schizophrenic is so eager to accept a degraded self-image we must keep in mind that schizophrenia is largely caused by a feeling of intense self-loathing, and when the schizophrenic recovers and looks back on his past folly, his self-hatred is redoubled. Like a guilt-ridden Christian who falls abjectly to his knees and confesses he is a miserable sinner, the schizophrenic emerging from his psychosis will in effect prostrate himself before what he perceives as the godlike authority of medical science, and confess he is a wretched sickie. Again like the Christian, the schizophrenic seeks redemption. Due both to his self-hatred and to his being led to believe that his ability to recognize that he is ill proves his sanity, the schizophrenic feels that by constantly berating himself and telling himself how sick he is he is making himself a saner person.

But complete sanity can only come through self-understanding. Unfortunately, many schizophrenic individuals do not want to have any awareness of the actual causes of their mental problems since such knowledge can be very painful. These individuals therefore cling to the medical model for much the same reason which had formerly induced them to cling to their delusional beliefs: to keep themselves from being aware of certain aspects of their personalities which they find thoroughly and dreadfully disturbing.

Not only does the medical model allow the schizophrenic to evade the burden of self-knowledge, it also allows him to evade the burden of responsibility. It permits the schizophrenic to disclaim all responsibility for his actions — to commit the most outrageous acts, and exclaim with a note of aggrieved innocence: "Don't blame me — my illness made me do it." The notion that the schizophrenic is the victim of a relentless disease over which he has no control also absolves him of all responsibility of making an honest and sustained effort to overcome his problems and justifies his leading a totally nonproductive parasitic existence.

Finally, the notion that schizophrenics suffer from an irreversible biological defect furnishes those people with a perfect pretext for spending the rest of their lives wallowing in self-pity.

But if those people don't have the presence of mind to reject all the vicious and dehumanizing nonsense coming from the psychiatric community, then they are pitiful persons indeed!

# APPENDIX A

# A NOTE ON HOW NEUROLEPTIC DRUGS WORK

In order to understand how neuroleptic drugs suppress schizophrenic symptoms we must first understand how schizophrenic symptoms are brought about.

The symptoms of schizophrenia are brought about by intense mental anguish or emotional pain: by a combination of such feelings as anxiety, panic, guilt, shame, self-loathing, and eerie awe. How such feelings produce schizophrenic symptoms is illustrated by the case history of an individual whom I will call Clyde.

Clyde is a largely recovered schizophrenic individual in his early thirties who on rare occasions is still symptomatic. Clyde works in a firm where most of the employees are women, many of whom are young and attractive.

While at work Clyde seldom talks to anyone and never smiles. He has, moreover, the bad habit of staring fixedly at the thighs of his female coworkers — a habit which makes him the butt of much ridicule and gossip.

Many of Clyde's coworkers openly mock him. Some of the women adopt sexually provocative poses whenever Clyde looks at them while they and their friends snicker contemptuously. The women constantly gossip about Clyde while the men constantly torment him with cruel jeering remarks.

Clyde can feel hostility and contempt radiating from his coworkers like heat from a stove. Every time he walks into the company cafeteria he feels excruciating emotional pain — pain which he feels deep down in his gut. In walking into that room he feels that he is totally vulnerable: that all his hidden weaknesses are known to everyone and are being openly discussed and laughed at.

In large part, Clyde's perception of the dislike and contempt in which he is held by his coworkers causes him pain because it activates his feelings of self-loathing. Clyde can never forgive himself for being a total failure with women. He can never forget the fact that he is over thirty years old and has never had a girlfriend in his entire life. That fact causes him to view himself as a "sex-starved loser" who has led "a meaningless, pitiful existence." Whenever he looks into the smirking, sneering faces of

233

his coworkers, his feelings of self-loathing become so intense that he is in a state of absolute agony. At such times he is in such emotional pain that in his mind the boundaries between his subjective feelings and external reality tend to become blurred.

Once while sitting at a table in the cafeteria in a state of great mental anguish, Clyde glanced over at a middle-aged woman who was reading an article in *Newsweek* magazine at a table next to his. The woman was holding the magazine so that its contents were clearly visible to him. When Clyde looked at the magazine the woman was reading, the title of the magazine article seemed to leap out at him: THE VALIDATION OF A SEX PERVERT.

For several seconds Clyde gaped at that weird magazine article title in utter astonishment, unable to fully believe what he was seeing was real. He was very much aware of the fact that he was under a great deal of emotional stress, and he had a strong feeling that his altered mental state was somehow distorting his perceptions. Moreover, the grim thought occurred to him that if only the emotional pain he was then experiencing was a little more intense, he would be totally convinced that that woman was holding the magazine for his benefit in order to tell him that she thought he was some kind of sex pervert.

After staring for several seconds at the bizarre title in the magazine the woman was holding, Clyde got up from his table and looked over the woman's shoulder directly down at the magazine. Upon coming closer to the magazine, he found that the title changed from THE VALIDATION OF A SEX PERVERT to THE VINDICATION OF A SEX PERVERT. After staring at that title for several seconds at close range, Clyde concluded somewhat reluctantly that what he was seeing must be real. However, to his utter dismay, upon picking up the July 18, 1983, issue of *Newsweek* magazine in the public library a few days later, Clyde found that the title of the article was THE VINDICATION OF A SEX PIONEER.

The above incident graphically illustrates how schizophrenic symptoms can be brought about by intense emotional pain. Clyde's intense feelings of anxiety, shame, and self-loathing caused his perceptions to be distorted to the point to where he saw the word pioneer as *pervert*. (Careful note should be taken of the following facts: Clyde had not been taking any recreational or psychiatric drugs, had perfect vision and superior intelligence, and had scrutinized that magazine article title for several seconds at very close range.) As Clyde himself realized, had his emotional pain been a little more intense his thinking would have been distorted to the point to where he would have firmly believed that that woman was holding that magazine in her hands for the express purpose of letting him know that she thought he was a sex pervert. Had his emotional pain been even more intense, Clyde would have assaulted that woman either physically or verbally.

Since I have explained how schizophrenic symptoms are brought about, I am now in a position to explain how neuroleptic drugs suppress these symptoms.

Neuroleptic drugs achieve their therapeutic affect by causing a flattening of emotion or psychic indifference (the classic lobotomy effect) by blockading or disrupting dopamine neurotransmission in the emotion-regulating centers of the brain.[1] These drugs suppress schizophrenic symptoms by reducing the intensity of such feelings as anxiety, guilt, shame, self-loathing, and so forth.

However, neuroleptic drugs do not cure schizophrenia, for they have no effect on the underlying causes of that disorder. Nor are those drugs unique in their ability to suppress schizophrenic symptoms. Like neuroleptic drugs, ethyl alcohol is also effective in reducing the individual's emotional pain. Furthermore, ethyl alcohol was successfully utilized by Harry Stack Sullivan in treating schizophrenic patients as long ago as the 1920s.

Finally, we must bear in mind that not all neuroleptic drugs have a sedative effect. Indeed, some neuroleptic drugs (Haldol, Prolixin) work by *increasing* the patient's mental anguish!

Paul, a schizophrenic friend of mine, explains how these drugs work:

> When they injected me with Prolixin I felt everything that was me — my ability to think, my ability to remember, and so forth — begin to dissolve. The only thing I was aware of was what God-awful *agony* I was in! Sure that drug cleared up my delusions all right. But they could have achieved the same effect had they shoved burning slivers of wood under my fingernails.

Paul's explanation seems perfectly plausible in view of the well-known fact that schizophrenic patients tend to shed their delusions whenever they are running a high fever. Patients running a high fever and patients taking such hellish drugs as Prolixin have something in common: both are in agony and must put their delusions on hold while they expend all their mental and physical energy just to hold themselves together.*

---

*As Chamberlin 1978 points out, much of the supposed "improvement" that takes place as a result of drug treatment in institutional settings stems from the sheer hideousness of the effects of these drugs and from the patients' conscious efforts to act in a way that will make a favorable impression on the staff so that the dosage of their medication will not be raised.

# APPENDIX B

## ON THE NOTION THAT SCHIZOPHRENIA IS NOT ONE BUT SEVERAL DIFFERENT DISEASES

In recent years the notion that schizophrenia is not one but several different diseases has become increasingly popular among psychiatric researchers. One of the leading proponents of this now fashionable view is T. J. Crow of Great Britain. In 1980, Crow published an article arguing that there are two different kinds of schizophrenia.[1] According to Crow, the first type of schizophrenia is caused by changes in dopaminergic neurotransmission, and is characterized by positive symptoms: delusions, hallucinations, and thought disorder. The second type of schizophrenia is caused by structural changes in the brain, and is characterized by negative symptoms: blunted emotions and poverty of speech. Unlike the first, this second type of schizophrenia is not responsive to treatment by neuroleptic drugs and may be irreversible.

Another more recent attempt to split schizophrenia into two distinct syndromes has been made by Martha E. Shenton and her associates at Harvard.[2] Believing schizophrenia to be caused by brain pathology localized in the temporal lobes, Shenton distinguishes between left and right temporal-lobe schizophrenia. According to Shenton, right temporal-lobe schizophrenics have more structural brain abnormalities, respond less favorably to neuroleptic drugs, and show more positive symptoms than do left temporal-lobe schizophrenics.

However, are the topologies of Shenton and Crow anything more than pseudoscientific fantasies? Note, for example, the inconsistencies in the data supporting the two topologies. In Shenton's topology, positive symptoms are associated with profound structural abnormalities in the brain and a poor response to neuroleptic drugs. It is the exact opposite in Crow's topology: positive symptoms are associated with the virtual absence of structural brain changes and a favorable response to neuroleptic drugs.

Numerous other arbitrary and whimsical attempts have been made to split schizophrenia into biologically distinct subtypes. Groups of schizophrenic patients have been differentiated from each other on the basis of such biological variables as platelet monoamine oxidase activity, urine phenylethylamine concentration, brain noradrenaline concentration, abnormalities on computerized tomography, lateralization asymmetries, and the presence or absence of tardive dyskinesia.[3]

However, the popular notion that schizophrenia consists of several distinct biological disorders has no solid empirical basis. Instead, all the available evidence clearly points to the unitary nature of schizophrenia. All the categories which have generally been used to discriminate different groups of schizophrenics, including the traditional subtypes of simple, hebephrenic, catatonic and paranoid, and the "process-reactive" dichotomy, have been shown to be nothing more than artificial abstractions. For example, it is well known that the four subtypes of schizophrenia are not stable: that catatonics sometimes become paranoids; paranoids, hebephrenics; and vice versa.[4] Likewise, seemingly "incurable" process schizophrenics — that is, individuals who have been schizophrenic for thirty or forty years — have been known to make complete recoveries.[5] Finally, individuals who had given every indication of being reactive schizophrenics — that is, exhibiting acute onset, good premorbid adjustment, and precipitating cause — have gone on to become chronic schizophrenics living a vegetative existence.[6]

Rather than being an overly broad category lumping together several distinct syndromes, there is reason to believe schizophrenia may be too narrow or restrictive a concept since no clear-cut distinctions can be drawn between it and other psychiatric disorders such as paranoia, reactive psychosis, multiple personality, and manic-depression.* The reasons for regarding schizophrenia and manic-depression as a single clinical entity are especially compelling. First, there are well-authenticated cases of one identical twin being schizophrenic while the other was manic-depressive.[7] Second, it is known that the diagnostic categories of schizophrenia and manic-depression are not stable: that schizophrenics sometimes become manic-depressive, and vice-versa.[8] Third, typical schizophrenic symptoms such as delusions and hallucinations,[9] catatonia,[10] paranoid ideation,[11] and blunted affect[12] are also to be found in manic-depressive patients. Fourth, there are studies which show there are no distinct boundaries between schizophrenia and manic-depression — that the two disorders tend to overlap and merge with each other.[13] In this regard, the first two editions of the *Diagnostic and Statistical Manual* recognized a clinical entity sharing features in common with both schizophrenia and manic-depression: schizoaffective schizophrenia. More recently, in DSM-III, schizoaffective is no longer recognized as a subtype of schizophrenia, but as an independent clinical entity midway between schizophrenia and manic-depression. However, DSM-III-R recognizes more than one type of schizoaffective disorder: one type which is closer to schizophrenia, and one type which is closer to manic-depression.

---

*Manic-depression is now often referred to as bipolar affective disorder.

Currently, in DSM-IV, these two subtypes of schizoaffective disorder have been changed to subtypes which have depressive and bipolar features — a change which in effect changes the schizoaffective disorder (originally a subtype of schizophrenia) to a subtype of manic-depression. Finally, there are studies which show that lithium, a drug used in treating manic-depression, is also effective in treating schizophrenia.[14] And there are also studies which show that the drugs used in treating schizophrenia — neuroleptic drugs — are equally effective in treating manic-depression.[15]

There are also striking similarities between schizophrenia and multiple personality disorder. Like schizophrenics, people with multiple personalities often have delusions and hallucinations.[16] Consequently, those people are often diagnosed as schizophrenic. For example, in *Multiple Personalities, Allied Disorders, and Hypnosis*, Eugene L. Bliss reports that out of a group of 35 patients diagnosed as schizophrenic, 20 were found to have multiple personalities.[17] Furthermore, Bliss also notes that many people with multiple personalities would also qualify for a DSM-III diagnosis of schizophrenia.[18]

Contrary to what most psychiatrists would have us believe, schizophrenics *do* have split personalities. The hallucinations of these individuals represent split-off portions of their personalities. Note, for example, the highly personalized hallucinatory experiences of my friend Paul: his escapades involving the seven spirits of the White Brotherhood and his relationship with the ethereal, Athena-like personage. Paul's hallucinatory companions had personalities every bit as distinct as any encountered in case histories of people with multiple personalities.

Finally, environmentally induced trauma and autohypnosis are important in the etiologies of both schizophrenia and multiple personality disorder.

To sum up: Not one shred of evidence supports the currently popular notion that schizophrenia is not one but several different psychiatric disorders. Furthermore, as I have shown, all the available evidence points to the unitary nature of schizophrenia. Moreover, since no clear-cut distinctions can be drawn between schizophrenia and a number of other psychiatric syndromes, such labels as schizophrenia, paranoia, manic-depression, and so forth, are mere artificial abstractions obscuring the unitary nature of madness. Indeed, I would go even further than that: the madness-sanity dichotomy is itself a mere artificial convention obscuring the fundamental unity of the human mind.

Trying to understand schizophrenia and its causes from a strictly medical or biological perspective will always fail: it is like trying to understand Judaism by analyzing blood or urine samples taken from Jews.[19]

The current popularity of the notion that schizophrenia is more than one disease reflects a profound crises in contemporary schizophrenia research. For more than one hundred years psychiatric researchers have been putting forth theories in regard to the biological causes of schizophrenia, and, as inexorably as the earth spins on its axis and the sun appears over the horizon each morning, those theories have always failed. Slowly and gradually the sobering realization has dawned upon the psychiatric community that any and all theories pertaining to schizophrenia *as a whole* must inevitably fail; for if any one biological defect is pointed to as *the* cause of schizophrenia, the overwhelming majority of schizophrenics will always be found not to manifest that particular defect. Since no one particular defect can possibly explain schizophrenia as a whole, the notion has arisen that schizophrenia must be many different diseases caused by a variety of biological defects.

According to the eminent philosopher of science, Karl R. Popper, what distinguishes a good scientific theory from metaphysics and pseudoscience is not so much that the former is capable of being verified, but rather the possibility of it being falsified or refuted. It is the testability or refutability of a theory that makes it possible for it to be replaced by a more adequate theory. Testability or falsifiability is therefore the essential element that makes scientific advance possible. As Popper points out, even an astrologer can make predictions that can be verified in a vague or general sort of way. But an astrologer will never allow his predictions to be falsified, for he will always have an explanation as to why his predictions didn't turn out. However, according to Popper, it is precisely the astrologer's refusal to allow his predictions to be falsified that marks him as a pseudoscientist.[20]

At present, due to the widely held doctrine that schizophrenia is not one but several different diseases, psychiatric researchers have rendered their theories about schizophrenia incapable of being refuted. For example, if I were to put forth the whimsical theory that schizophrenia is a brain disease caused by an allergy to cats, and some other researcher were to provide case histories of schizophrenics who had never been near cats in their entire lives, I could always save my theory from being refuted by merely claiming that some types of schizophrenia are caused by an allergy to cats and some are not.* There can therefore be as many types of schizophrenia as there are theories about schizophrenia.

---

*Of an equally whimsical hypothesis, T.J. Crow 1994 writes: "The hypothesis that prenatal exposure to influenza is the cause of schizophrenia is easy to test and, if in error, to eliminate. The hypothesis that some (but not all) epidemics of influenza are responsible for a proportion (unspecified) of schizophrenic illnesses (of indeterminate type) is not. It has generated confusion."

# NOTES

The complete facts of publication are contained in the Bibliography. Only shortened forms of reference will be given here — usually the author's surname and date of publication.

## PART I A RECIPE FOR MADNESS

## 1. THE ENVIRONMENT OF THE SCHIZOPHRENIC

1. Szasz 1976.

2. Laing and Esterson 1970.

3. Sarbin and Mancuso 1980.

4. Other authors who reject the medical model include: Becker 1964; Boyle 1990; Braginsky, Braginsky and Ring 1982; Breggin 1991; Chamberlin 1978; Chesler 1972; Cooper 1967; Foucault 1973; Fullinwider 1982; Goffman 1961; Hill 1983; Jenner, Monteiro, Zagalo-Cardoso, et al 1993; Leifer 1969; Rosenhan 1973; Scheff 1966; Schrag 1978; Siebert 1996; Ullman and Krasner 1975.

5. Meyer 1906.

6. Bateson, Jackson, Haley, et al 1956; Haley 1959.

7. Mishler and Waxler 1968.

8. Lidz, Fleek and Cornelison 1965.

9. Bowen 1960; Wynne, Ryckoff, Day, et al 1958.

10. Laing and Esterson 1970; Scott and Ashworth 1967.

11. Delay, Deniker and Green 1962.

12. Stierlin 1963.

13. Alanen 1966.

14. Laing and Esterson 1970 pp. 31-50.

15. Brody 1959 pp. 388-389.

16. Lidz, Fleck and Cornelison 1965 pp. 163-170.

17. Wynne and Singer 1963.

18. Singer and Wynne 1965.

19. Laing 1967.

20. Siirala 1963.

21. Mishler and Waxler 1968 p. 288.

22. Bateson, Jackson, Haley 1956 pp. 212-213.

23. Scott and Ashworth 1969 p. 13.

24. Ibid. p. 13.

25. Ibid. p. 13.

26. Ibid. pp. 15, 29.

27. Ibid. pp. 25-31.

28. Dr. Lidz has won the *Frieda Fromm-Reichmann Award* of the American Academy of Psychoanalysis, the *William C. Menninger Award* of the American College of Physicians, the *Stanley R. Dean Award* of the American College of Psychiatrists, and the *Van Giesen Award* of the New York Psychiatric Institute. He has also won the *Salmon Lecture Medal*.

29. Lidz 1973 pp. 7-8.

30. Lidz, Fleck and Cornelison 1965 p. 136.

31. Lidz 1973 p. 45.

32. Ibid. pp. 31-32.

33. Ibid. p. 100.

34. Ibid. p. 100.

35. Ibid. p. 100.

36.    Ibid. p. 100.

37.    Ibid. p. 48.

38.    Ibid. p. 48.

39.    Ibid. p. 33.

40.    Ibid. pp. 48, 75.

41.    Ibid. p. 74.

42.    Jackson and Weakland 1959; Hill 1955 pp. 125-129.

43.    Seales 1958.

44.    Wynne and Singer 1963 p. 197.

45.    Pines 1979 p. 57.

## 2. THE INNER WORLD OF THE SCHIZOPHRENIC

1.    My exposition of Sullivan's thought is derived from the following sources: Chapman and Chapman 1980; Mullahy 1967; Sullivan 1953; 1956.

2.    Mullahy p. 493.

3.    Sullivan 1953 p. 134.

4.    Although this is largely a description of my own experience I have also been influenced by Silvano Arieti's very eloquent description of prepsychotic panic. See Arieti 1974 pp. 120-121.

5.    Chapman and Chapman 1980 pp. 111-112.

6.    Hill 1955 pp. 46-47; Lu 1962 pp. 226-229.

7.    Chapman and Chapman 1980 p. 112.

8.    Ibid. p. 112.

9.    Fairbairn 1952 pp. 65-67.

10.    Guntrip 1968 p. 64.

11.    Ibid. p. 65.

12. I myself was virtually unable to get any sleep in the six or seven weeks immediately prior to the onset of my psychosis. Moreover, prolonged sleep deprivation has been the pattern in every schizophrenic person I have ever talked to and is mentioned in the autobiographies of various schizophrenics including: Boisen 1960; Schreber 1955; Sechehaye 1951; Vonnegut 1975.

    For understandable reasons it is extremely difficult to obtain hard scientific data on the sleep disorders of schizophrenics *prior* to the onset of their psychosis. Nevertheless, Kupfer and his associates have found significant sleep disorders in acute schizophrenics especially in the waxing period of their psychosis. See Kupfer, Wyatt, Scott, et al 1970.

13. Selye 1978, chapter 5.

14. "In humans . . . increasing brain catecholamines (dopamine, noradrenaline) decreases REM sleep, while decreasing brain catecholamines increases REM sleep." Quoted from Rubin and Poland 1977 p. 93.

15. Ibid. p. 95; Bliss, Clark and West 1959; Brauchi and West 1959.

16. Boisen 1971 p. 79.

17. Ibid. pp. 79-80.

18. Bateson, Jackson, Haley, et al 1956 p. 223.

19. Shor 1959 p. 585.

20. Ibid. p. 595.

21. Ibid. p. 596.

22. Ibid. p. 597.

23. Quoted in Fullinwider 1982 p. 144.

## PART II. THE MAKING OF A SCHIZOPHRENIC

## 1. MOTHER

1. Melges 1968 p. 105.

2. Trethowan 1968.

3. Melges 1968 pp. 100, 105-106.

4. During the first year of my life, my mother's social circumstances were very different from those prevailing in the first years of my siblings' lives. During the first year of my sister's life, my parents were living together; while a few weeks after my brother was born, my mother moved to Troy, Texas, near Camp Hood where my father was stationed. However, just prior to my birth, my parents were separated. This period of separation lasted for an entire year. During this period of separation my mother worried incessantly about my father: about his wild behavior which was always getting him into trouble, and about the constant possibility of his being sent into combat.

I think that during this anxiety-ridden year of my mother's life, many of the anxious feelings she had concerning my father were transferred onto me and that this had some kind of lasting effect. I believe this to be so because in later years whenever my father upset my mother, she would always begin worrying about *me*.

## 2. THE WITCH DOCTOR'S CURSE

1. Letter to author dated November 9, 1992.

## 9. I RECEIVE MY LABEL

1. Instead of having a tranquilizing effect, many neuroleptic drugs actually *increase* the patient's anxiety. This was true in my case. Taking Stelazine made me very nervous. However, in my naivete, it never occurred to me that my increased nervousness was caused by the drug I was taking. Rather, I thought I was taking that drug in order to control my nervousness. Consequently, I began to view myself as a "nerve case" — which certainly didn't help my self esteem.

## 10. RECAPITULATION, ANALYSIS, AND CONCLUSION

1. Arieti 1974 pp. 574-575.

2. Ibid. pp. 575-576.

3. Bick and Kinsbourne 1987.

4. Ibid. p. 225.

5. Ibid. p. 225.

6. Johnson 1978 pp. 53, 116.

7. Bentall and Slade 1985; Young, Bentall, Slade, et al 1986.

8.    Mott, Small and Anderson 1965.

9.    Johnson 1978 p. 53.

10.   Lidz 1973 pp. 57-58.

11.   American Psychiatric Association 1994 p. 285.

12.   Some of my favorite biblical self-contradictions are as follows. Mark 1:12, 13 tells us that Jesus was tempted in the wilderness: "And *immediately* [after his baptism] the spirit driveth him into the wilderness. And he was there in the wilderness forty days tempted of Satan." But John 2:1, 2 tells us that Jesus was *not* tempted in the wilderness: "And the *third day* [after his baptism] there was a marriage in Cana of Galilee. . . . And both Jesus was called and his disciples to the marriage." Some of the most serious contradictions are found in the four strikingly different accounts of Christ's resurrection. One such contradiction relates to what was found at Christ's sepulcher. Luke 24:4 states that *two* angels were seen at the sepulcher *standing up*, while Matthew 28:2, 5 tells us that *only one* angel was seen and he was *sitting down*. John 20:11, 12 tells us that *two* angels were seen within the sepulcher, while Mark 16:5 states that *only one* angel was seen within the sepulcher. Another contradiction relates to how the women reacted to the news of Christ's resurrection. According to Matthew 28:8 and Luke 24:9 the women immediately told the disciples the news of Christ's resurrection, while Mark 16:8 states: "And they . . . fled from the sepulcher; for they trembled and were amazed: *neither said they anything to any man*; for they were afraid." Some of these biblical self-contradictions are unbelievably blatant. For example, Exodus 33:11 states: "And the Lord spoke unto Moses face to face, as a man speaketh unto his friend" while only nine verses later in this very same chapter (verse 20) we read: "And he said, Thou canst not see my face: for there shall no man see me and live." From Matthew 19:26 we learn "with God all things are possible," while Judges 1:19 tells us that God "could not drive out the inhabitants of the valley, because they had chariots of iron." There are also innumerable doctrinal self-contradictions in the Bible. One of the most famous of these is Paul and James' clash over justification. Paul (Romans 3:28): "A man is justified by faith without the works of the law." James (James 2:24): "by works is a man justified, and not by faith only."

      That the Bible contains contradictions has been widely known for at least 250 years. Yet religious people will flatly deny that the Bible contains any contradictions. Clearly schizophrenics are not the only people who ignore reality!

## PART III. THE MEDICAL MODEL REEXAMINED

## 1. PSYCHIATRY'S GIANT STEP BACKWARD

1.  Quoted from Rodgers 1982 p. 85.

2.  For Thomas Szasz's views on the repressive nature of psychiatry see: Szasz 1970. For Szasz's views on schizophrenia see: Szasz 1976. For Szasz's views on mental illness in general see: Szasz 1974.

## 2. SCHIZOPHRENIA AS A BRAIN DEFECT

1.  Torrey and Peterson 1976.

2.  Donahue Transcript p. 5.

3.  Ibid. p. 14.

4.  Weinberger, Wagner and Wyatt 1983 p. 205.

5.  Of the twelve studies which reveal no differences in the ventricular size of schizophrenics and normal controls, eight of these studies involve the use of computerized tomography while the other four studies involve the use of magnetic resonance imaging. The eight studies utilizing computerized tomography include: Benes, Sunderland, Pearson, et al 1982; Coffman, Mefferd, Golden et al 1981; Glück, Radü, Mundt et al 1980; Jernigan, Zatz, Moses, et al 1982; Nasrallah, Jacoby and McCalley-Whitters 1981; Shima, Kanba, Masuda et al 1985; Trimble and Kingsley 1978; Yates, Jacoby and Andreasen 1987. The four studies utilizing magnetic resonance imaging include: Johnstone, Crow, MacMillan, et al 1986; Matthew and Partain 1985; Smith, Baumgartner and Calderon 1987; Smith, Calderon, Ravichandran, et al 1984.

6.  Jernigan, Zatz, Moses, et al 1982.

7.  Reveley 1985 p. 367.

8.  Maser and Keith 1983 p. 271.

9.  Ibid. p. 271.

10. Yates, Jacoby and Andreasen 1987.

11. Smith, Baumgartner and Calderon 1987; Smith, Calderon, Ravichandran, et al 1984.

12. Matthew and Partain 1985.

13. Johnstone, Crow, MacMillan, et al 1986.

14. Maser and Keith 1983 p. 268.

15. Geschwind and Galaburda 1985a p. 450.

16. Geschwind and Galaburda 1985b p. 521.

17. Andreasen, Olsen, Dennert, et al 1982.

18. Farmer, Jackson, McGuffin, et al 1987.

19. Nasrallah, Kuperman, Hamra, et al 1983.

20. Pandurangi, Dewan, Boucher, et al 1986.

21. Owens, Johnstone, Crow, et al 1985.

22. Obiols, Marcos and Salamero 1987.

23. Bankier 1985.

24. Owens, Johnstone, Crow, et al 1985 p. 36.

25. Obiols, Marcos and Salamero 1987 p. 201.

26. Pandurangi, Dewan, Boucher, et al 1986 p. 166.

27. Bankier 1985 p. 244.

28. Morihisa and Weinberger 1986.

29. Andreasen 1986.

30. Nasrallah 1986.

31. Cutting 1985.

32. For example, see: Adler and Waldo 1991; Scheibel and Conrad 1993; Torry 1991.

33. Mednick 1970.

34. Schmajuk 1987.

35.  Scheibel and Kovelman 1981; Kovelman and Scheibel 1984.

36.  Weinberger, Wagner and Wyatt 1983 p. 195.

37.  Altshuler, Conrad, Kovelman and Scheibel 1987.

38.  Winson 1985 p. 11.

39.  Ibid. pp. 11-12.

40.  Ibid. p. 13.

41.  PET studies which support the hypofrontal theory of schizophrenia include: Buchsbaum, Ingvar, Kessler, et al 1982; Farkas, Wolf, Jaeger, et al 1984.

42.  DeLisi, Buchsbaum, Holcomb, et al 1985.

43.  Ibid. p. 80.

44.  Ibid. pp. 80-81.

45.  Buchsbaum, DeLisi, Holcomb, et al 1984; Matthew, Meyer, Francis, et al 1980.

46.  There are at least ten PET scan studies in which no differences are found between schizophrenics and normal controls in regard to hypo-frontality. These ten studies include: Early, Reiman, Raichle, et al 1987; Gur, Gur, Skolnick, et al 1985; Gur, Resnick, Alavi, et al 1987; Gur, Skolnick, Gur, et al 1983; Jernigan, Sargent, Pfefferbaum, et al 1985; Kling, Metter, Riege, et al 1986; Sheppard, Gruzelier, Manchanda, et al 1983; Volkow, Brodie, Wolf, et al 1986; Widen, Bergstrom, Blomqvist, et al 1983; Widen, Blomqvist, Greitz, et al 1983.

47.  Sheppard, Gruzelier, Manchanda, et al 1983.

48.  Gur, Resnick, Alavi, et al 1987.

49.  Breggin 1983 pp. 39-43.

50.  Widen, Blomqvist, Greitz, et al 1983.

51.  Volkow, Brodie, Wolf, et al 1986.

52.  Wolkin, Jaeger, Brodie, et al 1985 p. 567.

53.  Geraud, Arné-Bès, Guell, et al 1987.

54.    Ibid. p. 11.

55.    Szechtman, Nahmias, Garnett, et al 1988.

56.    Allen 1991 p. 27.

57.    Solomon, Holzman, Levin, et al 1987 p. 31.

58.    Siever, Haier, Coursey, et al 1982 p. 1003.

59.    Brezinova and Kendell 1977.

60.    Quoted from Gould 1981 p. 51.

61.    Ibid. p. 69.

62.    Torrey 1983 p. 106.

## 3. SCHIZOPHRENIA AS A BIOCHEMICAL DEFECT

1.    Fink 1987 p. 672.

2.    Kety 1959 p. 1528.

3.    Graham, Booth, Boranga, et al 1982.

4.    Greden, Krofol, Garner, et al 1981; Meltzer, Fang, Tricou, et al 1982.

5.    Castro, Lamaire, Toscano-Aguilar et al 1983; Dewan, Pandurangi, Boucher, et al 1982; Herz, Fava, Molnar, et al 1985.

6.    Schweizer, Swenson, Winokur, et al 1986.

7.    Ceulemans, Westenberg and van Praag 1985.

8.    Shuchter, Zisook, Kirkorowicz, et al 1986.

9.    Bleuler 1978 pp. 495-496.

10.   Horwitt 1956 p. 429.

11.   In regard to Dr. Heath's career as a lobotomist see: Scheflin and Opton 1978 pp. 289, 334. For Heath's involvement with the military and the CIA see: Chavkin 1978 p. 12; Scheflin and Opton 1978 pp. 150-151, 337. For Heath's treatment of homosexuals and frigid women by brain implantation see: Scheflin and Opton 1978 p. 337; Schrag 1978 p. 172. For Heath's treatment of neurotics and schizophrenics with brain

implantation see: Heath 1977; Scheflin and Opton 1978 pp. 335-336.

12.    Heath, Martens, Leach, et al 1957; 1958.

13.    Kety 1959 pp. 1591-1592.

14.    Akerfeldt 1957.

15.    Kety 1959 pp. 1590-1591.

16.    An amusing account of the adrenaline-adrenochrome fiasco can be found in Snyder 1974 pp. 55-57.

17.    Smith and Sines 1960 pp. 185-187.

18.    Smith, Thompson and Koster 1969.

19.    Gordon, Smith, Rabinowitz, et al 1973.

20.    Smith and Sines 1960 p. 187.

21.    Woolley and Shaw 1954.

22.    Kety 1959 p. 1593.

23.    For example, Persson and Roos 1969; Post, Fink, Carpenter, et al 1975; and Rimon, Roos, Rakkolainen, et al 1971 found no significant differences in the levels of 5-hydroxyindoleacetic acid (5HIAA) — the major metabolite of serotonin — in the cerebrospinal fluids of schizophrenics and normal controls. However M.C. Bowers did find some correlation between CSF 5HIAA and "unusual thoughts." Bowers 1973 p. 312.

24.    Domschke, Dickschas, Mitznegg et al 1979 p. 1024.

25.    Ibid. p. 1024.

26.    Ibid. p. 1024.

27.    Davis, Bunney, DeFraites, et al 1977.

28.    Breggin 1983 pp. 18-20.

29.    Ibid. pp. 20-21.

30.    Ibid. pp. 21-23; Abbott 1982 pp. 41-48.

31.    Ibid. pp. 23-25.

32. Ibid. pp. 25-28.

33. Ibid. pp. 28-30.

34. Ibid.

35. Lennard et al 1971.

36. Davidson and Davis 1988; Davis, Davidson, Mohs, et al 1985; Pickar, Labarca, Doran, et al 1986.

37. Berger, Faull, Kilkowski, et al 1980; Bowers 1973; Gattaz, Riederer, Reynolds, et al 1983; Persson and Roos 1969; Post, Fink, Carpenter et al 1975; Rimon, Roos, Rakkolainen, et al 1971.

38. Burt, Creese and Snyder 1977.

39. Mackay, Iverson, Rossor, et al 1982; Reynolds, Reynolds, Riederer, et al 1980.

40. Wong, Wagner, Tune, et al 1986.

41. Farde, Wiesel, Hall, et al 1987; Farde, Wiesel, Stone-Elander, et al 1990; Hietala, Syvälahti, Vuorio, et al 1994. For a discussion of the significance of the divergent findings of Farde and Wong see: Andreasen, Carson, Diksic, et al 1988.

42. Martinot, Peron-Magnan, Huret, et al 1990.

43. Wong, Wagner, Pearlson, et al 1985.

44. Frankenhaeuser, Lundberg, Rauste-Von Wright, et al 1986 found that mental stress can cause increased dopamine turnover in normal individuals.

45. Selye 1978 pp. 111-114.

46. Davidson and Davis 1988; Karoum, Karson, Bigelow, et al 1987.

47. Chouinard and Jones 1978.

48. Snyder 1974 pp. 200-204.

49. Griffith, Cavanaugh, Held, et al 1972.

50. Ibid. p. 97.

51. Ibid. p. 99.

52. Kempf 1920 pp. 477-515.

53. Sullivan 1953 pp. 134-137.

54. Arieti 1974 pp. 120-121.

55. Connell 1958 p. 53.

56. Callaway 1959.

57. Connell 1958 p. 52.

58. Ellinwood 1967 pp. 275-277.

59. Connell 1958 pp. 49, 60, 62-64. Other authors who are of the opinion that amphetamine psychosis does not merely precipitate latent schizophrenia include: Griffith, Cavanaugh, Held, et al 1972; Snyder 1974 pp. 207-208.

60. Quoted from Jackson 1964 pp. 70-71.

61. Breggin 1983 p. 2.

62. Lehman and Hanrahan 1954 pp. 229-230.

63. Anton-Stephens 1954 p. 550.

64. I was prescribed first Stelazine, then Thorazine (chlorpromazine). I took Stelazine from 1960 to 1963, and Thorazine from 1963 to 1970. In 1963 a psychiatrist advised me to take 200 mg of Thorazine, a dose which I found totally intolerable. After taking 200 mg of Thorazine on an on and off basis for several weeks, I reduced the dosage to 75 mg, then to 50 mg in 1966, then to 25 mg in 1967. (Most often I obtained my prescription through a general practitioner. The last time I saw a psychiatrist — or any other mental health professional — was in 1963.)

65. Breggin 1983 p. 14.

66. Sterling 1979 p. 17.

67. Klerman 1970 p. 50.

68. Ibid. p. 50.

69. Breggin 1983 p. 57.

70. Ibid. pp. 57-58.

71. Ibid. pp. 57-58.

72. Other chemical substances for which antischizophrenic claims have been made include the experimental non-dopamine blocking drug *propranolol* (Yorkston, Gruzelier, Zaki, et al 1977) and *lithium* (Alexander, Van Kammen and Bunney 1979; Delva and Letemendia 1982; Donaldson, Gelenberg and Baldessarini 1983 pp. 507-512; Small, Kellams, Milstein, et al 1975) a drug which is used in treating manic-depression.

73. Sullivan 1962 p. 287.

74. Rappaport, Hopkins, Hall, et al 1978.

75. Ibid. p. 106.

76. Ibid. p. 105.

77. Easton and Link 1986-1987.

78. Gardos and Cole 1976.

79. Rifkin and Kane 1984.

80. Dion, Dellaril and Farkas 1982.

81. Hartlage 1965.

82. Breggin 1983 pp. 65-66.

83. Ibid. pp. 117-123.

84. Ibid. pp. 89-90.

85. Ibid. p. 89.

86. Ibid. pp. 78-82.

87. Abbott 1982 pp. 42-43.

88. Breggin 1983 pp. 151-152.

89. Andreasen 1984 p. 209.

90. Breggin 1983 pp. 90-91.

91. American Psychiatric Association 1980. According to this APA report, the latter figure (40 percent) represents the risk of elderly people developing tardive dyskinesia.

92. Tepper and Haas 1979.

93. Chouinard and Jones 1980.

94. Sale and Kristal 1978. Witschy, Malone and Holden 1984.

95. Chouinard, Annable and Ross-Chouinard 1986 p. 893.

96. Borison, Diamond, Sinha et al 1988. Ekblom, Eriksson and Lindstrom 1984.

97. Addonizio, Susman and Roth 1986.

98. Sternberg 1986 p. 1273.

99. Ibid. p. 1273.

100. Keck, Pope and McElroy 1987 estimate the prevalence of neuroleptic malignant syndrome at about .9 percent; while Pope, Keck and McElroy 1986 estimate its prevalence at 1.4 percent.

101. Addonizio, Susman and Roth 1986.

102. Breggin 1983 p. 71.

103. Ibid. p. 71.

104. Ibid. p. 71.

105. Ibid. p. 71.

106. Ibid. p. 71.

107. Ibid. p. 71.

108. Ibid. p. 71.

109. Ibid. p. 72.

110. These long-term follow-up studies of schizophrenic patients include those of: Bleuler 1978; Ciompi 1980a; 1980b; Harding 1984; Harding, Brooks, Ashikaga, et al 1987; Huber, Gross and Schüttler 1975; Huber, Gross, Schüttler, et al 1980; Tsuang, Woolson and Fleming 1979.

111.  Kornetsky 1976.

## 4. SCHIZOPHRENIA AS A GENETIC DEFECT

1.  Bassett 1988.

2.  Ibid. p. 800.

3.  Reuters 1988. Sherrington, Brynjolfsson, Petursson, et al 1988 p. 167 have also mentioned the possibility of instituting "genetic counselling in families where chromosome 5 linkage can be reliably established."

4.  Gottesman and Shields 1982 p. 104.

5.  Jackson 1960 p. 60.

6.  Ibid. pp. 65-71.

7.  For example Rosenthal (1962) p. 402 reports that male identical twins tend to be twice as discordant for schizophrenia as female identical twins. Furthermore, nearly all of the twin studies that have been done show a much higher rate of concordance for schizophrenia in females than in males. Gottesman and Shields 1982 pp. 113,115.

8.  Jackson 1960 p. 68.

9.  Pollin, Stabenau and Tupin 1965 pp. 73-75.

10.  Gottesman and Shields 1982 pp. 119-120; Pollin, Stabenau and Tupin 1965 pp. 70, 74-75; Wahl 1976 p. 98.

11.  Pollin, Stabenau and Tupin 1965 p. 74.

12.  Ibid. pp. 68, 73-74, 76.

13.  Pollin, Stabenau, Mosher, et al 1966 p. 499.

14.  Ibid. p. 507.

15.  Ibid. p. 495; Pollin, Stabenau and Tupin 1965 p. 68.

16.  Gottesman and Shields 1982 pp. 119-120; Wahl 1976 pp. 100-101.

17.  Allen and Pollin 1970.

18.  Heston 1966; Heston and Denny 1968.

19. Rosenthal, Wender, Kety, et al 1968; 1971.

20. Rosenthal, Wender, Kety, et al 1971 p. 308.

21. Lowing, Mirsky and Pereira 1983 p. 1167.

22. Ibid. pp. 1169-1170.

23. Wender, Rosenthal, Zahn, et al 1971.

24. Wynne, Singer and Toohey 1976 p. 436.

25. Ibid. pp. 437-438.

26. Singer and Wynne 1965 p. 210.

27. Ibid. p. 210.

28. Ibid. p. 210.

29. Ibid. p. 211.

30. Ibid. p. 211.

31. Ibid. p. 211.

32. Gottesman and Shields 1976 p. 367.

33. Gottesman and Shields 1982.

34. Higgins 1966; 1976; Wender, Rosenthal, Kety, et al 1974 p. 122.

35. Higgins 1966 p. 155; Wender, Rosenthal, Kety, et al 1974 p. 122.

36. Bleuler 1978 p. 420.

37. Hopkins 1988.

38. Bunzow, Van Tol, Grandy, et al 1988. Moises, Gelernter, Giuffra, et al, 1991 and Su, Burke, O'Neill, et al 1993 found no linkage between the $D_2$ dopamine receptor gene and schizophrenia; Sabaté, Campion, d'Amato, et al 1994 found no linkage between the $D_3$ dopamine receptor gene and schizophrenia; Macciardi, Petronis, Van Tol, et al 1994 found no linkage between the $D_4$ dopamine receptor gene and schizophrenia; and Persico, Wang, Black, et al 1995 found no linkage between the dopamine transporter gene and schizophrenia.

39.  Many schizophrenia researchers now believe that schizophrenia-susceptibility genes are located on at least five different chromosomes — on chromosomes 6, 8, 9, 20, and 22. See Moises, Yang, Kristbjarnarson, et al 1995.

40.  American Psychiatric Association 1994 pp. 662-665.

41.  Kagan, Reznick and Snidman 1988.

42.  Jonas and Jonas 1975; Leff 1976.

## 5. FACTS THE MEDICAL MODEL CANNOT EXPLAIN

1.  This is evident from the following autobiographical accounts: Barnes 1972; Jefferson 1948; O'Brien 1960. For a discussion of this phenomenon see: Cooper 1967; Laing 1967; Stern 1972 pp. 29-37.

2.  Harding 1984; Harding, Brooks, Ashikaga, et al 1987.

3.  Harding's subjects were retrospectively diagnosed by Yale University psychiatrists, John S. Strauss and Alan Breir. Drs. Strauss and Breir state they had access to excellent records containing detailed descriptions of conversations and behavior to assist their rediagnostic work. Harding, Brooks, Ashikaga, et al 1987 p. 732.

4.  Ibid. p. 730.

5.  Harding 1984 p. 43.

6.  Harding, Brooks, Ashikaga, et al 1987 p. 728.

7.  Bleuler 1978.

8.  Ciompi 1980a; 1980b.

9.  Huber, Gross and Schüttler 1975; Huber, Gross, Schüttler, et al 1980.

10.  Tsuang, Woolson and Fleming 1979.

11.  Geisen and Feuer 1984.

12.  Bleuler 1978 p. 490.

13.  Ibid. p. 453.

14.  Ibid. p. 191.

15. Ibid. pp. 223-234.

16. Ibid. p. 481.

17. Laing and Esterson 1970 pp. 214-215. The situational nature of catatonic symptoms has also been noted by Fromm-Reichmann 1959 p. 119; Ullman and Krasner 1975 pp. 353-354.

18. Torrey 1983 p. 42.

19. Quoted from Hayward and Taylor 1956 pp. 327-340.

20. Zarlock 1966 p. 71.

21. Ibid. p. 72.

22. Ibid. p. 74.

23. Braginsky, Braginsky and Ring 1982 p. 62.

24. Ibid. p. 71.

25. This has been recently confirmed by a 1994 study by Hyde, Nawroz, Goldberg, et al. In using a battery of neuropsychological tests known to be sensitive to cognitive impairment in progressive dementia, these authors were unable to find any evidence of intellectual decline in their chronic schizophrenic subjects.

26. Fleck 1960 p. 337.

27. Sarbin and Mancuso 1980.

28. Harding, Brooks, Ashikaga, et al 1987 p. 733.

29. Ennis 1972 p. 22.

30. Helfand 1956.

31. Ibid. p. 40.

32. Fromm-Reichmann 1959 pp. 174-175.

33. Stierlin 1959 p. 149.

34. Searles 1958 p. 576.

35. Coate 1965 pp. 21-22.

36.    Bowers and Freedman 1966 p. 241.

## 6. THE ANATOMY OF A DOGMA

1.    Mannheim 1985 p. 40.

2.    Breggin 1991 p. 113-115.

3.    Goldman and Murray 1943 p. 161.

4.    Talbott and Tillotson 1941.

5.    Fisher and Greiner 1960. See also: Hoen, Morell and O'Neill 1957.

6.    Himwich, Alexander and Lipetz 1938; Himwich 1952.

7.    Berman 1976.

8.    Diethelm 1939 p. 1174

9.    Himwich 1952 p. 565.

10.    Breggin 1979 p. 139.

11.    Quoted from Rodgers 1982 p. 85.

12.    Whitehead 1925; 1938 pp. 127-169. Forty years before the discovery of Bell's theorem, Whitehead was aware of the fact that the equations of quantum physics logically imply that the universe is an interconnected whole. This mysterious, instantaneous — and experimentally verified — action-at-a-distance is consistent with such things as sympathetic magic, voodoo and telepathy, and cannot possibly be reconciled with the mechanical world view.

13.    Burtt 1932.

14.    Marcuse 1964 pp. 144-169.

15.    Mumford 1967-1970. Mumford (Vol. 2, pp. 86-98) points out that the concept of the machine logically implies some kind of *purpose*: a machine is, after all, an instrument consciously designed for some preconceived end. This mechanical or teleological world view was thoroughly discredited by Charles Darwin in 1859.

# APPENDIX A

## A NOTE ON HOW NEUROLEPTIC DRUGS WORK

1.    Breggin 1983 pp. 118-123.

# APPENDIX B

## ON THE NOTION THAT SCHIZOPHRENIA
## IS NOT ONE BUT SEVERAL DIFFERENT DISEASES

1.    Crow 1980.

2.    Shenton, Ballinger, Marcy, et al 1989.

3.    Wyatt, Potkin, Kleinman, et al 1981.

4.    Arana 1978 p. 137; Bleuler, E. 1950 p. 227; Bleuler, M. 1978 p. 439; Kendler, Gruenberg and Tsuang 1985; Pao 1979 pp. 225-226.

5.    Bleuler 1978 pp. 223-234. The probands of Harding, Brooks, Ashikaga, et al 1987 could also be justifiably viewed as "process schizophrenics" yet they had a recovery rate of 45 to 68 percent.

6.    Vaillant 1978.

7.    A case history of identical twin brothers, one of whom had been diagnosed as schizophrenic and the other as manic by raters using strict DSM-III criteria, is provided by Dalby, Morgan and Lee 1986. A case history of identical triplets, two of whom were diagnosed as schizophrenic and the other as manic-depressive by blind raters, is provided by McGuffin, Reveley and Holland 1982. That this co-occurrence of schizophrenia and manic-depression in identical twins is by no means a rare phenomenon, is best illustrated by a 1987 study by Farmer, McGuffin and Gottesman. In studying 24 pairs of identical twins in which at least one twin was diagnosed as schizophrenic — the Maudsley twin series — these authors found five of these 24 twin pairs to have a manic-depressive member. These kinds of case studies are especially interesting in light of Rosenthal, Wender, Kety, et al 1968 p. 387 comments on the results of their adoption study: "Such data suggest that the inherited core diathesis is the same for both schizophrenia and manic-depressive psychosis."

261

8.  That schizophrenia can change to manic-depression has been documented by Sheldrick, Jablensky, Sartorius, et al 1977; and by Ziskind, Somerfeld and Jens 1971. In their long-term follow-up study, Harding, Brooks, Ashikaga, et al 1987 p. 730 found that some of their schizophrenic probands were exhibiting manic-depressive symptoms. That manic-depression can change to schizophrenia has been documented by Kendler and Tsuang 1982 in an interesting case history of identical twins who are first concordant for manic-depression but who later became concordant for schizophrenia.

9.  See "Clinical Description" in Goodwin and Jamison 1990 pp. 15-55.

10. In one study, Taylor and Abrams (1977) found that 28 percent of their 123 manic-depressive subjects showed clinical signs of catatonia. Ries (1985) has presented studies showing that catatonia is every bit as common in manic-depression as it is in schizophrenia.

11. Fry 1978.

12. Jampala, Abrams and Taylor 1985.

13. Kendell and Brockington 1980; Kendell and Gourlay 1970.

14. In a placebo-controlled double-blind study, Alexander, Van Kammen and Bunney (1979) found that 7 of their 13 schizophrenic subjects were less psychotic after receiving lithium. After lithium withdrawal, 4 of the 7 patients who had benefited from the drug relapsed. Other studies which have found lithium beneficial in treating schizophrenia include those of: Delva and Letemendia 1982; Donaldson, Gelenberg and Baldessarini 1983 pp. 507-512; Small, Kellams, Milstein, et al 1975.

15. In a controlled double-blind study, Wyatt and Torgow (1977) found neuroleptic drugs equally effective in treating schizophrenia and manic-depression. Lehmann and Hanrahan, the first researchers on the North American continent to utilize neuroleptic drugs to treat psychiatric patients, found that chlorpromazine had a more beneficial effect on manic patients than on schizophrenic patients. Lehmann and Hanrahan 1954 pp. 231-233. Finally, in a comprehensive controlled double-blind study, Prien, Caffey and Klett 1972 found chlorpromazine clearly superior to lithium in treating highly active manic patients.

16. Bliss 1986 pp. 150-151, 170-171.

17. Ibid. pp. 172-173.

18. Ibid. p. 173.

19.  There are many parallels between Nazi pseudoscience and psychiatric pseudoscience. For example, just as Nazi physiognomists believed they could spot a Jew by the shape of his head or the slope of his nose, some contemporary psychiatric researchers such as Guy, Majorski, Wallace, et al 1983 believe they can spot a schizophrenic by certain minor physical anomalies such as: hair that will not comb down or stay combed (electric hair); malformed, asymmetrical, or soft and pliable ears; eyes with epicanthus folds; hands with curved fifth fingers; and so forth. In each case, social or cultural phenomena — Judaism, schizophrenia — are regarded as forms of biological degeneracy.

20.  Popper 1959; 1963.

# BIBLIOGRAPHY

Abbott, J.H. (1982) *In the Belly of the Beast: Letters From Prison*. New York: Vintage Books.

Ackerfeldt, S. (1957) "Oxidation of N-N-Dimethyl-p-phenylenediamine by Serum with Mental Disease." *Science*, 125:117-119.

Addonizio, G., Susman, V.L. and Roth, S.D. (1986) "Symptoms of Neuroleptic Malignant Syndrome in 82 Consecutive Inpatients." *American Journal of Psychiatry*, 143:1587-1590.

Adler, L.E. and Waldo, M.C. (1991) "Counterpoint: A Sensory Grating — Hippocampal Model of Schizophrenia." *Schizophrenia Bulletin*, 17:19-24.

Alanen, Y.O. (1966) "The Family in the Pathogenesis of Schizophrenic and Neurotic Disorders." *Acta Psychiatrica Scandinavica*, 42:Suppl 189.

Alexander, P.E., Van Kammen, D.P. and Bunney, W.E. (1979) "Antipsychotic Effects of Lithium in Schizophrenia." *American Journal of Psychiatry*, 136:283-287.

Allen, J.S. (1991) "Schizophrenics Are People." *The Humanist*, May/June p. 26-27, 38.

Allen, M.G. and Pollin, W. (1970) "Schizophrenia in Twins and the Diffuse Ego Boundary Hypothesis." *American Journal of Psychiatry*, 127:437-442.

Altshuler, L.L., Conrad, A., Kovelman, J.A. and Scheibel, A. (1987) "Hippocampal Pyramidal Cell Orientation in Schizophrenia: A Controlled Neurohistologic Study of the Yakovlev Collection." *Archives of General Psychiatry*, 44:1094-1095.

American Psychiatric Association (1980) *Task Force Report: Tardive Dyskinesia* Washington, D.C.: APA.

American Psychiatric Association (1994) *Diagnostic and Statistical Manual of Mental Disorders*, Fourth Edition Washington, D.C.: APA.

Andreasen, N.C. (1984) *The Broken Brain: The Biological Revolution in Psychiatry*. New York: Harper & Row.

Andreasen, N.C. (1986) "Is Schizophrenia a Temporolimbic Disease?" In *Can Schizophrenia Be Localized in the Brain?* Ed. N.C. Andreasen. Washington D.C.: American Psychiatric Press, pp. 37-52.

Andreasen, N.C., Carson, R., Diksic, M., et al (1988) "Workshop on Schizophrenia, PET and Dopamine $D_2$ Receptors in the Human Neostriatum." *Schizophrenia Bulletin*, 14:471-484.

Andreasen, N.C., Olsen, S.A., Dennert, J.W., et al (1982) "Ventricular Enlargement in Schizophrenia: Relationship to Positive and Negative Symptoms." *American Journal of Psychiatry*, 139:297-302.

Anton-Stephens, D. (1954) "Preliminary Observations on the Psychiatric Uses of Chlorpromazine (Largactil)" *Journal of Mental Science*, 100:543-557.

Arana, J.D. (1978) "Schizophrenic Psychoses." In *Clinical Psychopathology: The Psychiatric Foundations of Medicine*. G.U. Ballis, L. Wurmser and R.G. Grenell Eds. Boston: Butterworth Publishers.

Arieti, S. (1974) *Interpretation of Schizophrenia*. (2nd ed.) New York: Basic Books.

Aschauer, H.N., Aschauer-Trieber, G., Isenberg, K.E., et al (1990) "No Evidence for Linkage Between Chromosome 5 Markers and Schizophrenia." *Human Heredity*, 40:109-115.

Bankier, R.G. (1985) "Third Ventricle Size and Dementia in Schizophrenia." *British Journal of Psychiatry*, 147:241-245.

Barnes, M. (1972) *Mary Barnes: Two Accounts of a Journey Through Madness*. New York: Harcourt Brace Jovanovich.

Bassett, A.S., McGillivray, B.C., Jones, B.D., et al (1988) "Partial Trisomy Chromosome 5 Cosegregating With Schizophrenia." *Lancet*, 1:799-801.

Bateson, G., Jackson, D., Haley, J., et al (1956) "Toward a Theory of Schizophrenia." In G. Bateson, *Steps to an Ecology of Mind*. New York: Ballantine Books, 1972, pp. 201-227.

Becker, E. (1964) *The Revolution in Psychiatry*. New York: The Free Press.

Benes, F., Sunderland, P. Jones, B.D., et al (1982) "Normal Ventricles in Young Schizophrenics." *British Journal of Psychiatry*, 141:90-93.

Bentall, R.P. and Slade, P.D. (1985) "Reliability of a Scale Measuring Disposition Towards Hallucination: A Brief Report." *Personality and Individual Differences*, 6:527-529.

Berger, P.A., Faull, K.F., Kilkowski, T. et al (1980) "CSF Monoamine Metabolites in Depression and Schizophrenia." *American Journal of Psychiatry*, 137:174-180.

Berman, S. (1976) "Fasting: An Old Cure for Fat, A New Treatment for Schizophrenia." *Science Digest*, Jan. pp. 27-29.

Bick, P.A. and Kinsbourne, M. (1987) "Auditory Hallucinations and Subvocal Speech in Schizophrenic Patients." *American Journal of Psychiatry*, 144:222-225.

Bleuler, E. (1950) *Dementia Praecox or the Group of Schizophrenias.* New York: International Universities Press.

Bleuler, M. (1978) *The Schizophrenic Disorders: Long-Term Patient and Family Studies.* Trans. by S.M. Clemens New Haven: Yale University Press.

Bliss, E.L. (1986) *Multiple Personality, Allied Disorders, and Hypnosis.* New York: Oxford University Press.

Bliss, E.L., Clark, L.D., and West, C.D. (1959) "Studies of Sleep Deprivation — Relationship to Schizophrenia." *A.M.A. Archives of Neurology and Psychiatry*, 81:348-359.

Boisen, A. (1960) *Out of the Depths.* New York: Harper & Row.

Boisen, A.T. (1971) *The Exploration of the Inner World: A Study of Mental Disorder and Religious Experience.* Philadelphia: University of Pennsylvania Press.

Borison, R.L., Diamond, B.I., Sinha, D. et al (1988) "Clozapine Withdrawal Rebound Psychosis." *Psychopharmacology Bulletin*, 24:260-263.

Bowen, M. (1960) "A Family Concept of Schizophrenia." In *The Etiology of Schizophrenia.* Ed. D.D. Jackson. New York: Basic Books, pp. 346-372.

Bowers, M.B. (1973) "5-Hydroxindoleacetic Acid (5HIAA) and Homovanillic Acid (HVA) Following Probenecid in Acute Psychotic Patients Treated with Phenothiazines." *Psychopharmacologia*, 28:309-318.

Bowers, M.B. Jr. and Freedman, D.X. (1966) "'Psychedelic' Experiences in Acute Psychoses." *Archives of General Psychiatry*, 15:240-248.

Boyle, M. (1990) *Schizophrenia: A Scientific Delusion?* London: Routledge.

Bracha, H.S., Wolkowitz, O.M., Lohr, J.B., et al (1989) "High Prevalence of Visual Hallucinations in Research Subjects with Chronic Schizophrenia." *American Journal of Psychiatry*, 146:526-528.

Braginsky, B.M., Braginsky D.D., and Ring, K. (1982) *Methods of Madness: The Mental Hospital as a Last Resort*. Lanham, MD.: University Press of America.

Brauchi, J.T. and West, L.J. (1959) "Sleep Deprivation." *Journal of the American Medical Association*, 171:11-14.

Breggin, P.R. (1979) *Electroshock: Its Brain-Disabling Effects*. New York: Springer Publishing Co.

Breggin, P.R. (1983) *Psychiatric Drugs: Hazards to the Brain*. New York: Springer Publishing Co.

Breggin, P.R. (1991) *Toxic Psychiatry: Why Therapy, Empathy, and Love Must Replace the Drugs, Electroshock, and Biochemical Theories of the "New Psychiatry."* New York: St. Martin's Press.

Brezinova, V. and Kendell, R.E. (1977) "Smooth Pursuit Eye Movements of Schizophrenics and Normal People Under Stress." *British Journal of Psychiatry*, 130:59-63.

Brodey, W.M. (1959) "Some Family Operations and Schizophrenia: A Study of Five Hospitalized Families Each with a Schizophrenic Member." *Archives of General Psychiatry*, 1:379-402.

Buchsbaum, M.S., DeLisi, L.E., Holcomb, H.H., et al (1984) "Anteroposterior Gradients in Cerebral Glucose Use in Schizophrenia and Affective Disorders." *Archives of General Psychiatry*, 41:1159-1166.

Buchsbaum, M.S., Ingvar, D.H., Kessler, D., et al. (1982) "Cerebral Glucography with Positron Tomography: Use in Normal Subjects and in Patients with Schizophrenia." *Archives of General Psychiatry*, 39:251-259.

Bunzow, J.R., Van Tol, H.H.M., Grandy, D.K., et al (1988) "Cloning and Expression of a Rat $D_2$ Dopamine Receptor cDNA." *Nature*, 336:783-787.

Burt, D.R., Creese, I. and Snyder, S.H. (1977) "Antischizophrenic Drugs: Chronic Treatment Elevates Dopamine Receptor Binding in Brain." *Science*, 196:326-328.

Burtt, A.E. (1932) *The Metaphysical Foundations of Modern Physical Science: A Historical and Critical Essay*. (2nd ed.) London: Routledge & Kegan Paul.

Callaway, E. (1959) "The Influence of Amobarbital (Amylobarbitone) and Methamphetamine on the Focus of Attention." *Journal of Mental Science*, 105:382-392.

Castro, P. Lamaire, M., Toscano-Aguilar, M., et al (1983) "Abnormal DST Results in Patients with Chronic Schizophrenia." *American Journal of Psychiatry*, 140:1261.

Ceulemans, D.L.S., Westenberg, H.G.M. and Van Praag, H.M. (1985) "The Effect of Stress on the Dexamethasone Suppression Test." *Psychiatry Research*, 14:189-195.

Chamberlin, J. (1978) *On Our Own: Patient-Controlled Alternatives to the Mental Health System*. New York: Hawthorn.

Chapman, A.H. and Chapman, M.C.M.S. (1980) *Harry Stack Sullivan's Concepts of Personality Development and Psychiatric Illness*. New York: Brunner/Mazel.

Chavkin, S. (1978) *The Mind Stealers: Psychosurgery and Mind Control*. Boston: Houghton Mifflin.

Chesler, P. (1972) *Women and Madness*. Garden City, N.Y.: Doubleday.

Chouinard, G., Annable, L. and Ross-Chouinard, A. (1986) "Supersensitivity Psychosis and Tardive Dyskinesia: A Survey in Schizophrenic Outpatients." *Psychopharmacology Bulletin*, 22:891-896.

Chouinard, G. and Jones, B.D. (1978) "Schizophrenia as a Dopamine-Deficiency Disease." *Lancet*, 2:99-100.

Chouinard, G. and Jones, B.D. (1980) "Neuroleptic-Induced Supersensitivity Psychosis: Clinical and Pharmacologic Characteristics." *American Journal of Psychiatry*, 137:16-21.

Ciompi, L. (1980a) "Catamnestic Long-term Study of the Course of Life and Aging of Schizophrenics." *Schizophrenia Bulletin*, 6:606-618.

Ciompi, L. (1980b) "The Natural History of Schizophrenia in the Long Term." *British Journal of Psychiatry*, 136:413-420.

Coate, M. (1965) *Beyond All Reason*. New York: Lippincott.

Coffman, J.A., Mefferd, J., Golden, C.J., et al (1981) "Cerebellar Atrophy in Chronic Schizophrenia" (letter) *Lancet*, 1:666.

Connell, P.H. (1958) *Amphetamine Psychosis*. London: Oxford University Press.

Cooper, D. (1967) *Psychiatry and Anti-Psychiatry*. New York: Ballantine Books.

Crow, T.J. (1980) "Molecular Pathology of Schizophrenia: More than one Disease Process?" *British Medical Journal*, 280:66-68.

Crow, T.J. (1994) "Prenatal Exposure to Influenza as a Cause of Schizophrenia." *British Journal of Psychiatry*, 164:588-592.

Crowe, R. R., Black, D.W., Wesner, R. et al (1991) "Lack of Linkage to Chromosome 5g11-g13 Markers in Six Schizophrenia Pedigrees." *Archives of General Psychiatry*, 48:357-361.

Cutting, J. (1985) *The Psychology of Schizophrenia*. New York: Churchill Livingstone.

Dalby, J.T., Morgan, D. and Lee, M.L. (1986) "Single Case Study: Schizophrenia and Mania in Identical Twin Brothers." *Journal of Nervous and Mental Disease*, 174:304-308.

Davidson, M. and Davis K.L. (1988) "A Comparison of Plasma Homovanillic Acid Concentrations in Schizophrenic Patients and Normal Controls." *Archives of General Psychiatry*, 45:561-563.

Davis, G.C., Bunney, W.E., DeFraites, E.G., et al (1977) "Intravenous Naloxone Administration in Schizophrenia and Affective Illness." *Science*, 197:74-77.

Davis, K.L., Davidson, M., Mohs, R.C., et al (1985) "Plasma Homovanillic Acid Concentration and the Severity of Schizophrenic Illness." *Science*, 227:1601-1602.

Delay, J., Deniker, P., and Green, A. (1962) "Le Miliea Familial des Schizophrenes: 3. Résultats et Hypothèses." *L'Encephale*, 51:5-73.

DeLisi, L.E., Buchsbaum, M.S., Holcomb, H.H., et al (1985) "Clinical Correlates of Decreased Anteroposterior Metabolic Gradients in Positron Emission Tomography (PET) of Schizophrenic Patients." *American Journal of Psychiatry*, 142:78-81.

Delva, N.J. and Letemendia, J.J. (1982) "Lithium Treatment in Schizophrenia and Schizoaffective Disorder." *British Journal of Psychiatry*, 141:387-400.

Detera-Wadleigh, S.D., Goldin, L.R., Sherrington, R., et al (1989) "Exclusion of Linkage to 5q11-13 in Families with Schizophrenia and other Psychiatric Disorders." *Nature*, 340:391-393.

Dewan, M.J., Pandurangi, A.K., Boucher, M.L., et al (1982) "Abnormal Dexamethasone Suppression Test Results in Chronic Schizophrenic Patients." *American Journal of Psychiatry*, 139:1501-1503.

Diamond, B.I. and Borison, R.L. (1986) "Basic and Clinical Studies of Neuro-leptic-Induced Supersensitivity Psychosis and Dyskinesia." *Psychopharmacology Bulletin,* 22:900-905.

Diethelm, O. (1939) "An Historical View of Somatic Treatment in Psychiatry." *American Journal of Psychiatry,* 95:1165-1179.

Dion, G., Dellaril, D. and Farkas, M. (1982) "The Relationship of Maintenance Neuroleptic Dosage Levels to Vocational Functioning in Severely Psychiatrically Disabled Clients: Implications for Rehabilitation Practitioners." *Psychosocial Rehabilitation Journal,* 29:29-35.

Domschke, W., Dickschas, A., Mitznegg, P., et al (1979) "C.S.F. Endorphin in Schizophrenia." (letter) *Lancet,* 1:1024.

Donahue Transcript #07203, Cincinnati: Multimedia Productions, 1983.

Donaldson, S.R., Gelenberg, A.J. and Baldessarini, R.J. (1983) "The Pharmacologic Treatment of Schizophrenia: A Progress Report." *Schizophrenia Bulletin,* 9:504-527.

Early, T.S., Reiman, E.M., Raichle, M.E., et al (1987) "Left Globus Pallidus Abnormality in Never-Medicated Patients With Schizophrenia." *Proceedings of the National Academy of Science of the United States of America,* 84:561-563.

Easton, K. and Link, I. (1986-1987) "Do Neuroleptics Prevent Relapse? Clinical Observations in a Psychosocial Rehabilitation Program." *Psychiatry Quarterly,* 58:42-50.

Ekblom, B., Eriksson, K. and Lindstrom, L.H. (1984) "Supersensitivity Psychosis in Schizophrenic Patients After Sudden Clozapine Withdrawal." *Psychopharmacology,* 83:292-294.

Ellinwood, E.H. (1967) "Amphetamine Psychosis: I. Description of the Individuals and Process." *Journal of Nervous and Mental Disease,* 144:273-283.

Ennis, B.J. (1972) *Prisoners of Psychiatry.* New York: Harcourt Brace Jovanovich.

Fairbairn, W.R.D. (1952) *An Object-Relations Theory of the Personality.* New York: Basic Books.

Farde, L. Wiesel, F.A., Hall, H., et al (1987) "No $D_2$ Receptor Increase in PET Study of Schizophrenia." *Archives of General Psychiatry,* 44:671-672.

Farde, L., Wiesel, F.-A., Stone-Elander, S., et al (1990) "D$_2$ Dopamine Receptors in Neuroleptic-Naive Schizophrenic Patients: A Positron Emission Tomography Study with ["C] Raclopride." *Archives of General Psychiatry*, 47:213-219.

Farkas, T., Wolf, A.P., Jaeger, J., et al (1984) "Regional Brain Glucose Metabolism in Chronic Schizophrenia: A Positron Emission Transaxial Tomographic Study." *Archives of General Psychiatry*, 41:293-300.

Farmer, A., Jackson, R., McGuffin, P., et al (1987) "Cerebral Ventricular Enlargement in Chronic Schizophrenia: Consistencies and Contradictions." *British Journal of Psychiatry*, 150:324-330.

Farmer, A.E., McGuffin, P. and Gottesman, I.I. (1987) "Twin Concordance for Schizophrenia: Scrutinizing the Validity of the Definition." *American Journal of Psychiatry*, 44:634-641.

Fink, G. (1987) "Highs and Lows." Review of S.H. Snyder's *Drugs and the Brain* in *Nature*, 325:671-672.

Fisher, K.J. and Greiner, A. (1960) "'Acute Lethal Catatonia' Treated by Hypyothermia." *Canadian Medical Association Journal*, 82:630-634.

Fleck, S. (1960) "Family Dynamics and the Origin of Schizophrenia." *Psychosomatic Medicine*, 12:333-344.

Foucault, M. (1973) *Madness and Civilization: A History of Insanity in the Age of Reason*. Trans. Richard Howard. New York: Vintage Books.

Frankenhaeuser, M., Lundberg, U., Rauste-Von Wright, M., et al (1986) "Urinary Monoamine Metabolites as Indices of Mental Stress in Healthy Males and Females." *Pharmacology Biochemistry and Behavior*, 24:1521-1525.

Fromm-Reichmann, F. (1959) *Psychoanalysis and Psychotherapy. Selected Papers of Frieda Fromm-Reichmann*. Ed. D.M. Bullard. Chicago: University of Chicago Press.

Fry, W.F. Jr., (1978) "Paranoid Episodes in Manic-Depressive Psychoses." *American Journal of Psychiatry*, 135:974-976.

Fullinwider, S.P. (1982) *Technicians of the Finite: The Rise and Decline of the Schizophrenic in American Thought 1940-1960*. Westport, Conn.: Greenwood Press.

Gardos, G. and Cole, J. (1976) "Maintenance Antipsychotic Therapy: Is the Cure Worse than the Disease?" *American Journal of Psychiatry*, 133:32-36.

Gattaz, W.F., Riederer, P. Reynolds, G.P., et al (1983) "Dopamine and Noradrenaline in the Cerebrospinal Fluid of Schizophrenic Patients." *Psychiatry Research*, 8:243-250.

Geisen, L. and Feuer, E. (1984) "The Treatment-Resistant Patient and the Need to Stay Crazy." *Psychiatric Quarterly*, 56:75-82.

Geraud, G., Arné-Bès, M.C., Guell, A., et al (1987) "Reversibility of Hemodynamic Hypofrontality in Schizophrenia." *Journal of Cerebral Blood Flow and Metabolism*, 7:9-12.

Geschwind, N. and Galaburda, A.M. (1985a) "Cerebral Lateralization: Biological Mechanisms, Associations, and Pathology: I. A Hypothesis and a Program for Research." *Archives of Neurology*, 42:428-459.

Geschwind, N. and Galaburda, A,.M. (1985b) "Cerebral Lateralization: Biological Mechanisms, Associations, and Pathology: II. A Hypothesis and a Program For Research." *Archives of Neurology*, 42:521-552.

Glück, E., Radü, E.W., Mundt, C., et al (1980) "A Computed Tomographic Prolective Trohoc Study of Chronic Schizophrenics." *Neuroradiolgy*, 20:167-171.

Goffman, E. (1961) *Asylums: Essays on the Social Situation of Mental Patients and Other Inmates*. Garden City, N.Y.: Doubleday Anchor.

Goldman, D., and Murray, M. (1943) "Studies on the Use of Refrigeration Therapy in Mental Disease with Report of Sixteen Cases." *Journal of Nervous and Mental Disease*, 97:152-165.

Goodwin, F.K. and Jamison, K.R. (1990) *Manic-Depressive Illness*. New York: Oxford University Press.

Gordon, S.G., Smith, K., Rabinowitz, J.L., et al (1973) "Studies of *Trans-3-*Methyl-2-Hexanoic Acid in Normal and Schizophrenic Humans." *Journal of Lipid Research*, 14:495-503.

Gottesman, I.I. and Shields, J. (1976) "A Critical Review of Recent Adoption, Twin, and Family Studies of Schizophrenia: Behavioral Genetics Perspectives." *Schizophrenia Bulletin*, 2:360-398.

Gottesman, I.I. and Shields, J. (1982) *Schizophrenia: The Epigenetic Puzzle*. Cambridge: University of Cambridge Press.

Gould, S.J. (1981) *The Mismeasure of Man*. New York: W.W. Norton & Company.

Graham, P.M., Booth, J. Boranga, G., et al (1982) "The Dexamethasone Suppression Test in Mania." *Journal of Affective Disorder*, 4:201-211.

Grayson, H.M. and Olinger, L.B. (1957) "Simulation of 'Normalcy' by Psychiatric Patients on the MMPI." *Journal of Consulting Psychology*, 21:73-77.

Greden, J.F., Krofol, Z., Garner, R., et al. (1981) "Neuroendocrine Evaluation of Schizoaffectives with the Dexamethasone Suppression Test." In *Biological Psychiatry*. Eds. C. Perris, G. Struwe and B. Jansson. Amsterdam: Elsevier/Biomedical Press.

Griffith, J.D., Cavanaugh, J., Held, J., et al (1972) "Dextroamphetamine: Evaluation of Psychomimetic Properties in Man." *Archives of General Psychiatry*, 26:97-100.

Guntrip, H. (1968) *Schizoid Phenomena Object-Relations and the Self.* New York: International Universities Press.

Gur, R.E., Gur, R.C., Skolnick, B.E., et al (1985) "Brain Function in Psychiatric Disorders: III. Regional Cerebral Blood Flow in Unmedicated Schizophrenics." *Archives of General Psychiatry*, 42:329-334.

Gur, R.E., Resnick, S.M., Alavi, A., et al (1987) "Regional Brain Function in Schizophrenia: I. A Positron Emission Tomographic Study." *Archives of General Psychiatry*, 44:119-125.

Gur, R.E., Skolnick, B.E., Gur, R.C., et al. (1983) "Brain Function in Psychiatric Disorders: I. Regional Cerebral Blood Flow in Medicated Schizophrenics." *Archives of General Psychiatry*, 40:1250-1254.

Guy, J.D., Majorski, L.V., Wallace, C.J., et al (1983) "The Incidence of Minor Physical Anomalies in Adult Male Schizophrenics." *Schizophrenia Bulletin*, 9:571-582.

Haley, J. (1959) "The Family of the Schizophrenic: A Model System." *Journal of Nervous and Mental Disease*, 129:357-374.

Harding, C.M. (1984) *Long-Term Functioning of Subjects Rediagnosed as Meeting the DSM III Criteria for Schizophrenia.* (Doctoral Dissertation). Burlington, University of Vermont.

Harding, C.M., Brooks, G.W., Ashikaga, T., et al (1987) "The Vermont Longitudinal Study of Persons With Severe Mental Illness, II: Long-Term Outcome of Subjects Who Retrospectively Met DSM-III Criteria for Schizophrenia." *American Journal of Psychiatry*, 144:727-735.

Hartlage, L.C., (1965) "Effects of Chlorpromazine on Learning." *Psychological Bulletin*, 64:235-245.

Hayward, M.L. and Taylor, J.E. (1956) "A Schizophrenic Patient Describes the Action of Intensive Psychotherapy." In *The Inner World of Mental Illness*. Ed. B. Kaplan. New York: Harper and Row, 1964. pp. 323-334.

Heath, R.G. (1977) "Modulation of Emotion with a Brain Pacemaker: Treatment for Intractable Mental Illness." *Journal of Nervous and Mental Disease*, 165:300-317.

Heath, R.G., Martens, S., Leach, B.E., et al (1957) "Effect of Behavior in Humans with the Administration of Taraxein." *American Journal of Psychiatry*, 114:14-24.

Hearth, R.G., Martens, S., Leach, B.E., et al (1958) "Behavioral Changes in Nonpsychotic Volunteers Following the Administration of Taraxein, the Substance Obtained from Serum of Schizophrenic Patients." *American Journal of Psychiatry*, 114:917-920.

Helfand, I. (1956) "Role Taking in Schizophrenia." *Journal of Consulting Psychology*, 20:37-41.

Herz, M.I., Fava, G.A., Molnar, G., et al (1985) "The Dexamethasone Suppression Test in Newly Hospitalized Schizophrenic Patients." *American Journal of Psychiatry*, 142:127-129.

Heston, L.L. (1966) "Psychiatric Disorders in Foster Home Reared Children of Schizophrenic Mothers." *British Journal of Psychiatry*, 112:819-825.

Heston, L.L. and Denny, D. (1968) "Interactions Between Early Life Experience and Biological Factors in Schizophrenia." In *The Transmission of Schizophrenia* Eds. D. Rosenthal and S.S. Kety. New York: Pergamon Press, pp. 363-376.

Hietala, J., Syvälahti, E., Vuorio, K., et al (1994) "Striatal $D_2$ Dopamine Receptor Characteristics in Neuroleptic-Naive Schizophrenic Patients Studied with Positron Emission Tomography." *Archives of General Psychiatry*, 51:116-123.

Higgins, J. (1966) "Effects of Child Rearing by Schizophrenic Mothers." *Journal of Psychiatric Research*, 4:153-167.

Higgins, J. (1976) "Effects of Child Rearing by Schizophrenic Mothers: A Follow-Up." *Journal of Psychiatric Research*, 13:1-9.

Hill, D. (1983) *The Politics of Schizophrenia: Psychiatric Oppression in the United States*. Lanham, Md.: University Press of America.

Hill, L.B. (1955) *Psychotherapeutic Intervention in Schizophrenia*. Chicago: University of Chicago Press.

Himwich, H.E. (1952) "Effect of Shock Therapies on the Brain." In *Biology of Mental Health and Disease*. Ed. H.E. Himwich, L. Kalinowsky, and W.E. Stone. New York: Hoeber, pp. 548-567.

Himwich, H.E., Alexander F.A.D. and Lipetz, B. (1938) "Effect of Acute Anoxia Producted by Breathing Nitrogen on the Course of Schizophrenia." *Proceedings of the Society for Experimental Biology and Medicine*, 39:367-369.

Hoen, T.I., Morello, A. and O'Neill, F.J. (1957) "Hypothermia (Cold Narcosis) in the Treatment of Schizophrenia." *Psychiatric Quarterly*, 31:696-702.

Hopkins, O. (1988) "Scientists Clone Gene Linked to Schizophrenia, Parkinson's." *Seattle Times*, Dec. 22, p. D12.

Horwitt, M.K. (1956) "Fact and Artifact in the Biology of Schizophrenia." *Science*, 124:429-430.

Huber, G., Gross, G. and Schüttler, R. (1975) "A Long-term Follow-up Study of Schizophrenia: Psychiatric Course of Illness and Prognosis." *Acta Psychiatrica Scandinavica*, 52:49-57.

Huber, G., Gross, G., Schüttler, R, et al (1980) "Longitudinal Studies of Schizophrenic Patients." *Schizophrenia Bulletin*, 6:592-605.

Hyde, T.M., Nawroz, S., Goldberg, T.E., et al (1994) "Is There Cognitive Decline in Schizophrenia? A Cross-Sectional Study." *British Journal of Psychiatry*, 164:494-500.

Jackson, D.D. (1960) "A Critique of the Literature on the Genetics of Schizophrenia." In *The Etiology of Schizophrenia*. Ed. D.D. Jackson. New York: Basic Books. pp. 37-87.

Jackson, D.D. (1964) *Myths of Madness: New Facts for Old Fallacies*. New York: Macmillan.

Jackson, D.D. and Weakland, J.H. (1959) "Schizophrenic Symptoms and Family Interaction." *Archives of General Psychiatry*, 1:618-621.

Jampala, V.C., Abrams, R. and Taylor, M.A. (1985) "Mania With Emotional Blunting: Affective Disorder or Schizophrenia?" *American Journal of Psychiatry*, 142:608-612.

Jefferson, L. (1948) "I Am Crazy Wild This Minute. How Can I Learn to Think Straight?" In *The Inner World of Mental Illness* Ed. B. Kaplan. New York: Harper and Row, 1964 pp. 3-42.

Jenner, F.A., Monteiro, A.C.D., Zagalo-Cardoso, J.A., et al (1993) *Schizophrenia: A Disease or Some Ways of Being Human?* Sheffield: Sheffield Academic Press Ltd.

Jernigan, T.L., Sargent, T., Pfefferbaum, A., et al (1985) "Fluorodeoxyglucose PET in Schizophrenia." *Psychiatry Research*, 16:317-329.

Jernigan, T.L., Zatz, L.M., Moses, J.A., et al (1982) "Computed Tomography in Schizophrenics and Normal Volunteers." *Archives of General Psychiatry*, 39:765-770.

Johnson, F.H. (1978) *The Anatomy of Hallucinations*. Chicago: Nelson-Hall.

Johnstone, E.C., Crow, T.J., MacMillan, J.C., et al (1986) "A Magnetic Resonance Study of Early Schizophrenia." *Journal of Neurology, Neurosurgery, and Psychiatry*, 49:136-139.

Jonas, A.D. and Jonas, D.F. (1975) "An Evolutionary Context for Schizophrenia." *Schizophrenia Bulletin*, No. 12:13-41, Spring.

Kagan, J., Reznick, J.S., and Snidman, N. (1988) "Biological Bases of Childhood Shyness." *Science*, 240:167-171.

Karoum, F., Karson, C.N., Bigelow, L.B., et al (1987) "Preliminary Evidence of Reduced Combined Output of Dopamine and its Metabolites in Chronic Schizophrenia." *Archives of General Psychiatry*, 44:604-607.

Keck, P.E., Pope, H.G., and McElroy, S.L. (1987) "Frequency and Presentation of Neuroleptic Malignant Syndrome: A Prospective Study." *American Journal of Psychiatry*, 144:1344-1346.

Kempf, E.J. (1920) *Psychopathology*, St. Louis: C. V. Mosby.

Kendell, R.E. and Brockington, I.F. (1980) "The Identification of Disease Entities and the Relationship Between Schizophrenic and Affective Psychoses." *British Journal of Psychiatry*, 137:324-331.

Kendell, R.E. and Gourlay, J. (1970) "The Clinical Distinction Between the Affective Psychoses and Schizophrenia." *British Journal of Psychiatry,* 117:261-266.

Kendler, K.S., Gruenberg, A.M. and Tsuang, M.T. (1985) "Subtype Stability in Schizophrenia." *American Journal of Psychiatry,* 142:827-832.

Kendler, K.S. and Tsuang, M.T. (1982) "Identical Twins Concordant for the Progression of Affective Illness to Schizophrenia." *British Journal of Psychiatry,* 141:563-566.

Kety, S.S. (1959) "Biochemical Theories of Schizophrenia: A Two-Part Review of Current Theories and the Evidence Used to Support Them." *Science,* 129:1528-1532, 1590-1596.

Klerman, G.L. (1970) "Clinical Efficacy and Actions of Anti-psychotics." In *Clinical Handbook of Psychopharmacology.* Ed. A. DiMaseio and R. Shrader. New York: Science House.

Kling, A.S., Metter, E.J., Riege, W.H., et al (1986) "Comparison of PET Measurement of Local Brain Glucose Metabolism and CAT Measurement of Brain Atrophy in Chronic Schizophrenia and Depression." *American Journal of Psychiatry,* 143:175-180.

Kornetsky, C. (1976) "Hyporesponsivity of Chronic Schizophrenic Patients to Dextroamphetamine." *Archives of General Psychiatry,"* 33:1425-1428.

Kovelman, J.A. and Scheibel A. (1984) "A Neurohistological Correlate of Schizophrenia." *Biological Psychiatry,* 19:1601-1621.

Kupfer, D.J., Wyatt, R.J., Scott, J., et al (1970) "Sleep Disturbance in Acute Schizophrenic Patients." *American Journal of Psychiatry,* 126:1213-1223.

Laing, R.D. (1967) *The Politics of Experience.* New York: Ballantine Books.

Laing, R.D. and Esterson A. (1970) *Sanity, Madness, and the Family: Families of Schizophrenics.* Baltimore, Md.: Pelican Books.

Leff, J.F. (1976) "Schizophrenia and Sensitivity to the Family Environment." *Schizophrenia Bulletin,* 2:566-574.

Lehmann, H.E. and Hanrahan, G.E. (1954) "Chlorpromazine: New Inhibiting Agent For Psychomotor Excitement and Manic States." *Archives of Neurology and Psychiatry,* 71:227-237.

Leifer, R. (1969) *In the Name of Mental Health: The Social Functions of Psychiatry.* New York: Science House.

Lennard, H.L., et al (1971) *Mystification and Drug Misuse: Hazards in Using Psychoactive Drugs.* New York: Harper & Row.

Lewontin, R.C., Rose, S.P.R. and Kamin, L.C. (1984) *Not in Our Genes: Biology, Ideology and Human Nature.* New York: Pantheon Books.

Lidz, T. (1973) *The Origin and Treatment of Schizophrenic Disorders.* New York: Basic Books.

Lidz, T., Blatt, S. and Cook, B. (1981) "Critique of the Danish-American Studies of the Adopted-Away Offspring of Schizophrenic Parents." *American Journal of Psychiatry*, 138:1063-1068.

Lidz, T., Fleck, S. and Cornelison, A.R. (1965) *Schizophrenia and the Family.* New York: International Universities Press.

Lowing, P.A., Mirsky, A.F. and Pereira, R. (1983) "The Inheritance of Schizophrenia Spectrum Disorders: A Re-analysis of the Danish Adoptee Study Data." *American Journal of Psychiatry*, 140:1167-1171.

Lu, Y.-C., (1962) "Contradictory Parental Expectations in Schizophrenia." *Archives of General Psychiatry*, 6:219-234.

Macciardi, F., Petronis, A., Van Toh, H.H.M., et al (1994) "Analysis of the $D_4$ Dopamine Receptor Gene Variant in an Italian Schizophrenia Kindred." *Archives of General Psychiatry*, 51:288-293.

MacKay, A.V.P., Iversen, L.L., Rossor, M., et al (1982) "Increased Brain Dopamine and Dopamine Receptors in Schizophrenia." *Archives of General Psychiatry*, 39:991-997.

Mannheim, K. (1985) *Ideology and Utopia: An Introduction to the Sociology of Knowledge.* Trans. L. Wirth and E. Shils. San Diego: Harvest/ Harcourt Brace Jovanovich.

Marcuse, H. (1964) *One-Dimensional Man: Studies in the Ideology of Advanced Industrial Society.* Boston: Beacon Press.

Martinot, J.-L., Peron-Magnan, P., Huret, J.-D., et al (1990) "Striatal $D_2$ Dopaminergic Receptors Assessed with Positron Emission Tomography and [$^{76}$Br] Bromospiperone in Untreated Schizophrenic Patients." *American Journal of Psychiatry*, 147:44-50.

Maser, J.D. and Keith, S.J. (1983) "CT Scans and Schizophrenia — Report on a Workshop." *Schizophrenia Bulletin*, 9:265-283.

Matthew, R.J., Meyer, J.S., Francis, D.J., et al (1980) "Cerebral Blood Flow in Depression." *American Journal of Psychiatry*, 137:1449-1450.

Matthew, R.J. and Partain, L.C. (1985) "Midsagittal Sections of the Cerebellar Vermis and Fourth Ventricle With Magnetic Resonance Imaging of Schizophrenic Patients." *American Journal of Psychiatry*, 142:970-971.

McGuffin, P., Reveley, A. and Holland, A. (1982) "Identical Triplets: Non-Identical Psychosis?" *British Journal of Psychiatry*, 140:1-6.

Mednick, S.A. (1970) "Breakdown in Individuals at High-Risk for Schizophrenia: Possible Predispositional Perinatal Factors." *Mental Hygiene*, 54:50-63.

Melges, F.T. (1968) "Postpartum Psychiatric Syndromes." *Psychosomatic Medicine*, 30:95-108.

Meltzer, H.Y., Fang, V.S., Tricou, B.J., et al (1982) "Effect of Dexamethasone on Plasma Prolactin and Cortisol Levels in Psychiatric Patients." *American Journal of Psychiatry*, 139:763-768.

Meyer, A. (1906) "Fundamental Concepts of Dementia Praecox." *British Medical Journal*, 2:757-760.

Mishler, E.G. and Waxler, N.E. (1968) *Interaction in Families: An Experimental Study of Family Process and Schizophrenia.* New York: John Wiley & Sons.

Moises, H.W., Gelernter, J., Giuffra, L.A., et al (1991) "No Linkage Between $D_2$ Dopamine Receptor Gene Region and Schizophrenia." *Archives of General Psychiatry*, 48:643-647.

Moises, H.W., Yang, L., Kristbjarnarson, H., et al (1995) "An International Two-Stage Genome-Wide Search for Schizophrenia Susceptibility Genes." *Nature Genetics*, 11:321-324.

Morihisa, J.M. and Weinberger, D.R. (1986) "Is Schizophrenia a Frontal Lobe Disease? An Organizing Theory of Relevant Anatomy and Physiology." In *Can Schizophrenia Be Localized in the Brain?* Ed. N.C. Andreasen, Washington D.C.: American Psychiatric Press, pp. 17-36.

Mosher, L.R. (1980) "Community Residential Treatment for Schizophrenia: Two-Year Follow-Up." *International Journal of Rehabilitation Research*, 3:393-395.

Mosher, L.R. and Menn, A. (1982) "Soteria: An Alternative to Hospitalization for Schizophrenia." *Current Psychiatric Therapies*, 21:189-203.

Mott, R.H., Small, I., and Anderson, J.M. (1965) "Comparative Study of Hallucinations." *Archives of General Psychiatry*, 12:595-601.

Mullahy, P. (1967) "Harry Stack Sullivan's Theory of Schizophrenia." *International Journal of Psychiatry*, 4:492-521.

Mumford, L. (1967-1970) *The Myth of the Machine*. (2 vol.) New York: Harcourt Brace Jovanovich.

Nasrallah, H.A. (1986) "Is Schizophrenia a Left Hemisphere Disease?" In: *Can Schizophrenia Be Localized in the Brain?* Ed. N.C. Andreasen. Washington D.C.: American Psychiatric Press, pp. 53-74.

Nasrallah, H.A., Jacoby, C.G., and McCalley-Whitters, M. (1981) "Cerebellar Atrophy in Schizophrenia and Mania." (letter) *Lancet*, 1:1102.

Nasrallah, H.A., Kuperman, S., Hamra, B., et al (1983) "Clinical Differences Between Schizophrenic Patients With and Without Large Cerebral Ventricles." *Journal of Clinical Psychiatry*, 44:407-409.

Obiols, J.E., Marcos, T., and Salamero, M. (1987) "Ventricular Enlargement and Neuropsychological Testing in Schizophrenia." *Acta Psychiatrica Scandinavica*, 76:199-202.

O'Brien, B. (1960) *Operators and Things: The Inner Life of a Schizophrenic*. London: Eleck Books.

Owens, D.G.C., Johnstone, E.C., Crow, T.J., et al (1985) "Lateral Ventricular Size in Schizophrenia: Relationship to the Disease Process and its Clinical Manifestations." *Psychological Medicine*, 15:27-41.

Pandurangì, A.K., Dewan, M.J., Boucher, M., et al (1986) "A Comprehensive Study of Chronic Schizophrenic Patients: II. Biological, Neuropsychological, and Clinical Correlates of CT Abnormality." *Acta Psychiatrica Scnadinavica*, 73:161-171.

Pao, P.-N. (1979) *Schizophrenic Disorders: Theory and Treatment From a Psychodynamic Point of View*. New York: International Universities Press.

Persico, A.M., Wang, Z.W., Black, D.W., et al (1995) "Exclusion of Close Linkage of the Dopamine Transporter Gene with Schizophrenia Spectrum Disorders." *American Journal of Psychiatry*, 152:134-136.

Persson, T. and Roos, B.-E. (1969) "Acid Metabolites from Monoamines in Cerebrospinal Fluid of Chronic Schizophrenics." *British Journal of Psychiatry*, 115:95-98.

Pickar, D., Labarca, R., Doran, A.R., et al (1986) "Longitudinal Measurement of Plasma Homovanillic Acid Levels in Schizophrenic Patients: Correlation With Psychosis and Response to Neuroleptic Treatment." *Archives of General Psychiatry*, 43:669-676.

Pines, M. (1979) "Superkids." *Psychology Today*, Jan. pp. 53-63.

Pollin, W., Stabenau, J.R., Mosher, L., et al (1966) "Life History Differences in Identical Twins Discordant for Schizophrenia." *American Journal of Orthopsychiatry*, 36:492-509.

Pollin, W., Stabenau, J.R., and Tupin, J. (1965) "Family Studies with Identical Twins Discordant for Schizophrenia." *Psychiatry*, 28:60-78.

Pope, H.G., Keck, P.E. and McElroy, S.L. (1986) "Frequency and Presentation of Neuroleptic Malignant Syndrome in a Large Psychiatric Hospital." *American Journal of Psychiatry*, 143:1227-1233.

Popper, K.R. (1959) *The Logic of Scientific Discovery*. New York: Harper Torchbooks.

Popper, K.R. (1963) *Conjectures and Refutations: The Growth of Scientific Knowledge*. New York: Harper Torchbooks.

Post, R.M., Fink, E., Carpenter, W.T., et al (1975) "Cerebrospinal Fluid Amine Metabolites in Acute Schizophrenia." *Archives of General Psychiatry*, 32:1063-1069.

Prien, R.F., Caffey, E.M. and Klett, J.C. (1972) "Comparison of Lithium and Chlorpromazine in the Treatment of Mania." *Archives of General Psychiatry*, 26:146-153.

Rappaport, M., Hopkins, H.K., Hall, J., et al (1978) "Are There Schizophrenics For Whom Drugs May Be Unnecessary or Contraindicated?" *International Pharmacopsychiatry*, 13:100-111.

Reveley, M.A. (1985) "CT Scans in Schizophrenia." *British Journal of Psychiatry*, 146:367-371.

Reuters. (1988) "Britons Report Schizophrenia Gene Discovery." *Seattle Times*, July 26, p. A5.

Reynolds, G.P., Reynolds, L.M., Riederer, P., et al (1980) "Dopamine Receptors and Schizophrenia: Drug Effect or Illness." (letter) *Lancet*, 2:1251.

Ries, R.K. (1985) "DSM-III Implications of Catatonia and Bipolar Disorder." *American Journal of Psychiatry*, 142:1471-1474.

Rifkin, A. and Kane, J.M. (1984) "Low Dose Neuroleptic Maintenance Treatment of Schizophrenia." In *Drug Maintenance Strategies in Schizophrenia*. Ed. J.M. Kane. The Monograph Series of the American Psychiatric Press.

Rimón, R., Roos, B.-E., Rakkolainen, V., et al (1971) "The Content of 5-Hydroxyindoleacetic Acid and Homovanillic Acid in the Cerebrospinal Fluid of Patients with Acute Schizophrenia." *Journal of Psychosomatic Research*, 15:375-378.

Rodgers, J.E. (1982) "Roots of Madness." *Science 82*, July/August, pp. 84-91.

Rosenhan, D.L. (1973) "On Being Sane in Insane Places." *Science*, 179:250-258.

Rosenthal, D. (1962) "Familial Concordance by Sex With Respect to Schizophrenia." *Psychological Bulletin*, 59:401-421.

Rosenthal, D., Wender, P.H., Kety, S.S., et al (1968) "Schizophrenic's Offspring Reared in Adoptive Homes." In *The Transmission of Schizophrenia*. Eds. D. Rosenthal and S. S. Kety. New York: Pergamon Press, pp. 377-391.

Rosenthal, D., Wender, P.H., Kety, S.S., et al (1971) "The Adopted-Away Offspring of Schizophrenics." *American Journal of Psychiatry*, 128:307-311.

Rubin, R.T. and Poland, R.E. (1977) "Human Sleep: Basic Mechanisms and Pathologic Patterns." Chapter 6 In *Biological Basis of Psychiatric Disorders*. Ed. A. Frazier and A. Winokur. New York: Spectrum Publications.

Sabaté, O., Campion, D., d'Amato, T., et al (1994) "Failure to Find Evidence for Linkage or Association Between Dopamine $D_3$ Receptor Gene and Schizophrenia." *American Journal of Psychiatry*, 151:107-111.

St. Clair, D., Blackwood, D., Muir, W., et al (1989) "No Linkage of Chromosome 5q11-q13 Marker to Schizophrenia in Scottish Families." *Nature*, 339: 305-309.

Sale, I. and Kristall, H. (1978) "Schizophrenia Following Withdrawal From Chronic Phenothiazine Administration: A Case Report." *Australian and New Zealand Journal of Psychiatry*, 12:73-75.

Sarbin, T.R. and Mancuso, J.C. (1980) *Schizophrenia: Medical Diagnosis or Moral Verdict?*. New York: Pergamon.

Scheff, T.J. (1966) *Being Mentally Ill: A Sociological Theory*. New York: Aldine.

Scheflin, A.W. and Opton, E.M. (1978) *The Mind Manipulators*. New York: Paddington Press.

Scheibel, A.B. and Conrad, A.S. (1993) "Hippocampal Dysgenesis in Mutant Mouse and Schizophrenic Man: Is There a Relationship?" *Schizophrenia Bulletin*, 19:21-33.

Scheibel, A.B. and Kovelman, J.A. (1981) "Disorientation of the Hippocampal Pyramidal Cell and Its Processes in the Schizophrenic Patient." *Biological Psychiatry*, 16:101-102.

Schmajuk, N.A. (1987) "Animal Models for Schizophrenia: The Hippocampally Lesioned Animal." *Schizophrenia Bulletin*, 13:317-327.

Schrag, P. (1978) *Mind Control*. New York: Pantheon Books.

Schreber, D.P. (1955) *Memoirs of My Nervous Illness*. London: William Dawson & Sons.

Schweizer, E.E., Swenson, C.M., Winokur, A., et al (1986) "The Dexamethasone Suppression Test in Generalized Anxiety Disorder." *British Journal of Psychiatry*, 149:320-322.

Scott, R.D., and Ashworth, P.L. (1967) "'Closure' at the First Schizophrenic Break-down: A Family Study." *British Journal of Medical Psychology*, 40:109-145.

Scott, R.D., and Ashworth, P.L. (1969) "The Shadow of the Ancestor: A Historical Factor in the Transmission of Schizophrenia." *British Journal of Medical Psychology*, 42:13-32.

Searles, H.F. (1958) "Positive Feelings in the Relationship Between the Schizophrenic and His Mother." *International Journal of Psychoanalysis*, 39:569-586.

Sechehaye, M. (1951) *Autobiography of a Schizophrenic Girl*. New York: Grune & Stratton.

Selye, H. (1978) *The Stress of Life*. (2nd ed.) New York: McGraw-Hill.

Sheldrick, C., Jablensky, A., Sartorius, N., et al. (1977) "Schizophrenia Succeeded by Affective Illness: Catamnestic Study and Statistical Enquiry." *Psychological Medicine*, 7:619-624.

Shenton, M.E., Ballinger, R., Marcy, B., et al (1989) "Two Syndromes of Schizophrenic Psychopathology Associated With Left vs. Right Temporal Deficits in P300 Amplitude." *Journal of Nervous and Mental Disease*, 177:219-225.

Sheppard, G., Gruzelier, J., Manchanda, R., et al (1983) "O Positron Emission Tomographic Scanning in Predominantly Never-Treated Acute Schizophrenic Patients." *Lancet*, 2:1448-1452.

Sherrington, R., Brynjolfsson, J., Petursson, H., et al (1988) "Localization of a Susceptibility Locus for Schizophrenia on Chromosome 5." *Nature*, 336:164-167.

Shima, S., Kanba, Y., Masuda, T., et al. (1985) "Normal Ventricles in Chronic Schizophrenics." *Acta Psychiatrica Scandinavica*, 71:25-29.

Shor, R.E. (1959) "Hypnosis and the Concept of the Generalized Reality-Orientation." *American Journal of Psychotherapy*, 13:582-602.

Shuchter, S.A., Zisook, S., Kirkorowicz, C., et al (1986) "The Dexamethasone Suppression Test in Acute Grief." *American Journal of Psychiatry*, 143:879-881.

Siebert, A. (1996) *Schizophrenia is Not A Disease or Illness — Psychiatry is Deluded*. Portland, OR: Practical Psychology Press.

Siever, L.J., Haier, R.J., Coursey, R.D., et al (1982) "Smooth Pursuit Eye Tracking Impairment: Relation to Other 'Markers' of Schizophrenia and Psychologic Correlates." *Archives of General Psychiatry*, 39: 1001-1005.

Siirala, M. (1963) "Schizophrenia: A Human Situation." *American Journal of Psychoanalysis*, 23:39-58.

Singer, M.T. and Wynne, L.C. (1965) "Thought Disorder and the Family Relations of Schizophrenics: IV. Results and Implications." *Archives of General Psychiatry*, 12:201-212.

Small, J.G., Kellams, J.J., Milstein, V., et al (1975) "A Placebo Controlled Study of Lithium Combined with Neuroleptics in Chronic Schizophrenia Patients." *American Journal of Psychiatry*, 132:1315-1317.

Smith, K. and Sines, J.O. (1960) "Demonstration of a Peculiar Odor in the Sweat of Schizophrenic Patients." *Archives of General Psychiatry*, 2:184-188.

Smith, K., Thompson, G.F. and Koster, H.D. (1969) "Sweat in Schizophrenic Patients: Identification of the Odorous Substance." *Science*, 166:398-399.

Smith, R.C., Baumgartner, R., and Calderon, M. (1987) "Magnetic Resonance Imaging Studies of the Brains of Schizophrenic Patients." *Psychiatry Research*, 20:33-46.

Smith, R.C., Calderon, M., Ravichandran, G.K., et al (1984) "Nuclear Magnetic Resonance in Schizophrenia: A Preliminary Study." *Psychiatry Research,* 12:137-147.

Snyder, S.H. (1974) *Madness and the Brain.* New York: McGraw-Hill.

Solomon, C.M., Holzman, P.S., Levin, S., et al (1987) "The Association Between Eye-Tracking Dysfunctions and Thought Disorder Disorder in Psychosis." *Archives of General Psychiatry,* 44:31-35.

Sterling, P. (1979) "Psychiatry's Drug Addiction." *New Republic,* Dec. 8, pp. 14-18.

Stern, P.J. (1972) *In Praise of Madness: Realness Therapy — The Self Reclaimed.* New York: W.W. Norton.

Sternberg, D.E. (1986) "Neuroleptic Malignant Syndrome: The Pendulum Swings." *American Journal of Psychiatry,* 143:1273-1275.

Stierlin, H. (1959) "The Adaptation to the 'Stronger' Person's Reality: Some Aspects of the Symbiotic Relationship of the Schizophrenic." *Psychiatry,* 22:143-152.

Stierlin, H. (1963) "Familie und Schizophrenie" *Nervenarzt,* 34:495-500.

Su, Y., Burke, J., O'Neill, F.A., et al (1993) "Exclusion of Linkage Between Schizophrenia and the $D_2$ Dopamine Receptor Gene Region of Chromosome 11q in 112 Irish Multiplex Families." *Archives of General Psychiatry,* 50:205-211.

Sullivan, H.S. (1953) *Conceptions of Modern Psychiatry.* New York: W.W. Norton.

Sullivan, H.S. (1956) *Clinical Studies in Psychiatry.* New York: W.W. Norton.

Sullivan, H.S. (1962) *Schizophrenia as a Human Process.* New York: W.W. Norton.

Szasz, T.S. (1970) *The Manufacture of Madness: A Comparative Study of the Inquisition and The Mental Health Movement.* New York: Delta.

Szasz, T.S. (1974) *The Myth of Mental Illness: The Foundations of a Theory of Personal Conduct.* (rev. ed.) New York: Harper & Row.

Szasz, T.S. (1976) *Schizophrenia: The Sacred Symbol of Psychiatry.* New York: Basic Books.

Szechtman, H., Nahmìas, C., Garnett, S., et al (1988) "Effect of Neuroleptics on Altered Cerebral Glucose Metabolism in Schizophrenia." *Archives of General Psychiatry*, 45:523-532.

Talbott, J.H. and Tillotson, K.J. (1941) "The Effects of Cold on Mental Disorders: A Study of Ten Patients Suffering from Schizophrenia and Treated with Hypothermia." *Diseases of the Nervous System*, 2:116-126.

Taylor, M.A. and Abrams, A. (1977) "Catatonia: Prevalence and Importance in the Manic Phase of Manic-Depressive Illness." *Archives of General Psychiatry*, 34:1223-1225.

Tepper, S.J. and Haas, J.F. (1979) "Prevalence of Tardive Dyskinesia." *Journal of Clinical Psychiatry*, 40:508-516.

Torrey, E.F. (1983) *Surviving Schizophrenia: A Family Manual.* New York: Harper Colophon Books.

Torrey, E.F. (1988) "Stalking the Schizovirus." *Schizophrenia Bulletin*, 14:223-229.

Torrey, E.F. (1991) "A Viral-Anatomical Explanation of Schizophrenia." *Schizophrenia Bulletin*, 17:15-18.

Torrey, E.F. and Peterson, M.R. (1976) "The Viral Hypothesis of Schizophrenia." *Schizophrenia Bulletin*, 2:136-146.

Trethowan, W.H. (1968) "The Couvade Syndrome — Some Further Observations." *Journal of Psychosomatic Research*, 12:107-115.

Trimble, M. and Kingsley, D. (1978) "Cerebral Ventricular Size in Chronic Schizophrenia." *Lancet*, 1:278-279.

Tsuang, M.T., Woolson, R.F. and Fleming, J.A. (1979) "Long-Term Outcome of Major Psychoses, I: Schizophrenia and Affective Disorders Compared With Psychiatrically Symptom-Free Surgical Conditions." *Archives of General Psychiatry*, 36:1295-1301.

Ullman, L.P. and Krasner, L. (1975) *A Psychological Approach to Abnormal Behavior.* (2nd ed.) Englewood Cliffs, N.J.: Prentice-Hall.

Vaillant, G.E. (1978) "A 10-Year Followup of Remitting Schizophrenics." *Schizophrenia Bulletin*, 4:78-85.

Volkow, N.D., Brodie, J.D., Wolf, A.P., et al (1986) "Brain Metabolism in Patients with Schizophrenia Before and After Acute Neuroleptic Administration." *Journal of Neurology, Neurosurgery and Psychiatry*,

49:1199-1202.

Vonnegut, M. (1975) *The Eden Express*. New York: Bantam Books.

Wahl, O.F. (1976) "Monozygotic Twins Discordant for Schizophrenia: A Review." *Psychological Bulletin*, 83:91-106.

Weinberger, D.R., Wagner, R.R. and Wyatt, J. (1983) "Neuropathological Studies of Schizophrenia." *Schizophrenia Bulletin*, 9:193-212.

Wender, P.H., Rosenthal, D., Kety, S.S., et al (1974) "Crossfostering: A Research Strategy for Clarifying the Role of Genetic and Experiential Factors in the Etiology of Schizophrenia." *Archives of General Psychiatry*, 30:121-128.

Wender, P.H., Rosenthal, P., Zahn, T.P., et al (1971) "The Psychiatric Adjustment of the Adopting Parents of Schizophrenics." *American Journal of Psychiatry*, 127:1013-1018.

Whitehead, A.N. (1925) *Science and the Modern World*. New York: Macmillan.

Whitehead, A.N. (1938) *Modes of Thought*. New York: The Free Press.

Widen, L., Bergström, M., Blomqvist, G., et al (1983) "Positron Emission Tomography Studies of Brain Energy Metabolism in Schizophrenia." In: *Positron Emission Tomography of the Brain*. Ed. W.E. Heiss and M.E. Phelps. Berlin: Springer-Verlag, pp. 192-195.

Widen, L., Blomqvist, G., Greitz, T., et al (1983) "PET Studies of Glucose Metabolism in Patients with Schizophrenia." *AJNR*, 4:550-552.

Winson, J. (1985) *Brain & Psyche: The Biology of the Unconscious*. New York: Vintage Books.

Witschy, J.K., Malone, G.L. and Holden, L.D. (1984) "Psychosis After Neuroleptic Withdrawal in a Manic-Depressive Patient." American Journal of Psychiatry, 141:105-106.

Wolkin, A., Jaeger, J., Brodie, J.D., et al (1985) "Persistence of Cerebral Metabolic Abnormalities in Chronic Schizophrenia as Determined by Positron Emission Tomography." *American Journal of Psychiatry*, 142:564-571.

Wong, D.F., Wagner, H.N., Pearlson, G., et al (1985) "Dopamine Receptor Binding of C-11-3-N-Methylspiperone in the Caudate in Schizophrenia and Bipolar Disorder: A Preliminary Report." *Psychopharmacology Bulletin*, 21:595-598.

Wong, D.F., Wagner, H.N., Tune, L.E., et al (1986) "Positron Emission Tomography Reveals Elevated $D_2$ Dopamine Receptors in Drug-Naive Schizophrenics." *Science*, 234:1558-1562.

Woolley, D.W. and Shaw, E. (1954) "A Biochemical and Pharmacological Suggestion About Certain Mental Disorders." *Science*, 119:587-588.

Wyatt, R.J., Potkin, S.G., Kleinman, J.E., et al (1981) "The Schizophrenic Syndrome: Examples of Biological Tools for Subclassification." *Journal of Nervous and Mental Disease*, 169:100-112.

Wyatt, R.J. and Torgow, J.S. (1977) "A Comparison of Equivalent Clinical Potencies of Neuroleptics as Used to Treat Schizophrenia and Affective Disorders." *Journal of Psychiatric Research*, 13:91-98.

Wynne, L.C., Ryckoff, I.M., Day, J., et al (1958) "Pseudo-Mutually in the Family of Schizophrenics." *Psychiatry*, 21:205-220.

Wynne, L.C. and Singer, M.T. (1963) "Thought Disorder and the Family Relations of Schizophrenics: I. A Research Strategy." *Archives of General Psychiatry*, 9:191-198.

Wynne, L.C., Singer, M.T. and Toohey, M. (1976) "Communication of the Adoptive Parents of Schizophrenics." In *Schizophrenia 75. Psychotherapy, Family Studies, Research*. Eds. J. Jorstad and E. Ugelstad. Oslo: University of Oslo Press, pp. 413-451.

Yates, W.R., Jacoby, C.G., and Andreasen, N.C. (1987) "Cerebellar Atrophy in Schizophrenia and Affective Disorder." *American Journal of Psychiatry*, 144:465-467.

Yorkston, N.J., Gruzelier, J.H., Zaki, S.A., et al (1977) "Propranolol as an Adjunct to the Treatment of Schizophrenia." *Lancet*, 2:575-578.

Young, H.F., Bentall, R.P., Slade, P.D., et al (1986) "Disposition Toward Hallucination, Gender and EPQ Scores: A Brief Report." *Personality and Individual Differences*, 7:247-249.

Zarlock, S.P. (1966) "Social Expectations, Language, and Schizophrenia." *Journal of Humanistic Psychology*, 6:68-74.

Ziskind, E., Somerfeld, E. and Jens, R. (1971) "Can Schizophrenia Change to Affective Psychosis?" *American Journal of Psychiatry*, 128:331-335.

# INDEX

VE *(See ventricular enlargement)*
Ventricular enlargement 165-168, 247, 266, 272, 279, 281, 284, 287
Wender, Paul H. 202, 203, 205, 257, 261, 283, 287, 288
Whitehead, Alfred North 229, 260, 288
Wynne, Lyman C. 11, 204, 241-243, 257, 285, 289
Zarlock, Stanley P. 212, 259, 289